MAX WEBER
AND POLITICAL
COMMITMENT

EDWARD BRYAN PORTIS

MAX WEBER
AND POLITICAL COMMITMENT

Science, Politics, and Personality

TEMPLE UNIVERSITY PRESS
Philadelphia

Temple University Press, Philadelphia 19122
Copyright © 1986 by Temple University. All rights reserved
Published 1986
Printed in the United States of America

Library of Congress Cataloging-in-Publication Data

Portis, Edward Bryan.
Max Weber and political commitment.

Bibliography: p.
Includes index.
1. Weber, Max, 1864–1920.
2. Weber, Max, 1864–1920—Personality.
3. Social sciences—Philosophy. 4. Social waves.
5. Politics, Practical.
I. Title. H59.W4P67 1986   301'.092'4   86-14442
ISBN 0-87722-445-5 (alk. paper)

CONTENTS

PREFACE   vii

CHAPTER ONE: Social Science and Politics   3

CHAPTER TWO: Max Weber Becomes a
Scientist   21

CHAPTER THREE: Commitment and
Personality   49

CHAPTER FOUR: The Scientific Personality   68

CHAPTER FIVE: Personal Identity and Social
Theory   89

CHAPTER SIX: The Political Function of Social
Science   114

CHAPTER SEVEN: Max Weber Becomes a
Politician   145

NOTES   171

BIBLIOGRAPHY   227

INDEX   241

v

PREFACE

A mbitious books inevitably raise more issues than can be explored adequately in a volume of reasonable length. There is little prospect that this relatively thin work might have escaped this fate. My primary intent is to affirm the proposition that social science and politics are antithetical activities that cannot be seriously pursued by the same individuals. I do not expect most readers to be favorably disposed toward this proposition at the onset, but I hope that the theoretical argument advanced in its support will be found at least challenging. Even more troublesome for some readers, however, will be the picture of Max Weber that emerges from my analysis of his work and aspects of his personal experience. I believe that as a social scientist he was without peer. Yet many who would agree with this assessment have a much more grandiose vision than do I (or did Weber) of what a social scientist can be. Exaggerating the distinction, one might say that my interpretation replaces Weber the tragic prophet with Weber the political eunuch. Social science has no need of prophets, and I am of the opinion that my characterization of the man is nonderogatory as well as factually valid.

Let me emphasize, however, that this characterization does not constitute a complete biography. It is a one-dimensional accentuation meant to illustrate the theoretical argument and place much of Weber's scholarly work in perspective. More specifically, I do not claim that my account of his nervous disorders is complete. There were undoubtedly additional factors at work that conditioned those elaborated here. I maintain only that the elements to which I refer were of considerable importance, and I believe that the facts of the matter support this limited claim.

I have been writing this book for more years than I care to acknowledge. Portions of the following journal articles can be found within the text, although significantly altered or in a much different context:

"Citizenship and Personal Identity," *Polity*, 1986.
"Max Weber and the Unity of Normative and Empirical Theory," *Political Studies*, 1983.
"Max Weber's Theory of Personality," *Sociological Inquiry*, 1978.
"Political Action and Social Science: Max Weber's Two Arguments for Objectivity," *Polity*, 1980.
"Social Theory and Policy Evaluation," *Public Administration Quarterly*, 1987.
"Theoretical Interpretation from a Social Scientific Perspective: An Example from Max Weber," *Social Science Quarterly*, 1985.

My intellectual debts have accumulated over the years, and and I could not possibly mention all those who helped me in the course of this project. Professor Wolfgang J. Mommsen generously gave me some of his valuable time and advice at an early stage, Professor Horst J. Helle of the Max Weber Institute provided access to valuable information, and Richard Critchfield helped with the translation of a number of passages. The following individuals critically read parts of the evolving manuscript: Frederick Bergerson, Jon Bond, George Edwards, Robert Grady, Robert Grafstein, George Graham, Scarlet Graham, Robert Harmel, Richard Hartwig, David Large, Les Levine, Michael Levy, Don Moon, Avery Leiserson, L. L. Portis, Lawrence Scaff, Terry Scheid-Cook, and Frank Thompson. Two anonymous reviewers carefully read the entire manuscript for Temple University Press, making a number of very useful suggestions. All of these readers have contributed to whatever strengths are to be found in the present study. Of course, none can be held responsible for its deficiencies, especially since few would be likely to wholeheartedly concur in its conclusions.

I owe an intellectual debt of a much more diffuse but no less real nature to my former mentors, Joyotpaul Chaudhuri and Avery Leiserson. Jane Cullen of Temple University Press has been an invaluable source of editorial and managerial wisdom. Without John McDermott's encouragement and sage advice, this work might not have been published. Finally, I must express appreciation to my wife, Susie, and daughters, Maggie, Libby, and Katie, for offering the essential distractions that encourage a sense of perspective.

MAX WEBER
AND POLITICAL COMMITMENT

CHAPTER ONE

Social Science and Politics

The possibility of social science, as generally perceived today, was not seriously entertained until the Enlightenment and only became manifest in the latter years of the nineteenth century. It was the product of a new, or at least newly ascendent, view of knowledge. The new view replaced the notion of natural law with that of positive law. Natural law is based upon the premise that a transcendental order must be approximated if temporal existence is to display a degree of stability.[1] Positive law can also be considered to rest upon a conception of order, but only in the sense of "uniformity." Far from being transcendent, this order is imminent in experience because it expresses the determinant structure by which the entities of reality interact.[2]

Having radically different views of knowledge, these two general outlooks also have different views of the scholar's task and its meaning for political life. For the classical proponents of natural law philosophy and their contemporary heirs, the savant seeks through disciplined logical discourse, alone or aided by observation of the general tendencies of temporal affairs, to discover the universal rules of order in which humanity fulfills the end that defines it.[3] From this perspective politics should be concerned primarily with the adaptation of these general rules to particular circumstances, and as such has a distinctly ethical dimension. Conversely, the job of the modern social scientist is usually seen as the discovery, through reduction and systematic observation, of the elementary, uniform processes that explain the apparent diversity of experience. Once achieved, such knowledge enables a degree of prediction and potential control, and an informed politics will use such knowledge to minimize threats to social order and prosperity. While all politics may presume some sort of social commitment, its goals are primarily instrumental rather than ethical.

Despite their differences, these two general approaches to the nature of social knowledge are alike in assigning an essentially secondary status to politics. However important it may be in assuring stability or achieving other ends, politics should at some level be a process of applying or adapting one sort of wisdom or another.[4] The problems of social order are amenable to intellectual diagnosis and prescription because social order is subject to the laws of nature, however conceived. Fundamental problems of political conflict are caused by ignorance and, therefore, subject to amelioration by the dissemination of social knowledge. Since both orientations view politics as a derivative activity, both tend to treat in an offhand fashion the question with which this study is primarily occupied.

I am concerned with the extent to which social scientists can participate in political affairs without undermining the integrity of their scientific work. Put differently, I am concerned with the compatibility of political activity with social scientific objectivity. Irrespective of how expressed, the dimensions of the question must remain somewhat obscure at this initial stage of analysis. My primary conclusion, however, can be stated without equivocation. Overt political action always tends to compromise the social scientist's objectivity because science and politics are simply incompatible forms of activity, each requiring mutually exclusive personal characteristics. I am not asserting that politically motivated individuals, including misguided academics, could not arrive at important theoretical insights into the nature of social and political phenomena, nor even that they are less likely to do so than genuinely committed social scientists. My assertion is that such individuals cannot be genuinely committed social scientists because they must accept their insights on faith. No matter how sophisticated or consciously sincere their efforts to seek evidence or explore logical implications, difficulties encountered in this endeavor to support supposed insights are unlikely to ever call into question their validity.

I am referring to general or theoretical conceptions of social reality, not to assessments of specific situations. Quite clearly, an inability to assess and reassess the latter would be a severe handicap in politics, and I do not doubt that most politicians are quite sensitive to cues from their social environment and capable of great flexibility in responding to them. However, I think they are much less likely than those committed to science to change their fundamental perceptions of social reality. In fact, I will argue that it would be fatal for them as politicians to do so. Such an inability would be politically disadvantageous only if proper assessment of particular circumstances is somehow dependent upon possession of general truths. This is exactly the implication of the dominant trends in both the natural law and positive law conceptions of social knowledge. Political ends are realistic only if compatible with the inherent laws of social life, regardless of whether these are held to be transcendental or elemental, and only a knowledge of what could conceivably be accomplished can effectively guide the assessment of particular events.

As both imply the importance of a theoretically informed politics, the advocates of both traditions are not disposed to postulate the political incompetence of those capable of providing theoretical knowledge. Not being inclined to see difficulties, they are not likely to raise my question seriously. Indeed, within the classical tradition, the question is not whether philosophers could engage in politics but what incentives could possibly induce them to do so.[5] I am not, however, interested in philosophers, and I cannot claim that my thesis is applicable to those who see their task as the articulation of natural law doctrines discovered long ago or the interpretation of current affairs in terms of such majestic truths. Although I suspect that scholars of any kind will be hampered in their work if too involved in its social implications, my argument applies only to those who attempt to affirm their beliefs about social reality through empirical analysis. It is applicable, in other words, only to social scientists.

Initially, the advocates of a science of society were not really social scientists but rather moralists who saw such a science as a force for social reform. Consequently, they were not likely to see its political role as problematic. Social science was a product of the Enlightenment, with its faith in social progress through rationality. Of course, faith in human reason was nothing new. But the Enlightenment hero was a Promethean rather than Socratic figure. He did not seek to understand "nature" in order to submit to it, but to acquire, the tools to construct a harmonious society in which all individuals would be able to make their own decisions based upon their own autonomous intellects. Perhaps best epitomized by Condorcet, the Enlightenment thinkers saw in the advance of science the inevitable emancipation of the individual from the evils of prejudice and privilege.[6]

This Enlightenment faith contained a contradiction that forced the following generation of social scientific ideologues to alter it radically. Its two most basic tenets were individualism and scientific progress. Since the model of a successful science was provided by Newton's monumental achievement, progress in social science was seen as the attainment of a similarly unified theory for human affairs. The elementary principles of such a theory were sought in the laws of the intellect itself, and social progress was seen as the inevitable result of the evolution of the mind into a more complex and powerful instrument. But the measure of progress was increasingly seen in terms of the harmonious social unity to be made possible by scientific theory rather than the individual autonomy prized by the eighteenth century publicists. For individual autonomy in any meaningful sense is exceedingly difficult to reconcile with the subservience of the intellect to positive law. For the same reason, these early ideologues of a science of society were even less likely than their Enlightenment forebears to consider the political capacity of social scientists seriously. Precluded from attributing much importance to individual agency by the assumption of positive law, they naturally depreciated the influence of political effort upon the course of human affairs.[7]

Contemporary social scientists, at least in the West, typically justify their enterprise in terms much close to those of the Enlightenment publicists than those of the scientific ideologues who followed them. Affirmations of both the possibility of predictive knowledge and its relevance to public policy occur frequently. Yet Western social scientists remain firmly committed to some version of the democratic creed, reflecting a commitment to both determinism and individualism.

While an occasional social scientist is driven by the force of consistency to reject individualism, modern social scientific optimism has proved more resilient than its eighteenth century counterpart.[8] Part of the reason, no doubt, is that we are now dealing with real scientists, more concerned with empirical demonstration than formulating a comprehensive theoretical system. As John Stuart Mill pointed out, the greatest of the post-Enlightenment ideologues, Comte, did not really do sociology, however much he talked about it.[9] An empirically oriented individual is not likely to be bothered by an apparent logical necessity that cannot be empirically demonstrated. For example, the philo-sophically inclined Comte could dismiss psychology as a "mere branch" of physiology, while the modern empiricist Mill could dismiss Comte's claim with the observation that such a connec-tion was completely beyond human understanding. For the fore-seeable future, any demonstrable knowledge in this area would have "to be sought in the direct study . . . of the mental succes-sions themselves."[10]

It would be unfair, however, to say that contemporary social science has, by and large, escaped the agonies of contradiction of being oblivious to the requirement of consistency. Mill himself devoted an entire chapter of *A System of Logic,* "Of Liberty and Necessity," to the question. Although he formulated a challeng-ing argument for the compatibility of necessity and "freedom," he skirted the issue of the compatibility of positive law and indi-vidual agency. But contemporary social scientists have generally opted for another philosophical expedient to avoid the contra-diction, one with which Mill was not particularly comfortable. This is the doctrine often referred to as the "fact-value dichoto-my," and it is especially relevant to my primary concern, the rela-tionship between political activity and scientific objectivity.

The fact-value dichotomy can be defined as the assertion that propositions of "ought" cannot be deduced from propositions of "is." There are, of course, many versions of the doctrine, differing primarily on the exact meaning, if any, of ethical discourse.[11] In general, however, the doctrine allows social scientists to avoid the contradiction between individualism and necessity by implicitly accepting a distinction between an objective realm of human de-cision subject to the laws of science and a subjective realm imper-vious to scientific explanation. While this latter realm renders the laws of social science more "probabilistic" than those of physical science, the extent to which social science can provide an ade-quate basis for prediction and social control could only be determined by its successes and frustrations. But regardless of its degree of success, the existence of individual agency cannot be threatened by the progress of social science, however circumscribed by necessity it may come to be seen.

Since normative commitments cannot, according to this doctrine, be derived from what one believes to be true of reality, social scientists cannot scientifically define the ultimate goals that politicians should pursue. Yet social knowledge is bound to have tremendous instrumental value to political actors, and the fact-value dichotomy allows social scientists to use their expertise deliberately in support of politicians with whom they share normative commitments. In other words, it allows social scientists, qua social scientists, to engage in political activity. It does so because thought can be compartmentalized into subjective and objective components. In fact, scientific objectivity requires such a compartmentalization in order to eliminate the influence of subjective predilections. This is supposedly accomplished through intersubjectivity, which will be discussed further in another chapter. For the present I only want to note that if the role of normative commitments can be confined to the selection of "relevant" topics, social scientists are free to conduct their studies with political goals in mind without fear of compromising their scientific activity.

Max Weber has often been considered one of the foremost advocates of the fact-value dichotomy in social science.[12] In reality, his analysis of the relationship between social science and politics is more complex than this doctrine would allow and fundamentally incompatible with it. He denied that objectivity would be equated with impersonality or that it was possible for thought to be compartmentalized into normative and objective categories. As a consequence, he came to argue that the social scientist could not engage in political activity if his or her effort to test propositions through confrontation with reality is to be genuine. Weber

9

arrived at entirely different conclusions because he approached the problem from an entirely different perspective. It is this unique and largely unappreciated perspective that has led me to focus this study upon Weber's life and work. Although his analysis differs in a number of respects from mine, I have, for the most part, attempted to establish my thesis by building upon or modifying his arguments whenever possible.

For my purposes, the most salient feature of Weber's perspective is the autonomy of politics from science—in principle as well as practice. This autonomy follows from the refusal to assume the existence of either natural or positive law. Weber argued that the existence of either would have only marginal relevance for social science because neither type of generalization would be very useful in the explanation of human action, and therefore, neither could be scientifically confirmed. The categories through which social phenomena are perceived must be radically subjective, derived from priorities that the investigator brings to work rather than universal laws discovered through systematic observation or disciplined reflection. Because these priorities are antecedent to social scientific analysis, social problems cannot be scientifically resolved.

Both science and politics proceed from subjective assumptions. They differ, however, in the way behavior is rendered compatible with these subjective beliefs. The politician attempts to realize them socially or legislate them. The social scientist attempts to justify them, even though they can never be conclusively confirmed, by demonstrating their ability to achieve a coherent view of experience that can withstand empirical test and criticism. Weber defined science, like politics, as a form of action rather than a certain type of procedure or belief. Consequently, he saw the problem of the relationship between social science and politics as the compatibility between two types of activity rather than between comprehension and activity or theory and practice.

Each type of activity, he argued, necessarily imposes a separate ethos upon its practitioners, and only those with a definite set of personal characteristics are likely to conform consistently to the appropriate ethos. Yet the personal characteristics required by social science are mutually exclusive of those required by politics. It is *logically* impossible to pursue both simultaneously, and any effort to do so must result in the corruption of genuine commitment to at least one.

Just what these sets of personal characteristics are, and the reasons they are mutually exclusive, will be topics of later chapters. Weber came to see the problem in these terms because of historical developments that led to a serious personal predicament. As mentioned, social science only developed into a significant social phenomenon, as opposed to an idea or a hope, in the latter part of the nineteenth century. Before then, there were no university departments of social science, no social scientific journals, no professional organizations, and no generally recognized career opportunities in social science. Few, if any, individuals could have considered themselves social scientists in such an environment.

What in retrospect might be characterized as social scientific work in nineteenth century Germany was done within the faculties of history and, somewhat later, economics. Even most economists were in fact, if not in name, historians. In 1883, however, the Austrian economist Carl Menger published an attack on the historical approach in which he defended, in the name of science, the rationalistic, analytical methods usually associated with the early English economists. This attack began a long and multifarious exchange of polemics that became known in Germany as the "*Methodenstreit,*" drawing combatants from among both economists and historians. The controversy persisted at least until the 1920s and, like most academic wars, was never really resolved. But out of the *Methodenstreit* emerged a self-consciousness that contributed a great deal to the development of academic social science in Germany.[13]

Weber received his advanced training in legal and economic history during the initial stages of this dispute, which raged throughout his academic and scholarly career. As a matter of fact, his early academic career was probably enhanced to some extent by the increasing self-consciousness of social science. His first permanent appointment was to a chair in "political economy" at Freiburg, followed soon by a similar position at the more prestigious university at Heidelberg. Although his rapid advancement was surely due primarily to his brilliance, it would appear that he was particularly sought after because his work profitably synthesized the historical and analytical approaches.[14] He used rationalistic, analytical models to explain rather than merely describe historical processes; the result is recognizably social scientific even by today's more exacting standards. Indeed, just before receiving the offer from Heidelberg, he declined an attractive offer to organize and direct a new and heavily financed "Institute for the Social Sciences."[15]

Successful as he was in scholarship, Weber was not enthusiastic at the prospect of a career in higher education. As a young man, he considered scholarship as little more than a hobby. His conscious goal was a career in public service, and his advanced education was originally intended to be primarily in law. He took advantage of academic opportunities only after convincing himself of their compatibility with his aspirations for political involvement. But as he became increasingly immersed in his academic duties, he found it more and more difficult to participate actively in public affairs. His academic career came to an abrupt end, however, when he suffered a devastating nervous collapse that prevented any sort of sustained activity for a number of years. Although he was able to pursue scholarship during a long convalescence, he could not either actively participate in politics or teach until the last years of his life.

I will argue in the following pages that Weber's breakdown was at least in part a result of the tensions created by simultaneous commitments to both scientific and political careers. For him, the relationship between social science and politics was an intensely personal problem. His early methodological essays, written at the beginning of his convalescence, were in large part derived from efforts to restore clarity, perspective, and balance to his personal life—to restore, as will be seen, a sense of personal identity. His identity was shattered when he discovered that he was not what he wanted to be, planned to be, and thought he ought to be. Weber wanted to be a politician, yet he became a scientist. His inability to reconcile the two precipitated an exacting search for the personal requisites of each and for a relationship between them that would not compromise either.

He succeeded in isolating the personal requisites of each type of activity, discerning their incompatibility, and formulating general principles of social scientific organization that might encourage both scientific inquiry and informed public policy. Yet he apparently could not understand his inability either to repress completely his urge toward political involvement or to satisfy this urge through intermittent participation in public affairs. For this reason, a complete explication of my thesis is not to be found in Weber's work. He explained why social science and politics could not be pursued simultaneously but could not explain why they could not be compartmentalized. He only knew, as a personal fact, that each required a commitment so total as to constitute a distinct type of "personality."

His inability to understand his need to engage in only one type of action was due to his failure to establish the necessity of his conception of personality. He defined the concept as the coherence or continuity achieved through the ordering of behavior about ultimate commitments. Since science and politics are distinct ways by which behavior can be ordered, each is the basis for a distinct type of personality. Because they are among a finite set of ways to order behavior *rationally,* they are more than just culturally defined roles. They could occur in any social or cultural context, although their frequency is certainly conditioned by environmental factors. For Weber, the function of personality is to make possible self-understanding. Only if one gives oneself continuity through some sort of consistency can one see oneself as something to be understood. Yet he could not argue that such understanding is necessary, since he apparently believed that it became culturally prescribed during the Reformation. In other words, he seems to conclude that the need for personality was the result of a cultural development unique to the West.

This conclusion was bound to be personally unsatisfactory and is, in any case, incorrect. Weber's concept of personality is similar to, and certainly compatible with, the concept of "personal identity" and "self-conception" used by a number of latter-day psychologists and philosophers. They have persuasively demonstrated the necessity of self-consciousness for symbolic communication. Consequently, far from being the product of a particular cultural development, some form of personal identity would seem to be a prerequisite for culture itself.[16] Furthermore, the adverse psychological effects of a complete or partial loss of identity have been amply documented by modern psychologists. In the absence of a coherent personal identity, one's ability to integrate behavior and cope with the environment is inevitably impaired.

I will argue that Weber's own crisis to a significant extent was due to his consciousness of incompatible elements within his self-conception. Until he accepted himself as a scientist and forswore active political involvement, he was for a time incapable of persistently pursuing any goal. But even after this acceptance, he could not repress his interest in political affairs and was irresistibly drawn to the study of politics itself. Because of his intense interest in politics, an activity in which he could not allow himself to engage, he was forced to be continually vigilant. The tenacity, seriousness, and, at times, insensitivity with which he asserted his views on the role of "value-judgments" in social science were a manifestation of their personal urgency.

While the necessity of a coherent self-conception can account for Weber's inability to compartmentalize his activity consciously, his continued attraction to political affairs presents a more intractable problem. The only way he could reconcile his continued interest in politics with his identity as a scientist was to make politics the focus of his scholarly efforts. Whatever the specific topics of his investigations in the post-breakdown period, they were intended to discern the factors encouraging or inhibiting effective politics. If he could not engage in it, he could at least study it. Politics became the "value" about which Weber, the scientist, oriented his action. It ceased to be a behavioral option and became instead the priority that led to his most important and famous social conceptualizations.

He did not pretend to be able to explain the ultimate origins of this or any other commitment. Although not accepting the doctrine of the fact-value dichotomy, he believed it impossible to justify ultimate values scientifically. He presumed that they were derived from the metaphysical commitments that define one's general outlook, but he did not know how or why. I argue that ultimate commitments are necessarily derived from self-identity because it is a prerequisite for deliberation and action. Indeed, the very act of choosing presumes commitment to one's self-conception. Weber was to a great extent correct in believing that ultimate commitments were derived from general views of reality that cannot be conclusively confirmed by empirical analysis. Yet he was mistaken in believing that the "values" derived from these views are the basis of "personality." Instead, aspects of personal identity are derived from general views of social reality and are valued because they are aspects of identity rather than aspects of identity because they are valued.

Weber was able to combine commitments to both science and politics only because every self-conception has two types of components. One is the substantive commitments that give focus to activity, and the other is the way the individual believes he or she is able to render behavior consistent with these foci. For most individuals these two types are merged into a diffuse and imprecisely ordered set of roles. For Weber, they had to be quite distinct. He was able to forge a coherent conception of self only after he had consciously distinguished his scientific activity from his commitment to politics. The former, the "capability" aspect of his identity, was the result of his personal experience. The latter, the "functional" aspect, was entailed in his general conceptualization of social reality. Any comprehensive social outlook must incorporate, however implicitly, a conception of human nature and, therefore, defines to some extent its advocates. One's species is by definition a component of one's self-concept. It need not be the dominant component, as perhaps attested by the frequency with which humans willfully do away with recognized members of the species because of differing national, ethnic, religious, or class identities. Yet given Weber's conscious elaboration of theoretical assumptions, it is to be expected that the most fundamental among them would be the dominant component of his identity; and he identified humanity by politics, properly understood. Consequently, he was necessarily committed to an activity in which he lacked the capacity to engage. The resulting tension rendered his self-conception inherently unstable, even if logically coherent.

The implications of this analysis of personal identity for the relationship between social science and politics are far reaching. Despite the incompatibility of political and scientific activity, there is a necessary connection between social thought and political commitment. Since self-conception, to which one is necessarily committed, is in part determined by one's view of social reality, any comprehensive or fundamental social theory necessarily prescribes social "values." Consequently, to the extent that social science is able to call into question general theories of social reality, it has implications for politics that go far beyond the production of useful facts.

Yet this relationship between social theory and political commitment considerably complicates the problem of social scientific objectivity. Empirical analysis is only possible within a framework of fundamental theoretical assumptions. For this and other reasons, it is, strictly speaking, inconclusive; neither proof nor falsity can be demonstrated beyond doubt by empirical tests.[17] Nevertheless, the systematic confrontation of expectation and reality can be considered the most efficient and perhaps the only way to rid oneself of false conceptions. This is true, however, only if the individual seriously entertains the possibility that frustrated expectations might be indicative of conceptual invalidity. This would be possible if the individual can detach himself or herself from conceptual assumptions. But since at least part of one's fundamental conception of social reality is an integral part of self-conception, and self-conception necessarily entails commitment, such detachment is impossible in the case of general social theory. Given this impossibility, only an individual who cannot accept his or her fundamental social beliefs as given could be driven to reject them by frustrated expectations. Only such an individual might feel compelled to justify beliefs *to himself or herself* by demonstrating their ability to survive scrutiny and test. This is the essence of the scientific personality, which is the burden of chapter four.

In arguing that this scientific personality cannot be maintained in the face of serious political involvement, I realize that almost every reader will be able to provide apparent refuting examples. The most obvious candidate, of course, is Marx. Not only did he articulate an opposing view of the relationship between social science and political commitment, but he also devoted a great deal of effort over a number of years to realizing political goals derived from his scholarly insights. Although the analysis in the following pages builds upon Weber's insights, his example serves only as illustration. As I do not rest my case upon an empirical instance, I hope that its plausibility will not be assessed on the basis of widely shared assumptions concerning other instances. If my analysis is correct, such assumptions will have to be modified. I personally think that Marx was a great scholar but an ineffectual politician, and I suspect that this was the case because his sense of scholarly integrity tended to undermine his political acumen. Be this as it may, it is essential that participation in either political events or the forms of scientific inquiry not be confused with an inclination for such activity.

I am perhaps inviting misinterpretation by resorting occasionally to biographical narrative in developing my argument. While a work of art is often enhanced by understanding the psychological tensions that tormented its creator, a system of thought tends to be depreciated when traced to psychic disorders. The author of a theoretical system claims that his assertions are valid rather than emotionally satisfying. For this reason, psycho-biography probably lends itself too easily to polemic to ever be accepted as an entirely respectable enterprise. In any event, I am not engaged in such a project. My interest is not to depreciate Weber's work, but to extend it.[18]

While biographical facts can be useful for interpretive work, they are incapable of confirming theoretical points. In fact, my theoretical analysis justifies some of my inferences concerning relevant aspects of Weber's life rather than vice versa. My purpose in writing this book is to determine the implications of social theory for political commitment and the logical compatibility of commitments to both scientific and political activity. I have focused my attention on Weber's work because I believe that he came close to answering these questions. Of course, I have had to complement his analysis with my own, and I have not hesitated to conclude that he was mistaken when neither his words nor the context in which they were written allow him to be interpreted as presenting a defensible argument. Yet I usually have been able to interpret him in such a manner as to remove apparent inconsistency, perhaps seeing aspects or possibilities in his work not previously recognized.

Accepting that individual experience and psychological need are logically irrelevant to the assessment of theoretical validity, I deny the inverse. I am not arguing that Weber's thought can be explained by reference to his personal problems but that these problems were to some extent the result of his thought. For if personal identity is a source of ultimate commitment and is itself derived from beliefs about the nature of social reality and personal capabilities, then changes in such beliefs can potentially undermine the plausibility of one's self-conception. Given the importance of a secure identity for self-control, it is possible that the origin of some mental infirmity may be found in thought and perception rather than the reverse. In Weber's case, I believe that the initial crisis was brought on by his recognition that he was living a life incommensurate with his self-conception. Finding it impossible to change his course toward what he believed to be the suitable direction, his condition rapidly deteriorated. Partial recovery was the result of his acceptance of a paradoxical identity—a scientist of political life. Complete recovery came at the end of his life, when he was able to escape the paradox through self-deception. Just as knowledge shattered his mental stability, delusion restored it.[19]

Theoretically, the biographical dimensions of this study can contribute no more than the clarification of Weber's intentions. Yet it serves a very important purpose. Weber's experience illustrates, even dramatizes, the indispensability of personal commitment in social scientific inquiry, as well as its profound nature. For this commitment is far more than a mere willingness to abide by the rules that make empirical tests and intersubjectivity possible. It is an integral, indeed dominant, aspect of one's being.[20] It cannot be the result of calculation and choice, nor even of a sincere wish to better one's fellows through knowledge. Paradoxically, social scientific objectivity is the result of a thoroughly subjective orientation. In an age that has accepted a sharp distinction between the objective and the subjective, the personal meaning of most things tends to be obscure. The biographical dimension is intended to emphasize the personal meaning of social science.

CHAPTER TWO

Max Weber Becomes a Scientist

In 1898 Max Weber was a very successful young man. Appointed professor of political economy at the University of Freiburg, in 1894, he had accepted a similar position from the prestigious university at Heidelberg in 1896, when he was thirty-one years old. Although it is unusual in our educational system for full professors to be in their early thirties, the German university professor at the turn of the century enjoyed considerably more status than the twentieth century American counterpart.[1] Most academics at the time never attained a university professorship, and those who did typically were required to wait years. Yet Weber received his Freiburg appointment less than two years after he began teaching.

The rapid advancement of Weber's academic career was more than matched by its sudden demise. As described by his wife, Weber suffered a collapse after experiencing exhaustion and anxiety in preceding weeks.

> When during Whitsunweek, he wished to avoid the usually welcome visit of a friend and went walking in the Odenwald by himself, the glory of May was veiled by a dark curtain. He was extremely exhausted, his solid frame was weakened, and his tears welled up. Weber felt himself at a turning point.[2]

He certainly was at a turning point. After several unsuccessful attempts to resume his teaching duties, he eventually resigned from his position and did not accept another until twenty years later. In a sense, however, this was the beginning of a new career, for it marked the beginning of his truly great theoretical work. All of the influential studies for which Weber is famous were formulated after his academic career was destroyed.

Neither the breakdown nor the new phase of scholarship occurred in an instant. This chapter is primarily concerned with the development of some of the fundamental tensions within Weber's personality that eventually led to his collapse. As such, its subject matter is almost entirely biographical. Its purpose is to demonstrate that Weber became a social scientist, both by profession and in terms of habitual inclination, in spite of his conscious intention to pursue a life of action rather than scholarship. Consequently, this chapter is important in providing the context for the theoretical interpretation and argument of subsequent chapters.

The only detailed analysis of Weber's mental problems applies Freudian assumptions rather rigidly, attributing his neurosis to repressed hatred of his father and the unconscious guilt engendered by this hatred. According to orthodox Freudian doctrine, all men have such feelings toward their fathers because all men suffer from an oedipal complex. But most are able to cope with it in one way or another. Weber could not cope with it, so the argument goes, because the guilt feelings generated in him were especially severe because of the circumstances of his father's death. On the surface, these circumstances appear tailor made for orthodox Freudian analysis. The son, after a long period of financial dependence upon the father, during which he must suppress his rage over the manner in which the father treats the mother, at last achieves worldly success and independence. The mother wishes to visit the son periodically in order to escape her domineering husband, who, in turn, cannot understand his wife's behavior. The son vents his long pent-up rage at the father and orders him out of the son's house so that the mother can enjoy the son's company. The father dies shortly after. The son has a severe case of guilt, exacerbated by a stringent superego instilled at an early age by an exceedingly moralistic mother.[3]

This sequence of events fits a mechanical version of the Freudian perspective on mental pathology very well. The main problem is that this sort of Freudian perspective does not fit the actual facts, or at least the evidence, very well. For instance, there is absolutely no evidence that Weber felt responsible for his father's death, either at the time or over twenty years later—a very thorough job of repression.[4] Also, there is evidence that Weber was suffering some anxiety even during his years as a professor, before his break with his father, the years in which he should have been secure in his newly acquired independence.[5] The psychic tensions probably existed before the incident with his father, and this suggests that the incident itself was as much a symptom as a cause.[6]

Although causes are rather difficult to isolate in these matters, it will be argued here that one factor that can be considered a "sufficient" cause of Weber's breakdown is his success in academics. To put this success in its proper perspective, it must be understood that Weber did not plan on an academic career, and he certainly did not intend to become a scholar: "If I have achieved success in my academic career to which I did not aspire or lay claim, this leaves me rather cold and in particular gives me no answer to the question as to whether this career is the activity that is suitable for me."[7] Actually, in his student years Weber had already decided that a life of practical activity, rather than reflection, was most suitable for him, and for this reason he had aimed at becoming a lawyer. The law, he believed, was the field in which he could best launch himself upon a course that would lead to a career devoted to public affairs,[8] and during his brief exposure to the practice of law he found it exciting and rewarding.[9] As Weber put it, he possessed "an extraordinary yearning for a practical field of activity."[10] Weber's disinclination toward scholarship was based on more than an aversion to academic life style. He seriously doubted its practical importance to human affairs because he believed that theoretical considerations had limited impact on behavior and little meaning for the individual.[11]

Why, then, did Weber finally commit himself to pursuing an academic career? Part of the answer probably lies in the encouragement of his mentors, who could not have failed to recognize the tremendous potential of their student.[12] More important, however, was Weber's desire to achieve financial independence and to get started on a career of any kind. The reason that financial independence was so important to Weber will be discussed in following pages. The important point in the present context is that an academic career "opened up" to Weber quite by accident, and he merely took advantage of his opportunities after assuring himself that they would not preclude a life devoted to public service.[13]

In fact, these opportunities derived largely from his political activity. Weber made his early reputation as a scholar through an analysis of a political issue presented to a largely political organization. Weber joined the *Verein fur Sozialpolitik* because he sensed a political affinity with its younger members, most of whom were academics.[14] Apparently, he did not see the organization's primary purpose as the advancement of scholarship, and there is no reason why he should have. The *Verein* was founded in the 1870s by "reform minded men," many of whom were academics, who regarded the organization "part professional association, part pressure group."[15] Its purpose was to conduct studies on matters of public policy and to debate proposals for the resolution of public problems. In the first decade of its existence, it would adopt policy stands by majority vote. Its explicitly political nature, combined with its reformist nature and large propor-

tion of academics, led to the characterization of its members as
"*Katheder Sozialisten*" (socialists of the chair). In the 1880s,
however, internal divisions began to threaten the existence of the
organization, and its survival depended on abandoning the practice of adopting policy stands.[16] Not surprisingly, the organization's membership came to be even more dominated by academics, and the association became for all practical purposes the
professional organization for social science in Germany. But it
remained highly political, representing a reform orientation
clearly manifested in the topics chosen for investigation. The
leaders of the *Verein* supported studies of these topics, arranged
for their publication, and appointed "reporters" to interpret the
findings at the meetings of the *Verein*. "Success at these meetings
was of some importance in a man's academic career."[17]

Weber was among a number of reporters selected to present
the findings of a survey sponsored by the *Verein* on the condition
of agrarian workers in the eastern part of Germany. This was a
politically explosive issue because of its widely recognized implications for the financial interests of the large landowners of the
area, the "*Junkers*," who were the politically dominant class in
Germany.[18] Weber demonstrated that existing policies and social
conditions were driving German peasants and small farmers
from the area and that their place was being taken by low paid
Polish workers. This situation was economically advantageous to
the Junkers, but Weber argued that it weakened the nation both
internationally and economically. In effect, Weber argued that
the nation was subsidizing an anachronistic class for the sole purpose of maintaining that class in power. His analysis was, of
course, unpopular with the political right, and he became a life
long enemy of agrarian conservatism. But his unpopularity with
the right did not endear him to the left, elements of which reportedly attacked him fiercely from the floor of the meeting and
eventually left in protest;[19] their hostility was probably provoked

by his recommendation that the government support through economic measures the development of a class of small farmers in the area in order to strengthen the eastern border against possible Russian influence. Nevertheless, the vast majority of the *Verein,* including its leaders, were quite impressed with Weber, and he became, in effect, the *Verein's* expert on this important subject.[20] The important point for the present is that Weber's scholarly reputation was established by what was, quite consciously, a politically motivated study of a policy issue. Only the nature of the *Verein,* part political and part professional, enabled Weber to achieve fame as a scholar by an analysis, brilliant as it was, of a political issue.

Despite his sudden fame, Weber might still have avoided an academic position if he had not been offered a professorship in the field of political economy. As his wife tells it, the new subject appealed to him because "it was on the borderline of a number of scholarly fields" and "it was more fruitful for a political and sociological orientation than the more formal problems of legal thought."[21] In fact, Weber indicated at one point that he considered giving up scholarship because of his skepticism of the practical utility of jurisprudence, only to have his interest rekindled through his encounters with the political economists of the *Verein.*[22] Political economy was a relatively new and largely undefined field. The seminars in the subject, which were offered at most German universities, were concerned with issues of contemporary policy, especially their administrative and financial ramifications. Other than this, no real consensus existed on the purpose of the field, and each of the approximately sixty academic political economists was free to define the subject for himself. Given the lack of a tradition of social science, it is not surprising that "only a fraction of them" took "an active interest in social research."[23]

Shortly after he undertook his duties at Freiburg, Weber gave the customary inaugural address, in which he explained in some detail his conception of the subject. Unlike many of his colleagues, Weber was interested in social research but certainly not for its own sake: "The science of political economy is a political science. It is a servant of politics: not that of the daily politics of the moment which prevails for powerholders and classes, but of the consistent power interests of the nation."[24] Political economy, as defined by Weber, was the *application* of scholarship to an overriding political end. His acceptance of an academic career need not preclude an active, practical life devoted to public affairs. Weber established his reputation as a political economist while engaged in what he considered to be political activity, and it was only natural for him to conclude that political economy is a form of political activity, especially since the *Verein* was tacitly based upon this assumption and its leaders were all political economists.[25] Of course, an academic career also involves teaching, but Weber apparently enjoyed this aspect of his duties and, according to his wife, was quite good at it.[26] According to his own testimony, he found teaching more satisfying than scholarship because the former was a practical activity[27]—an activity closely associated in Weber's field with political preaching.[28]

Weber did not, however, confine his practical activity to the classroom. During his years as professor he was actively engaged in politics in a number of capacities. His inaugural address at Freiburg was a case in point.[29] In this speech Weber did more than outline his conception of the field; he also argued that questions of public policy should be considered from a nationalistic rather than an altruistic viewpoint.[30] This argument had a lasting impact on Friedrich Naumann, who was a publicist, a political activist, a leader of the Evangelical Social Union, and Weber's major link to the world of politics for most of their lives. The Evangelical Social Union was a reform oriented Protestant group that was intended in general to make Christianity socially meaningful and in particular to offer the working class an alternative to Marxism. Weber associated himself with this group largely for political reasons and perhaps also to please his mother, who was an active supporter.[31] Influenced by Weber's argument for the primacy of national interests, Naumann changed his approach and began demanding social reform for the sake of national unity rather than Christian charity, even going so far as to found a National Socialist Association, which he intended to become a political party.[32] Naumann generated many opportunities for Weber to give his views on the political issues of the day, which Weber supplemented by a number of political speeches to various other groups with which he was affiliated. He also published several polemical newspaper essays,[33] one of which, an attack upon a new law concerning the stock exchange, led to his appointment in 1896 to a legislative committee investigating the impact of the law. He enjoyed this experience immensely.[34] In general, the evidence indicates that Weber was succeeding in living a life devoted to public affairs, and in early 1897, after one of his political speeches, he was even invited to run for a legislative seat.

That year, however, saw a significant decline in Weber's political activity. He was not reappointed to the stock exchange committee,[35] and he was forced to decline to run for office because he accepted a very attractive professorship at Heidelberg. A limitation upon his political activity might have been a condition of that appointment; in any case, Weber recognized that the move to Heidelberg meant the end of his ability to play an active political role.

> I myself scarcely know whether I should hope for the offer. Mainly because I would like to put off for a number of years the decision with which I would be faced: to remain here [in Freiburg] and further involve myself in politics so far as the opportunities and inducements present themselves, or to accept a greater position which naturally would entail the obligation to give up all other activity. This limita-

tion I myself believe would be obviously necessary because of the greater duties. I know very well that if the choice were put before me right now, when politics, including the hopeless project of Naumann's, offers no real prospects for me, that I would unconditionally choose the increased academic activity. But I do not know if I would not regret this in the future, and then it would be too late.[36]

As will be seen in the next chapter, Weber did regret his decision, and by then it was too late, not in the sense that he meant—to be stranded in an academic career—but in the sense that it became impossible to pretend that he was something that he was not.

To this point the discussion has been concerned with Weber's career goals and how he tried to achieve them. We turn now to what in later years Weber referred to as the "inner calling." We have already seen that Weber believed his "inner calling" was to a practical, political life and that he did his best to heed this call. But his best wasn't really adequate, and Weber's behavior often contradicted his explicit goal. For instance, Weber knew that at Heidelberg he would have to limit his political activity, but his wife asserts that one of the reasons he decided upon the move was that "there he would feel less out of touch politically than in Freiburg."[37] Why did he accept a position that he knew would preclude the active political life that was so important to him? The reason he gave, and no doubt believed, was that the configuration of political parties offered little hope of realization for his political goals, and consequently, his activity would be futile. However, by Weber's own analysis of the requirements of effective political action, which demands the acceptance of both struggle and compromise, this is a very unpolitical excuse for his withdrawal from politics. But even more paradoxical is the fact that at the very moment Weber was lecturing the first gathering of Naumann's party on these requirements of politics, he was violating them himself. While events proved that Weber was correct in his prediction of a dismal future for Naumann's National Socialist Party, it was politically naive of him to lecture them on their political naivete: what better way to isolate oneself and minimize one's credibility with those he wishes to influence?[38]

Although a brilliant political analyst, Weber simply was not a politician. It is true that his "scientific activity was always a counterpart to his practical political concerns,"[39] but it is just as true that his practical concerns always became scholarly theses. Even in his youth Weber habitually related particular political issues to a larger context, attempting to determine wider implications unforeseen by the political combatants.[40] Mommsen correctly asserts that Weber, despite his occasional intemperance, was not a "fighter." He saw too much, was too much a qualifier, to commit himself to a specific, narrow task.[41] Conversely, when he was convinced that he was correct, he was too impatient with the folly of others to compromise, to tolerate their ignorance by adapting himself to it. Weber, despite his low opinion of scholarship for its own sake and despite his clear intention to avoid a career based on scholarship, was a scholar.[42]

How Weber became a scholar is the subject to which we now turn. Anticipating the pages to follow, we may say that Weber became a social scientist—the type of scholar he was—in order to protect himself from his mother. Despite the tendency to transform psychoanalytical analysis of the relation of boys to their fathers into dogma, the dominant influence on Weber's personal development was his mother, not his father. The greatest task facing a young human being is the formulation of an independent personal identity, and Weber's mother was a serious threat to his. Max Weber, Sr., on the other hand, was not much of a psychological threat to anyone, in spite of his propensity to order people about. It has even been suggested that the elder Weber felt threatened by his wife's stronger personality and that his aggressive behavior was a defensive response to this threat.[43]

Helene Weber's relationship with her husband was in accord

with a family pattern. Her mother before and at least one of her sisters (Ida Baumgarten) had similar problems with their husbands. Although these women were deeply religious, all three married men who did not share their spiritual interests. Reflecting back near the end of her life, Helene describes the process by which she and her husband became estranged:

> I had to fight for my belief in God and my interest in all religious development, an interest he did not share. In those days I regarded it as being considerate, as God-ordained resignation, that I bore my sorrow alone and did not force him against his nature to go along— and yet it was cowardice, fear of being misunderstood in these most difficult and most private concerns. I had no idea that the consequence would be our growing apart inwardly.[44]

There can be little doubt that Helene Weber felt herself morally superior to her husband, especially given that the lasting rift between them was provoked by the death of their fifth child, a four year old daughter. It seems that Max, Sr., wanted to get on with the business and pleasures of life after a respectable period of mourning, while Helene felt the need to bear her grief a good deal longer.[45] Even in different circumstances, however, it just was not her nature to "live and let live," particularly with moral and religious matters. Her sense of moral superiority was probably disguised by a stoic acquiescence to duty. Her husband probably dimly recognized, or felt, her true feelings and was thereby placed on the defensive in dealing with her. His defense seems to have consisted of the adoption of the attitude that his wife was a hopelessly impractical visionary, from which it naturally followed that it was up to him to take charge and manage the practical aspects of life by himself. Unfortunately, this defense rendered him something of a tyrant.[46]

What Helene could not impress upon her husband, she was obviously determined to impress upon her children. While any analysis of the estrangement between husband and wife must remain highly conjectual because of the dearth of information, there can be no doubt of Helene's deep concern for the spiritual development of her offspring.[47] In order to understand the relationship between Weber and his mother, it must be understood that she would have been satisfied only by assurances that her children's inner convictions measured up to her stringent standards of piety and charity; she was not to be satisfied by mere external compliance.[48] At one point she even arranged with her nephew, Fritz Baumgarten, who had befriended the younger Weber, to surreptitiously read her son's letters in order to ascertain his innermost thoughts.[49]

Although Helene Weber followed the same pattern with all her children, there are reasons to believe that Max received more attention than his siblings. First, he was the eldest and, therefore, an only child during his early years. Second, the Webers' next child died in infancy, perhaps increasing Helene's devotion to her first. Third, at the age of four or five Weber became very ill with "unilateral meningitis," and he required a great deal of care from his mother.[50] Finally, and most important, Weber became a "problem child." He withdrew from his mother at an early age and to a much greater extent than his brothers did. While she attempted to mold his innermost being, he presented to her an uncommunicative facade of acquiescence. He did not argue with her, complain to her, or confide in her. Her efforts, it seems, created a self-defeating cycle: the more she persisted, the more he withdrew; the more he withdrew, the more she persisted.[51]

Most children in modern society go through a process of withdrawal from their parents. The conditions of life in these societies, in which the parents usually cannot assure the place or future of their offspring, demand a degree of personal autonomy from the family.[52] This autonomy is usually achieved in a long and often painful period, when the child increasingly identifies with larger social units and activities, such as occupations.[53] This withdrawal can occur from a number of different ways. Perhaps the most typical path is through identification with peer groups in early adolescence. The peer groups then exercise an independent influence upon the values and aspirations of their members, reinforcing or countering those encouraged in the family.[54] Family influence does not end but exists increasingly as a residue, so to speak, gradually declining. Parents may still offer role models, but these are likely to become defined in social terms, such as occupation or creed, rather than in family terms.[55]

Weber's withdrawal from his mother was unusual in two respects. The first is that it began long before his adolescence.[56] His mother's constant concern that he live up to her exacting standards of devotion and selflessness, standards that no child is likely to meet, could only have caused her son to become self-conscious before he had formulated a clear self-identity.[57] Because he had no clear self-identity, rebellion was impossible; he was simply too vulnerable. Weber could have surrendered to his mother and tried his best to be what she wanted him to be. The cost of this response would have been the suppression of the hostility that her domination would inevitably have evoked, as well as serious feelings of inferiority caused by continually failing an impossible task.[58] The only other alternative would seem to be a withdrawal from his mother, in a sort of "holding action," until he could find some refuge by identifying himself with some other code of life. As we have seen, Weber followed this latter path.[59]

If he had been older, perhaps Weber could have sought refuge by identification with a peer group. This, however, was not possible for him, and the lack of peer group identification is the second aspect in which Weber's withdrawal is atypical. Middle-class families were more extended in nineteenth century German society than in our own, and Weber did not have access to potential peer groups when he needed them. Almost all social interaction for Weber during his childhood occurred with relatives.[60] Even as Weber grew older he avoided social activities with his peers,[61] and he certainly did not identify with them.[62] This later aversion to his peers was an indirect consequence of the means he substituted for peer groups in forming an identity.

Pressed by his mother, it was only natural for Weber to seek an identity in whatever alternative existed. The only accessible alternative for the young Weber was that represented by his father. Being unable to identify with a peer group, Weber achieved a self-identity by identifying with his father's world. The occupation of Max Weber, Sr., was a blend of public service and politics, in that he was very active in the National Liberal Party, even holding office, but he also held several high administrative positions throughout his life. According to his wife, Weber and his brothers considered it a privilege "to pass out cigars at dinners for the deputies," and he and his brother Alfred "became familiar with political problems at an early age and received a graphic presentation of the special character of political life."[63] Although Weber was withdrawing from his mother, it would be a mistake to believe that he was moving closer to his father.[64] Max Weber, Sr., was apparently largely inaccessible to his family except for occasional trips with his sons, perhaps partly to atone for his neglect of them otherwise.[65] Not only was he rarely at home, but his brusque, unreflective, and extroverted manner was hardly compatible with the reserved and sometimes moody bearing of his eldest son.[66] At any rate, there is absolutely no evidence that the youthful Weber lionized his father.

It was his father's world, the world of politics, rather than his father that provided Weber with a source of identity. Politics for him was a male's world, alien to his mother's code of life, where great and important things were accomplished by heroic deeds. Weber's internalization of this code of life is reflected in a number of his adolescent letters. For instance, he explained to his older cousin that he did not care as much for Virgil as Homer because the "purpose of a heroic epic" is "the utmost glorification of the hero," and Virgil just did not accomplish this to the satisfaction of the young Weber.[67] But he was ready to place "Ossian" above Homer because he preferred the "sentimental, misty, stormy outlook of the aged poet of the northland" to the "naive, sunny, calm writing of the old Southerner."[68] He disliked Cicero because he considered him to be a poor politician, "without appropriate resolve and energy, without skill, and without the ability to wait for the right moment."[69]

Most adolescent boys are susceptible to the lure of hero worship. Most try either to be their heroes in play or, at an older age, to imitate them through role taking.[70] There is no evidence that Weber imitated a particular political figure, or even that he inordinately esteemed any. Without a peer group to appreciate the role and validate, by recognition, the identity, the satisfaction gained by hero worship and imitation would be minimal. More important, it can be assumed that his mother would have quickly made the boy conscious of the fact of imitation, thereby deflating any youthful pretensions. In other words, these typical means by which youths experiment with new identities were not available to Weber because they offered him no protection from his mother.

Through single-minded preparation through study, Weber affirmed the reality of his identity as a politician. Study served the same psychological function as play or imitation; both are modes of vicarious participation that can give credibility to a new identity. Weber's mode had the great advantage for him of being immune from his mother's criticism. In fact, he could proudly present his youthful studies of political history to his parents with the safe expectation that they would bring praise.[71] Another advantage of this mode of affirming his identity was that it provided Weber with a weapon by which he could force his mother to keep her distance.[72] She could not become intimate, get close to his real feelings and aspirations, if she could not speak in an informed manner about his acknowledged interests. The effectiveness with which Weber used this weapon can be seen in the large number of his mother's complaints.[73]

As often happens, especially with interpersonal relations, the solution to one set of problems creates others. Weber's aversion to social activities with his peers has already been mentioned. During his youth and early manhood he did not form close friendships,[74] and he appears to have been frightened of young ladies.[75] Part of the problem may simply have been that Weber's single-minded concern with the adult world of public affairs put him at a disadvantage in attracting attention from his peers. There is some evidence that his vast store of historical knowledge was a bit frightening to some his age,[76] and others may have been more amused than impressed. But the problem was actually more serious. As Weber himself recognized, he found it extremely difficult to reveal his feelings to anyone, either within or outside the family.[77] Since his mother's efforts were constant, he could never neglect his defenses. As far as his peers were concerned, their youthful distractions probably threatened to undermine the commitment upon which he had based his identity, and he therefore avoided contact with them. As he grew older, however, Weber felt himself isolated, not only from those his own age but from life itself. He described this feeling with remarkable frankness in a letter to his cousin:

> I think you recognized from my earlier letters that in these last years, whose disagreeable barrenness I remember with horror, I had abandoned myself to such utter resignation, a resignation that was not without a certain bitterness, that, apart from a certain melancholy glow which some rich and beautiful memories of earlier years brought into my bookish existence, I was completely absorbed in what I would call the automatic continuation of my obligatory professional work—very much to my mother's chagrin, as you can imagine.[78]

Because of this manner in which he was forced to affirm his identity, this sense of "resignation," a feeling that his activity was incomplete or somehow ineffective, was unavoidable. He was preparing for a life that would be lived in some indeterminate future; he was not living for the present. But despite what the future holds, one exists in the present. Weber wanted to be a politician, but he realized that he was only preparing for a political life, not living one. This rather obvious observation is extremely important for the thesis of this chapter. One cannot *be* a potential politician. One can be a "political trainee" or an "apprentice politician," but one cannot *be* a potential anything. Many psychologists have seen the contribution that a secure self-identity makes to the stability of the personality, and many have seen the origin of much mental pathology in problems encountered in either formulating or maintaining an identity.[79] Weber could not have defined himself as a politician unless he was able and willing to detach himself from reality.[80] None of the evidence indicates that this was the case. Consequently, Weber must have seen himself as "one who prepared for politics." "Resignation" necessarily entails recognition.

What does "preparing for politics" mean? What activity does it require? Weber certainly did not confine his reading to practical subjects that would be of obvious use in his prospective life. Nor did he attempt to develop skills that might be required of an actual politician. Weber's commitment to politics was singularly cerebral. He typically sought to determine the origins of political problems rather than possible solutions or, more significantly, ways to implement solutions. While believing that he was preparing for an active, practical life, he was actually developing the style and habits of a scholar. He was becoming, in spite of his intentions, a social scientist.

To repeat, resignation necessarily entails recognition. Weber did not believe that he was a politician. He believed that he was in the process of becoming one. But there are no guidelines, no clearly recognized steps by which one is initiated into the world of politics. Nor is it likely that Weber consciously formulated in his own mind exactly what kind of politician he wanted to be, let alone how he was going to transform himself to this ideal. People are rarely completely conscious of their self-identities, and the term *self-image* is probably just as appropriate in most cases. During early adolescence, dreams of future conquests and accomplishments are probably sufficient to maintain one's belief in one's self. But as a youth grows older and the future draws near, something more tangible than dreams is required. The individual must begin making commitments, must actually pattern behavior in accordance with a self-image. Consequently, the self-image must become more specific. Weber appears to have specified his self-image in the usual, only partially conscious way—he appears to have identified with a role model.[81] For this he turned to his uncle, Hermann Baumgarten.

An active politician until Bismarck's deft maneuvers deprived him of prospects, Baumgarten was an academic historian and political critic during his later years. He was obviously a frustrated man, who could accept his forced retirement from politics only by becoming extremely pessimistic about Germany's political future. Although Weber could not share this pessimism,[82] Baumgarten's influence on Weber's political thinking is beyond question.[83] Moreover, both evidence and logic point to the conclusion that this older man who had befriended the young Weber, treated him as an equal, and shared his interests had a tremendous personal impact as well. If so, then Weber identified with a rather ambiguous role model: an unwilling scholar whose real interests were in politics.[84] Nothing could have been more conducive for the unconscious equating of "becoming a politician" with "being a scholar of social things." That such an equation is absurd will be demonstrated in the next three chapters. But as long as Weber was unaware of its absurdity, and probably only vaguely conscious of it anyway, the formula provided him with a secure self-identity during the long years of "resignation."

Two other members of the Baumgarten family indirectly helped Weber to resolve his emotional problems partially. During Weber's obligatory military service, he was stationed at Straus-bourg, the home of the Baumgartens. He was a frequent visitor and involved himself extensively in the family's life. His Aunt Ida possessed the same orientation toward life as his mother, only more forcefully and assertively.[85] Her forceful advocacy allowed Weber to explain explicitly to his mother that her way was not his own.[86] With Weber's achievement of a secure self-identity, his mother was no longer a threat. He could accept her for what she was, even attempting to humor her by sharing some of her in-terests.[87] Now, using his aunt as a point of reference, he could implicitly, and probably unconsciously, invite his mother to ac-cept him for what he was. Fortunately, she was sufficiently satis-fied with what he had become to do this, even soliciting his ad-vice on the development of his younger brothers. Recognizing that she and her son proceeded "from very different points of view," she was thankful that she could, at long last, really talk to him.[88]

More difficult to surmount than his estrangement from his mother was his sense of isolation. He did join a fraternity during his second year as a university student (after his cousin Otto Baumgarten was no longer in attendance), but fraternity life at that time was rigorously formal, not designed to satisfy a need for intimacy.[89] A more effective expedient was his liaison with yet another member of the Baumgarten family. He became engaged to his cousin Emmy. They never married, both because she be-came increasingly subject to nervous disorders and because he found someone more appealing. For a number of years, however, he wrote her letters expressing his feelings on a wide range of subjects. While never charged with emotion, these letters were affectionate and frank, indicating that Weber was trying his best to be intimate. The sense of resignation remained, but Emmy at least partially satisfied his need to feel close to someone.

In general, it appears that the fundamental difficulties of Weber's youth had been weathered. He emerged from his adolescence with a secure self-identity, sufficiently congruent with his needs to allow for personal stability. This is not to say that Weber was happy. He was probably miserable. He was still plagued with that sense of "resignation," which, as previously discussed, was a necessary consequence of his identity. More pressing, however, were the difficult conditions of living at home. For six years he prepared for a law career and continued his studies while living in his parents' house, financially dependent upon his father. Young men are typically dissatisfied with such arrangements, but it was particularly tormenting to Weber because the rift between his parents was growing deeper. The awkward situation was worsened by Helene's practice of complaining to her son about his father's insensitivity and overbearingness.[90] The dutiful son, of course, was required to console his distraught mother.

It would be a mistake, however, to conclude that Weber "accumulated a vast but inexpressible loathing for" his father "and a deep sympathy for his maltreated mother."[91] Weber was certainly sympathetic toward his mother, and insofar as he found it necessary to get involved, he stood with her.[92] But his partisanship was highly ambiguous. As shown by the suggestions he offered her concerning the upbringing of his brothers, he did not forget the difficulties she caused him.[93] More to the point, he placed some of the responsibility for his father's behavior on his mother. By her failure to assert her rights forcefully, Weber believed that his mother was encouraging his father at the very moment she was putting him in the wrong by "sacrificing" herself. As

Marianne Weber later pointed out, the sacrifice was accompanied by "secret rebellion" and only aggravated the situation.[94]

Rather than accumulating a tremendous rage at his father, Weber became increasingly impatient for his "real" life to begin. He did not want to become involved in the irresolvable dispute between his parents. He wanted out, and he knew that the only way out was a home and income of his own.[95] These became his main goals. He achieved them both at approximately the same time. First was his marriage to Marianne Schnitger, a distant cousin, closely followed by the offer from Freiburg. From Weber's perspective, these developments marked the beginning of the life for which he had been preparing himself. His belief that he had been delivered from his resignation is clearly reflected in his letter of proposal to Marianne:

> The tidal wave of passion runs high, and it is dark around us—come with me, my high minded comrade, out of the quiet harbor of resignation, out onto the high seas, where men grow in the struggle of souls and the transitory is sloughed off. *But bear in mind:* in the head and heart of the mariner there must be clarity when all is surging underneath him. We must not tolerate any fanciful surrender to unclear and mystical moods in our souls. For when feeling rises high, you must control it to be able to steer yourself with sobriety.[96]

This passage is also noteworthy in that the three elements that Weber later identified with a genuine "calling" for politics (passion, responsibility, and objectivity) are all present. His resignation, caused by his life of preparation, he now believed to be finished. He was embarking, he believed, upon a life of practical politics, and his years at Freiburg fully confirmed this belief.

On the surface it appears that events had turned out very well for Weber. He had established a home of his own, achieved success in a profession, and, most important, possessed the opportunity to be what he always wanted to be: a man of politics. But his success in solving his early problems and escaping his life of resignation created a much more serious difficulty. Painful as it was, his life of resignation had its advantages. It gave him meaning without requiring that he translate that meaning into action. Unpleasant as preparation for a future may be, it can provide one with a cheap identity—an identity that does not have to be purchased with real decisions and real risks. Weber's commitment to politics is beyond question. But people are a combination of what they want to be and what they must be. Mental stability is possible only if these two elements are compatible with one another, and mental health probably requires that they be reinforcing.[97] Weber became a scholar under the erroneous impression that the best way to prepare for a life of politics is to study politics. Perhaps Weber was not completely conscious of this belief, but as he himself pointed out, "An individual is apt to make a decision that may be decisive for his entire future intellectual course without having surveyed the question, to make a choice without even knowing that he is choosing."[98]

Yet nothing in Weber's early years appears to have foreordained his devastating collapse. Had he remained at Freiburg, helping Naumann with his quixotic projects and blaming the political climate for his inability to devote himself completely to politics, perhaps he could have continued indefinitely his life of "preparing for politics." Perhaps he could have eventually accommodated himself to the vicarious politics of his uncle, becoming an academic critic of the political scene. But at Heidelberg even this vicarious politics was severely restricted. It is my belief that Weber's move to Heidelberg made it increasingly difficult for him to pretend that he was engaged in meaningful political activity. He was eventually forced to admit to himself that he was a fraud, that he was not what he pretended to be. This recognition precipitated his initial breakdown. As his subsequent inability to extract himself from his "false life" became evident, he slipped deeper and deeper into the abyss. Partial recovery came only with his acceptance of himself as a scientist and the recognition of the inherent incompatibility between scientific and political activity.

In addition to the empirical assertions concerning Weber's particular case, this interpretation of his experience entails a number of general assumptions that I intend to demonstrate. Two of these, the logical incompatibility of scientific and political activity and the necessity of distinct personalities appropriate to each, will be the concern of a later chapter. The next chapter is devoted to an assumption crucial for all that follows. I believe that Weber came to consider his psychological dilemma to be primarily an intellectual problem. Moreover, I think he was correct. I will eventually demonstrate (although not in this chapter) that the logical difficulties of beliefs can have profoundly disturbing consequences for mental stability if the beliefs in question are incorporated into one's self-conception. Weber thought he could achieve a political life through a career in scholarship. He was wrong about this, as well as his own proclivities, and he paid the price.

According to the Freudian based analysis to which I have previously referred, Weber's breakdown was the result of the relationships he had established with his parents, combined with the guilt caused by the circumstances of his father's death. I have tried to show that this interpretation ignores some important facts and misconstrues the actual relationships between Weber and his parents.[99] It could be that his father's death hastened the breakdown in that it may have occasioned an increased degree of introspection or perhaps abruptly removed a scapegoat that Weber relied upon to vent his frustrations.[100] These frustrations, however, predated the altercation between father and son. Weber apparently suffered anxiety attacks long before this incident, which would indicate that his father's death may have exacerbated in some way the tensions that eventually became uncontrollable, but the tensions were already there.[101]

My interpretation of Weber's breakdown is at variance with much psychoanalytical theory in that it suggests that the immediate cause was an *increased* consciousness of an internal tension, and a logical tension at that. According to what might be called the orthodox psychoanalytical view, neurotic symptoms are caused either by the "damming up" of impulses that cannot be allowed conscious expression or "discharge" because they are prohibited by the superego or by the ego's efforts to avoid guilt feelings engendered by the superego as a consequence of satisfying such impulses.[102] In either case, the pathological consequences are attributed to the unconscious nature by which the impulses are vented or the guilt avoided. As the ego cannot consciously cope with these demands, the subject loses control over part of behavior normally directed by conscious intent. The subject invariably suffers from anxiety because this is the means by which the unconscious part of the ego is warned to activate its defense mechanisms.[103]

I do not wish to deny the tremendous contribution that Freud and his followers have made to the understanding of the processes by which unconscious mental phenomena affect behavior. However, the assumption that all neurotic behavior is the result of "damming up" of instinctual desires[104] is incompatible with the argument being presented here. That some, perhaps even most, cases of neurosis can be attributed to such a cause is almost indisputable. But there are a number of problems with any attempt to explain all behavior, pathological or otherwise, solely in terms of the reconciliation of instinctual drives with the necessity to adapt to the particular environment of the individual in question. The argument presented here precludes the acceptance of such a thoroughgoing "Freudianism,"[105] although it does not require the denial of the utility of psychoanalytical concepts in describing the repercussions of unconscious and unfulfilled wishes. Indeed, I have found the work of a number of modern psychoanalytically oriented scholars very helpful in formulating this argument.

According to my interpretation, Weber's breakdown was the result of frustrations caused by a logically contradictory self-identity rather than repressed guilt feelings occasioned by an unconscious superego. The only real incompatibility between this interpretation and orthodox psychoanalytical theory concerns the unconscious or conscious nature of that part of the mind called the superego. For Freud, the superego is formed by infantile identification with parents, which is the only way the young child can cope with the limitations imposed by the absolute, external authority of the adult. The child incorporates, or "introjects," the commanding figure into its own personality. Because the identification occurs at such an early age—before the child's ego has clearly developed—this part of the mind is unconscious, expressed as a number of rigid moral taboos.[106] But if the concept of the superego is expanded to include potentially conscious commitments to certain ideals that provide the individual with a sense of identity, or self-conception, then a third source of neurosis becomes possible.[107] A crisis of identity could result from commitment to mutually exclusive ideals, a crisis that would become more severe as the individual became more aware of the incompatibility. Recovery would be possible to the extent that the subject is able to reconcile the two commitments *rationally*, to repress one, or to free oneself from one. As we shall see, Weber at different times attempted all three alternatives, with varying degrees of success.

Symptoms of the initial stages of Weber's illness can certainly be accounted for in psychoanalytical terms, probably because Weber had repressed from consciousness any doubts he may have had about the real nature of his political life. When anxiety is caused by unconscious factors, the victim has no other recourse than to rely upon defense mechanisms that are at least partially unconscious, and therefore uncontrollable, in order to avoid anxiety.[108] When carried to such an extreme that they become exaggerated, uncontrolled behavior, these defensive mechanisms become the symptoms of a neurotic disorder. Weber's chronic habituation to work, which predated his breakdown by several years, is clearly such a defense mechanism. In Horney's words, one defense against anxiety is to "narcotize it," and one way of doing this it "to drown it in work."[109] Several years before his breakdown, Weber himself recognized the indispensable contribution of constant activity to his emotional stability,[110] although only in the midst of the breakdown could he see his need for work as a pathological symptom:

> Like John Gabriel Borkmann I could say "An icy hand has let go of me," for in the past years my sickly disposition expressed itself in a convulsive clinging to scholarly work as to a talisman, without my being able to say what it was supposed to ward off. As I look back upon it this is quite clear to me, and I know that sick or healthy, I shall never be like that again. The *need* to feel myself succumbing to the load of work is extinguished.[111]

That Weber's breakdown was the result of unconscious factors is also indicated by his obvious perplexity about his own condition.[112] Indeed, some of his symptoms followed the pattern of a "traumatic neurosis." As listed by Fenichel,[113] the first of these is the "blocking of or decrease in various ego functions." Actually, neurosis can broadly be defined as the inability of the ego to integrate and control behavior,[114] and there can be little doubt that this applies to Weber. He even lost the ability to read with ease, and he found it impossible to lecture.[115] There is ample evidence that Weber was also subject to the second symptom, "uncontrollable emotions, especially of anxiety and frequently of rage," as well as the third, severe disturbances of sleep.[116] That Weber's collapse was brought on by inner tensions rather than a traumatic event, however, is indicated by the fact that he also displayed symptoms following the pattern of an "anxiety neurosis." As is typical in such cases, Weber developed hysterical symptoms such as extreme exhaustion, back pain, and perhaps temporary partial paralysis.[117] As is also common with anxiety neurosis, his symptoms tended to be associated with specific situations; in other words, Weber developed phobias.[118] Initially, the inability to speak loudly or to read without severe repercussions was the most obvious of these phobias.

Anxiety neurosis is not distinguished from traumatic neurosis so much by its symptoms as by its causes. The sudden collapse of Weber's defenses against his inner conflict, giving the appearance of a traumatic neurosis, cannot be explained with the information available. We can conjecture, however, that Weber found it increasingly difficult to convince himself that he was playing a meaningful political role. The more successful he became and the longer he remained in his academic post, the more immeshed he became in the purely academic and scholarly expectations of his students and colleagues. Finally, he reached a point at which he realized, probably only dimly at first, that he was at a dead-end and he was not what he thought he was. As Erikson points out, identity must be relevant to commitment and activity if it is to survive:

> The ego gains strength *in practice*, and *in affectu* to the degree to which it can accept at the same time the total power of the drives and the total power of conscience—provided that it can nourish . . . that particular combination of work and love which alone verifies our identity and confirms it. . . . We are able to manage and creatively utilize our drives only to the extent to which we can acknowledge

their power by enjoyment, by awareness, and through the activity of work. If the ego is not able to accomplish these reconciliations, we may fall prey to what Freud called the "id."[119]

Weber's political life became, in effect, a fantasy, and he was too inquisitive, too honest with himself, to be able to repress the recognition of this fact completely. Given Weber's identification with politics, this recognition could have led only to what Erikson calls "metaphysical anxiety" or "ego-chill" and what Laing calls "ontological insecurity."[120] The loss of faith in one's own identity inevitably leads to the disorganization of the personality, which, in turn, results in "panic," when all "organized activity is lost" and "all thought is paralyzed."[121] Weber was reduced to a state in which he could do nothing other than sit quietly and pick at his fingernails.[122]

CHAPTER THREE

Commitment and Personality

M uch of the preceding analysis of the causes, or at least some of the causes, of Weber's illness is obviously conjectural. It is supported, however, by the road Weber took to partial recovery, as well as by the nature of his initial theoretical thinking after he was once again able to work. If recovery was to a great extent due to a recognition of the incompatibility of simultaneous commitments to both science and politics, one would expect to find significant evidence of this increasing awareness during the initial stages of recovery in both his behavior and his thought. This is indeed the case. As he began to improve, Weber increasingly shunned any form of direct political involvement. More important for my theoretical thesis, his new scholarly work explicitly explored the relationship between "personality" and commitment.

Weber began to regain control over himself during a transition period made possible by extensive travel. Even before his breakdown, he found that he could achieve temporary relief from anxiety by distracting himself through travel. Referring to a trip to Scotland and Ireland, taken after their first year in Freiburg, Marianne Weber asserted that "Weber relaxed completely only when he was traveling and looking."[1] A month after his father's funeral, apparently plagued with anxiety, he took a trip to Spain. As Weber explained, it was not a mere sight-seeing excursion:

> As long as work was out of the question for me, I could not have stood it in *one* place. . . . One can simply expose oneself to the whole profusion of the powerful impressions, so that one may, first of all, regain one's full nervous strength and then be capable of objectively processing everything that one has experienced.[2]

But it was only after his breakdown, when he was no longer able to narcotize his anxiety with work, that he relied extensively upon travel. In late 1900, the worst year of his illness, he went to Corsica. From there, in the spring of the next year, he traveled to Rome, then to southern Italy, then back to Rome. In the summer he went to Switzerland, then returned to Rome. In the spring of 1902 he moved to Florence. He finally returned that year to Heidelberg, much improved. But in December he felt much worse, complaining he stayed too long in Heidelberg,[3] and took a short trip to the Riviera. During the spring of 1903 he again visited Rome, adding Holland and Belgium in the summer. In August, 1904, he embarked on a trip to the United States, which lasted until winter. He enjoyed this long and arduous trip immensely, and both he and his wife testified to its therapeutic value.[4]

Travel was therapeutic because it distracted Weber from his understandable preoccupation with himself and perhaps gave him the distance from himself needed to place his personal problems in perspective. Travel might also have given him a clue as to his real nature, in that it may have presented him with observations that he found interesting to integrate into their historical context.[5] This dependence upon travel, like the need for constant work, was a response to anxiety, but the substitution of distraction for narcotization marked a qualitative change in the nature of Weber's illness. The need for work was obviously compulsive;

Weber had no control over it and could not explain it. On the other hand, he understood very well the distracting function of travel. Rather than compulsive, travel was something Weber consciously prescribed for himself. The change in defenses reflects a greater degree of control on Weber's part and indicates the beginning of his effort to understand and resolve his own psychic tension.

His hysterical symptoms soon disappeared. The latest evidence of debilitating physical infirmity is Weber's reference to back pains in April, 1902.[6] However, he was not entirely free from physical distress after this time. For over a decade Weber was subject to overexcitation, resulting in sleeplessness that in turn led to exhaustion. Indeed, exhaustion may have caused his back pains, indicating an even earlier demise of hysterical symptoms.[7] In any case, during this period he led a secluded life, carefully structured to avoid situations that might tax his nerves and destroy his sleep.[8] Since hysterical symptoms are often associated with phobias, it is not surprising that the latter ended with the former. Weber continued to avoid certain situations that caused him stress and anxiety, but his discomfort became associated with social context rather than with particular types of behavior. For instance, in the first years after his breakdown he found it impossible to address groups of any size that would require the raising of his voice, and he could read only with difficulty. The nature of the group or the material to be read apparently made little difference; it was the activity rather than the context that seems to have aroused anxiety and interfered with his self-control. In later years he avoided certain contexts, but his ability to engage in the previously impaired activities was restored.[9] This increased specificity is evidence of Weber's greater awareness of the sources of anxiety, since unconscious ego defenses are like conditioned reflexes, incapable of differentiation.[10]

More important for the substantiation of my interpretation is the change in the nature of the situation that Weber learned to avoid. It was obvious that his hysterical symptoms were activated by his academic duties, and despite his wife's reluctance, he became convinced at an early stage that he had to give up his position at Heidelberg. In fact, one receives the impression that Weber wanted out of academics altogether.[11] Yet even as his self-control was collapsing he affirmed his intention to engage in partisan political activity.[12] During these first years of illness, the only material he occasionally could read was the political news, and he apparently had his wife read this to him when he was unable.[13] He violently refused, on the other hand, to let his wife bring anything connected with academic affairs to his attention during this period.[14] In sum, the evidence strongly suggests that the period immediately after the first collapse, during which his condition became progressively worse, was associated with a conscious effort to disengage from academics in the hope of devoting himself to politics.

In late 1901, however, Weber's respective attitudes toward politics and scholarship changed completely. At that time he read his first book in years, a history of art, which was followed by a number of other volumes seemingly outside his field. Perhaps these first books served the same function as travel. By early 1902, he had developed a voracious appetite for scholarly reading and began regularly to visit a couple of colleagues attached to a historical institute in Rome.[15] In 1902 he both wrote a book review for a scholarly journal and agreed to write a methodological treatise.[16] In early 1903, during a conference of historians, he engaged in serious scholarly discussions (although he did not participate in the formal proceedings). At this conference he arranged for a non-teaching, honorary professorship at Heidelberg. He became extremely upset when, because of an apparent misunderstanding, it developed that he was not granted the formal faculty status required for voting at faculty meetings.[17]

Even more significant is that, at the same time as he was involving himself in scholarly activity, he was drawing away from active political involvement. Indeed, during the early stages of this transformation, even political discussion seems to have caused attacks of anxiety. For instance, a visit by Naumann was followed by several days of sleeplessness and depression.[18] Earlier, in late 1901, Marianne wanted to reply in print to an anti-feminist essay by a fellow named Gerlach. Initially Weber urged her on, but as his mother describes it, he hesitated when he thought he himself might become involved:

> [Marianne] wrote Naumann that she would send him a rejoining article as soon as possible. The post card had hardly been sent when Max became quite excited: she did not have permission to commit herself to a deadline, for the fear now seized him that, however much he would like to see how she formulates it politically, at any time he could be feeling poorly and then he would not be able even in the least degree to read, listen or speak. We told him that Naumann would accept an undetermined due date or even the omission of the political aspects, and the rest Marianne could write without him: "No, if something against Gerlach's view is to be written, it must be comprehensive, otherwise better nothing at all." Marianne said that she would write something and if he felt good enough he would look at it but otherwise she would put it aside. After a couple of days he himself again wished that she would write it. One afternoon we went to catch a breath of air and he decided not to go with us because of the long climb in the three story building; when we returned he had read the rejoinder and said that now I will dictate a few sentences to you, so you can approximately formulate the final section. After ten minutes of sharp, clear thoughts, which apparently came to him effortlessly, he suddenly said with obvious exhaustion and anxiety [Seelenangst]: the rest you must do. I can't do any more. Now my nerves are again so disturbed that regular sleep tonight will be impossible.[19]

Although he gradually regained the ability to discuss and write letters informally on political matters, Weber did not attend a political conference for a period of ten years. When he finally did go to such a meeting in 1908, it was only as a favor to a friend. Although he had resolved beforehand to remain silent, he became "infuriated" with some of the remarks and spoke twice with "controlled passion and force."[20] He did not consent to address a political gathering until after the outbreak of World War I. In 1903 he had the opportunity to edit a political journal with Naumann and his brother Alfred. He refused, but in the next year he committed himself to the collaboration with Jaffe and Sombart on the *Archiv fur Sozialwissenschaft und Sozialpolitik,* a decidedly scholarly enterprise.[21] Finally, it should be noted that the one academic activity that Weber considered practical activity, teaching, was the one aspect of academics in which he still could not engage. All of the evidence indicates that Weber's emergence from the depths of mental inanition was closely associated with a *conscious* rejection of political activity and with increased commitment to scholarship.

Conceivably, this reversal in Weber's willingness to engage in politics, and the inverse change in regard to scholarship, could be accounted for within orthodox psychoanalytical assumptions. Such an explanation would presume that change must have occurred in some symbolic meaning associating these activities with repressed impulses. Yet the facts of the matter are not auspicious for the success of any such explanation. First, as will be seen in later chapters, Weber did not change his affective orientation toward political affairs. He continued to be vitally interested in politics and to consider political life an admirable vocation for those capable of it. Second, his attitude toward scholarship, which did change, was not symbolic or affective, but rather conscious and cognitive. His analysis of the nature of social science is one of the reasons he is famous.

If, as I believe, Weber finally accepted himself as a social scientist and then came to realize through painful experience that political activity was incompatible with his new identity, it is to be expected that he would turn the full force of his formidable intellectual powers toward the understanding of what it was to be a social scientist, and why it precluded political activity. I believe that this is exactly what he did. Significantly, the first issues that engaged his attention after he was once again able to conduct research were difficult and abstract methodological questions that he undertook reluctantly, only because he felt he had to clarify what he was about.[22] In clarifying the nature of social science, however, Weber simultaneously raised the more general question of the nature of individual identity, of what it is to be a "person." The first two works completed after his period of inaction contain explicit discussions of the concept of "personality," even though one is an abstract methodological treatise and the other an essay on the cultural impact of Protestantism.[23] Accordingly, I will now turn away from biographical analysis in order to concentrate on the results of Weber's new theoretical orientation.

By "personality," Weber did not mean a set of habitual mannerisms, or an integrated pattern of behavioral propensities. He used the term to indicate the reason it makes sense to refer to a "person." Basically, Weber's concept of personality corresponds to the ideas of "personal identity" currently popular among many psychologists. He concluded that personality, in this sense, could exist only through commitment to ultimate values: " 'Personality' is a concept that finds its 'essence' in the consistency of its intimate relationship to certain ultimate 'values' and 'meanings' of life. These values and meanings have their effect by being forged into purpose and thereby translated into rational-teleological action."[24] In other words, one can be a person only if his or her behavior is rendered "responsible" by being in some way consistent with his or her ultimate values.[25]

On the surface, this assertion might strike one as arbitrary. In fact, it is logically entailed in Weber's conception of social reality, and Mommsen is quite correct in arguing that the concept of personality is the "keystone of Max Weber's thinking."[26] Weber was generally disinclined to bare his soul publicly or privately.[27] Consequently, his published work focuses upon issues that he thought relevant to potential readers. But whatever the explicit aims of his first historical and methodological studies after he was once again able to write, they resulted from his attempt to clarify the nature and evolution of the need for personal identity. This effort led to a thorough examination of the nature of social reality and the necessary assumptions of social science. The results of this examination must be understood before the implications of Weber's concept of personality can be grasped.

Given his psychological difficulties, we should not be surprised that Weber focused his attention upon the problem of "meaning," in the sense of significance or purpose. History is replete with tormented souls who have turned to contemplation or art to find something worth living for. But Weber was neither an artist nor a philosopher; he was a scientist. As such, he was more concerned with the consequence of meaning than with its discovery. Science, as conceived by Weber, must deal with observable events, and meaning can fall within its scope only insofar as it affects behavior.[28] For Weber, social science is concerned with the behavioral manifestations of meaning. It is, in short, the science of "action," of consciously motivated behavior.[29] Not all behavior, obviously, qualifies as action. Weber certainly did not suggest that unconscious, habitual, or externally conditioned behavior is either infrequent or irrelevant to social science. Its relevance, however, is determined by its effect on the progression and organization of action.[30]

Action is an undeniable fact of experience, science itself being one of its manifestations. Consequently, Weber was undeniably justified in choosing to study it scientifically. But he was not being arbitrary in positing action as the fundamental unit of analysis for social science. He argued that any social science that attempts to reduce action to mere behavior, explained by determinant laws rather than volition, must remain incomplete. To comprehend a course of action, one must, according to Weber, understand the particular goals or values that motivated the actors. All social causation is ultimately reducible to human meaning, to the varied and at times conflicting motives and decisions found among the individuals who constitute a society—regardless of the divergence of events from any or all of these motives or the extent to which the decisions have been conditioned by physiological, behavioral, or even ecological factors.[31]

These assertions are not due to Weber's acceptance of any notion of "free will." The assumption that motives cause behavior does not entail the further assumptions that one chooses one's values or that a particular individual could have resisted the force of a prospective goal.[32] Explanation by motive does entail, however, an idiographic, rather than a nomological, social science. Weber did not deny that determinant laws of human behavior might exist, but he argued that such laws could have only limited usefulness for social science because they could never give an adequate account of a specific act. Behavioral laws might enable one to isolate certain "semi-conscious dispositions" that influence action, but a general disposition can never explain why an act occurs. More precisely, the existence of a general disposition, which by definition lacks a specific objective, cannot explain a particular act, which by definition does have one or more specific objectives unique to the context in which the act takes place. Knowledge of an inherent, law-like disposition might be useful in explaining why an act was performed in a certain manner, but not why it occurred.[33]

Let me give a couple of examples to illustrate Weber's argument. In the nomological sciences, such as physics and chemistry, causation is based on universal determinant laws. *If* iron is exposed to moisture under certain conditions, *then* oxidation occurs. Of course, chemistry has advanced far beyond this point, and the statement could be expressed by similar "if-then" statements in terms of molecular theory. The important point is that both the laws and the conditions of their applicability can be expressed in universal terms. It makes no difference if one refers to a nail on the garage floor or the girders of a bridge; an explanation of rusting need not refer to a particular context, since all relevant factors (for example, density of the iron, extent of moisture, temperature) can be expressed in universal terms once they are isolated and measured.

Such is not the case with action. It is extremely difficult even to find if-then statements concerning action that would qualify as laws. Our effort to acquire food, for instance, is usually caused by actual or anticipated hunger pains, but the universal statement, "*If* suffering hunger pains, an individual will *then* attempt to acquire food," is clearly false. Persons known to be famished often refuse food for one reason or another. Weber's argument, however, does not rest upon the difficulty of formulating universal laws of motivation, but rather upon their inability to explain action really. Even if the universal statement concerning hunger were true, it could not account for action motivated by hunger, because action is necessarily contingent upon its particular context: The goal may in every case be food, but there is no universal definition of "food." To define it as "whatever is eaten to satisfy hunger" renders the universal statement tautological, while to define it as "whatever is considered eatable" merely underlines the inability of the general law to explain consciously motivated behavior. What is food to one individual may be disgusting to another, and their food-seeking action will differ accordingly.

If action is to be explained, it is necessary to "understand" the subjective meanings of the individuals and groups in question, for this is the basis of causation in social affairs. This empathizing understanding represents an advantage that the social scientist enjoys over the natural scientist, for the latter is forever limited to the discovery of formulas that merely express the constant conjunction of events.[34] The natural scientist may be able to explain some laws in terms of others but can never hope to understand why the "ultimate" laws hold. They simply express "the nature of things." On the other hand, social science cannot hope to attain the degree of unity, prediction, and demonstrability displayed in the more advanced nomological sciences. Not only does the concrete, idiographic focus of social science preclude the development of such highly abstract and unified theories as Newton's or Einstein's, but also the contingent relationship between value or desire and behavior dictates that explanations in terms of motive cannot be as conclusively confirmed as those explained by constant conjunction of events. The mere possession of the same motive does not always result in the same course of action.[35]

There are, of course, uniformities in social science, and Weber did not believe that social science was confined solely to the explanation of particular events. Indeed, he later distinguished between history and sociology on the basis of the latter's concern with "typical modes of action."[36] These uniformities in action, however, do not result from determinant laws of nature but from the mutual advantages of cooperative behavior and, especially, cultural values.[37] Weber argued that an understanding of a society's cultural values and ideas was an essential first step in the scientific investigation of any aspect of that society, and he frequently referred to the social sciences as "cultural science."[38] Even in modern societies, where much social action does not conform to cultural prescriptions, all persistent patterns of acting are in some way conditioned by cultural context. As Weber put it, even a thief orients his action on the basis of social expectations, "in that he acts surreptitiously." Although action might be determined by interest and values, which may or may not correspond to cultural ideals, cultural ideals cannot be ignored—by either the participants or the social scientist who is concerned with their behavior.[39]

Beyond the mere fact of social expectations and coercion, Weber assumes that human beings must have meaning in life, to some extent feel justified,[40] and culture is the main source of this justification: "The transcendental presupposition of every *cultural science* lies . . . in the fact that we are *cultural beings,* endowed with the capacity and the will to take a deliberate attitude towards the world and to lend it significance."[41] Most individuals derive their meaning from their cultural contexts, which have traditionally rested upon religious beliefs. Of course, only a select few attempt to mold their lives with a strict consistency upon a cultural ideal; the vast majority always makes concessions to the demands and pleasures of everyday life. Nonetheless, the ideal and its rationale provide meaning even to those who do not "live up" to it, and most organized religions even provide procedures by which the irresolute can easily atone for their earthly weaknesses. It is, however, those select few, the religious or ethical "*virtuosi*" demanding consistency between belief and life, who set or alter the standards that others follow with varying degrees of fidelity and consciousness.[42] We are not at this point interested in the intricacies of Weber's analysis of the interrelationship between cultural ideals and various forms of expediency or in the extent to which each has influenced the course of particular societies.[43] The important point for the present discussion is that Weber believed the need for personal identity became almost universal in modern society as a result of the manner by which one type of religious *virtuoso* in the West reconciled belief and life.

Only some form of either "mysticism" or "puritanism" has enabled such individuals to attain this consistency.[44] Both alternatives lead to asceticism, but the puritan, unlike the mystic, does not "prove himself . . . against action in the world," but rather by action in the world. He either strives to do God's will on earth or, more likely for his imitators, attempts to find evidence of God's grace through success in a useful wordly endeavor, that is, through a "vocation" (*Beruf*).[45] Only in the West did puritanism become a dominant cultural orientation. Consequently, only in the West did it become generally expected that individuals would be "personalities," would establish identities that justified their existence in this world.

> To put it in our terms: The Puritan, like every rational type of asceticism, tried to enable a man to maintain and act upon his constant motives, especially those which it taught him itself against the emotions. In this formal psychological sense of the term it tried to make him into a personality.[46]

Of course, even in cultures based upon some form of mysticism there have always been numerous individuals who have striven for meaning in this life.[47] But only in the West did the need to justify rather than escape earthly existence become culturally sanctioned.

According to Weber's famous thesis, this need to prove the fact of God's grace on earth created the frame of mind that encouraged an extensive degree of capital accumulation and the eventual development of capitalistic economies. Once firmly established as the mechanism of modern societies, however, capitalism no longer required the support of religious asceticism. But even with the decline of its religious basis, the cultural influence of Western puritanism persists. "The idea of duty in one's calling (*Beruf*) prowls about in our lives like the ghost of dead religious beliefs."[48] Although the values that puritanism taught may no longer be dominant, individuals in an increasingly secular world still require justification and have no other choice than to attempt to establish identities based upon whatever value they can find meaningful.

In the present context, the historical accuracy of Weber's analysis of the development of the need for personal identity is an irrelevant question. His explanation involves, however, two assumptions that are highly relevant to the analysis of the relationship between social science and politics. The first is that human beings require some sort of meaning in life. The second is that personal identity can be achieved only through the embodiment of ultimate values in action. Weber apparently accepted the first assumption simply on the basis of his own observation and experience, offering no argument for its logical necessity. In Chapter Five, I will argue that all individuals capable of action must have an identity that justifies their existence. Although there are probably significant differences in the types of "personality" associated with mysticism and puritanism, I believe that Weber was incorrect in maintaining that the general need for identity derived from Western puritanism.

On the other hand, Weber did present a convincing argument for the second assumption, concerning the nature of personal identity. "Personality," according to Weber, cannot be something in the "undifferentiated, vegetative 'underground' of personal life," which we can only discover and "feel" through experience.[49] Social and personal phenomena simply do not exist unless posited by someone. All objects, of course, must be posited by the apprehending agent. One's apprehension of them as objects is dependent upon selection from among an infinite variety of "sensations" and "experience."[50] If personality were identical with an immediate experience, such as "will," then we would quite literally be nonexistent to ourselves because we would have no knowledge of this will. "When one begins to think, *first-person* experiences are replaced by reflections upon third-person experiences which are conceived as an 'object.' "[51] Experiences or sensations cannot in themselves be anything, they must be made into objects. In the process they will acquire "perspectives and interrelationships which were not 'known' in the experience it-self."[52] Individuals must objectify themselves, as they must objectify anything else that occupies the mind, before they can even begin to view themselves as a problem to be understood.[53]

Weber's thesis concerning the status of social and personal phenomena, however, goes far beyond the necessity of mental positing. He asserts that such phenomena exist only as mental projections. For the crucial question that naturally follows from the necessity to posit objects mentally involves the criteria that the agent will use in selecting, or "screening," the experiences or sensations from which he or she structures an object. Weber probably accepted Kant's delineation of universal categories by which individuals order sensations into perceptions. But he explicitly rejected the idea that such categories might exist for social reality as well.[54] Social objects, although perhaps isolated through various physical manifestations such as individual behavior, visual art, or printing, are *cultural* phenomena rather than physical. This means that they exist only in the sense that they "embody" values, either as behavioral means to valued ends, such as organizations, or as values in themselves, such as status or communal groups.[55] In other words, human beings literally create their social environment from their cultural values. The same is true even of those social entities "discovered" by social scientists, such as "capitalism" or, in Weber's case, "the spirit of capitalism."[56] The only difference between the two types of social objects is that the former embodies cultural values while the latter embodies a social scientist's values. The conceptual entities of the social scientist embody his or her values in that these entities are instrumental in illuminating a problem that is personally important.[57] In all types of social entities, however, values provide the categories that structure the social environment.

Social conceptualization must be "ideal-typical," in this sense,[58] because social reality is composed of action, and action ensues only from an individual agent.[59] One never encounters a "pure" instance of "puritanism," "status group," "class," "community," or any other collective concept. This is not because of technical limitations upon the social scientist's ability to measure such phenomena but because any collective concept "represents a series of *conceptually* constructed events,"[60] not an ontologically independent entity.

> An ideal type is formed by the one-sided *accentuation* of one or more points of view and by the synthesis of a great many diffuse, discrete, more or less present and occasionally absent *concrete individual* phenomena, which are arranged according to these one-sidedly emphasized viewpoints into a unified [mental] construct. In its conceptual purity, this mental construct cannot be found empirically anywhere in reality. It is a *utopia.*[61]

Social concepts are merely mental constructions that individuals use to focus attention on those patterns of action deemed either worth doing or worth knowing. These intellectual abstractions are absolutely necessary. Without them, we would lack the necessary categories for regarding some acts in the almost infinite maze as "relevant," allowing us to ignore the rest. But because the collective concepts of social science do not correspond to or describe real objects, social knowledge cannot be knowledge of their properties and interactions. The only question about these ideal-types that can be answered through systematic observations is the degree to which social reality approximates or diverges from them. Empirical social knowledge can be nothing more than the knowledge of the extent to which social reality does not conform to the intellectual constructions with which we approach it.[62]

Returning to the topic at hand, personal knowledge can be nothing more than the knowledge of conformity to ideal type for exactly the same reasons. Just as the concepts by which we apprehend society are ideal-typical, our conceptions of ourselves and one another as distinct personalities are dependent upon values. Without reference to values "we" are nothing more than a collection of diffuse and meaningless "dispositions." "We" are given coherence through the *consistency* of the values that direct our behavior and, as personalities, can only be defined in terms of these values. Individual personalities are entities "synthetically produced by a value relationship";[63] "we" are a "complex of 'constant motives' ".[64]

But just as social concepts are not really descriptive of reality because of their ideal-typical nature, so too is an individual more than the constant motives in which he or she finds identity. Although Weber does not discuss most of the questions that modern psychologists find important, he certainly appreciated the impact of unconsciously learned inclinations and biological factors upon behavior. In fact, Weber assumed that most behavior is unconscious in the sense that the subjects themselves rarely reflect upon its purposes while actually doing it, and that the social scientist gives it a rational interpretation for reasons of methodological convenience.[65] The reason that the social scientist finds this procedure convenient, even necessary, is that it is the only way he or she can "understand" behavior as meaningful action, as intentional, and thereby explain patterns of action. The extent to which the social scientist cannot explain behavior as rational action and must, therefore, attribute it to the effects of "irrational" biological or psychic factors is the limit of his or her ability to see this behavior in functional terms.[66] Such behavior is simply meaningless from the social scientist's perspective, merely the external effect of an external cause, senseless in itself. Since social phenomena exist only through value relevance, such meaningless events are not "social," irrespective of their influence upon social phenomena.

What applies to the social scientist attempting to understand social phenomena also applies to the individual attempting to understand himself.[67] *Only insofar as he can see his behavior as rationally consistent with certain values can he establish a sense of personal identity.* Weber certainly did not deny that irrational, nondeliberative elements that have no apparent relation to values often determine behavior. He only pointed out that such behavior is often considered pathological just because it is not integrated with the subject's intentions. The individual's inability either to control or to understand this behavior is what defines him or her as a neurotic.[68] In order for one to attain a sense of identity, the individual must suppress those emotional desires and drives that are incompatible with the values that give his or her behavior consistency. Weber was well aware that suppression could lead to "repression," which, in turn, could lead to hysteria, compulsions, phobia, or other neurotic symptoms. Regardless of the dangers, however, emotional suppression is a requirement of personal identity.[69]

It is not the only such requirement. Above all, the mentally healthy and secure individual cannot directly seek to be a "personality," that is, to consciously play a role. Self-identity can only be achieved by the "whole-hearted devotion to a 'task' whatever it (and its derivative 'demands of the hour') may be."[70] Anyone at anytime can decide that it would be admirable to be identified with certain "ultimate values," but such a decision means nothing in itself. Simple desire cannot give an individual a secure sense of identity. Human beings give themselves substance by embodying their ultimate values in action. Only through genuine commitment, tested by adversity (including the acceptance of necessary drudgery), can the individual really "understand" himself or herself and attain a secure sense of identity.[71] An individual who devotes oneself to the realization of ideals has not only a greater sense of personal identity and a higher degree of self-esteem than one whose direct goal is to establish an identity, but he actually is also a more substantial "person" because he "is more than his mere appearance."[72]

Many implications of this conception of personal identity remain to be developed, and no doubt many questions remain to be answered. Its necessity, however, is a consequence of Weber's argument that ideal-types, mental constructions lacking ontologically independent referents, are necessary for understanding social reality. Now one can without self-contradiction assert the existence of social and physical entities, such as Durkheim's "social representations" or Freud's "id," which dominate individual consciousness in a determinant law-like manner. But in light of the impossibility of explaining action without reference to individual meanings, the ideal-type character of at least some personal and collective concepts cannot be denied. For if explanations of action are necessarily dependent upon individual intentions, then some collective concepts can only refer to patterns of action that result from shared or complementary goals.

Readers will have to answer for themselves the metaphysical question of whether social entities exist, as well as the question of the extent to which such entities might determine individual behavior.[73] For present purposes, it is sufficient that personal identity is based upon the commitments that the individual embodies in his or her behavior. In a later chapter, I will establish the need for such an identity and in a sense confirm or at least reinforce Weber's conception of personality. In the following chapter, I turn to Weber's analysis of the distinctive personal requisites of scientific and political action. In his view, each required not only certain personal attributes but also a total commitment—the type of commitment that could be maintained only as the basis of one's personal identity.

CHAPTER FOUR

The Scientific Personality

M ost individuals accept, with varying degrees of consciousness, culturally prescribed values and the conventional rules of behavior that supposedly embody or advance
those values. Consequently, any society is likely to be characterized by a set of typical "personalities" (or "identities") resulting from conscious fulfillment of social roles. Because these personality types are the result of socially imposed expectations,
they can be understood only in the context of the particular society and culture in question.[1]

According to Weber, non-elites in traditional societies typically
find meaning in the promise of some sort of life after death offered by religion.[2] Simultaneously, and increasingly in modern
societies, non-elites find meaning through identification with
communities of which they are a part, since almost any group,
regardless of its original purpose, can become meaningful in itself to its members and provide them with "ethnic honor."[3]
Elites, on the other hand, have an additional source of meaning
and identity. However, rationalized by metaphysical system or
religious doctrine, meaning for these strata of society is made
possible by what Weber called "status honor." In traditional societies, in which elites tend to be aristocratic in nature, their

"sense of self-esteem rests on their awareness that the perfection of their life pattern is an expression of their underived, ultimate, and qualitatively distinctive being."[4] In modern society the elite strata tend to be professional in nature. Their self-esteem rests not upon a distinctive life style that embodies certain cultural ideals but upon the dutiful performance of a concrete function.[5] In both cases, individuals give meaning to their lives by fulfilling a socially prescribed role, which, either because it embodies cultural values or because of its direct or indirect contribution to their maintenance, is endowed with status and is meaningful.

Before his breakdown, Weber could have derived a good deal of meaning and self-esteem from his professional position had he been so inclined. But status is social meaning, and the individuals who derive their sense of identity and self-esteem from this source usually do so without intellectual reflection. They tend to be unconcerned with intellectual questions, uncritically accepting their given social environment and its cultural ideals.[6] Weber was not likely, therefore, to find much personal security in his professional role. In light of the prestige enjoyed by the German university professor at the turn of the century, it was no doubt difficult to avoid completely the self-satisfaction made possible by his position. Given Weber's conscious priorities, we may conjecture that his difficulties were compounded by a sense of guilt or inadequacy at having occasionally succumbed to the temptation of status. But he could never have found his "calling" in his professional life before his breakdown.

Still less could professional status have provided a secure identity after his breakdown. Neither esteem of colleagues and students nor belief in the social benefits of his profession could have been sufficiently meaningful. Once a person of Weber's intellect and temperament had raised the question of his purpose in life, he could hardly have been assured by social convention. For Weber was, to broaden the range of his own concept, an intellectual "virtuoso." He required a thorough, rational consistency between belief and life. Indeed, he once distinguished between "average" and "hero" ethics; the former type takes humanity's supposed natural tendencies as its maxims, while the latter type requires individual struggle for the occasional achievement of some ultimate good. According to Weber, only "hero ethics" qualified as genuine "idealism."[7] The need for a thorough consisteny between belief and life can only result from a similarly thorough commitment to ultimate ends. A virtuoso could never be satisfied with an "average ethic."

More important than the fact of Weber's idealism is the fact that an individual can be a "person" only to the extent that a "hero ethic" is followed. For such an ethic demands that behavior be directed in some way by an ultimate value, and this is exactly the definition of personal identity. Consequently, a typology of "hero ethics" is a typology of personalities, and the rudiments of such a typology can be found in Weber's work. This typology is possible because the ways in which action can be *logically* consistent with any ultimate value are finite in number, even though the potential variety of ultimate values is unlimited. In other words, there are a certain number of ideal-typical personality types that appear with varying frequencies in every society during every historical period. What is typical in these individuals is not the values they pursue (which vary with culture, circumstance, and the individual) but the way they pursue them. Each type of personality is defined in terms of its own logic, and each presupposes personal characteristics compatible with its logic.

Although Weber did not develop a complete typology, he explicitly discussed three personality types.[8] We may call these three types the "saint," the "politician," and the "scientist." These should not be confused with social roles; those colloquially referred to as devout, political, or scientific or those associated with organizations that have religious, political, or scientific goals do not necessarily correspond to these ideal-typical personalities. Indeed, Weber's efforts to reform social scientific organization, to be discussed in Chapter Six, would lead one to suspect that he felt the social scientific enterprise suffered greatly from lack of a sufficient proportion of scientific personalities among the political economists of his day, and he was extremely concerned with the consequences of political leadership in Germany by persons without genuine political orientations.

Weber's analysis of the personal attributes suitable for political life is fairly straightforward and generally well known. Near the end of this chapter, I will discuss these attributes and contrast them with those required by science. But it must first be demonstrated that Weber did in fact establish that science required a specific personality, based upon a distinctive orientation toward values. Perhaps because he wished to avoid both tension with his colleagues and self-disclosure, he was far from straightforward in presenting this assertion. It is, however, entailed in his discussion of the validity, or "objectivity," of social science. Weber came to believe that empirical methods, at least in social science, could only hope to distinguish between true and false beliefs when researchers took a distinct orientation toward their own ultimate values.

Neither before nor after his breakdown did he believe it possible to eliminate the influence of the investigator's values from social science.[9] In his inaugural address at Freiburg, he articulated the view that political economy was a "political science," in the sense that it must proceed from a value perspective. Its purpose was to make possible informed evaluations relevant to policy needs.[10] Although Weber did not delve into the philosophical details, his view at this point was perfectly compatible with the doctrine of the fact-value dichotomy. Values may serve (necessarily for Weber) to focus our attention upon those facts relevant to our goals, but once they have performed this function it is imperative that their influence be eliminated from scientific research. This elimination is achieved through intersubjectivity. Its supposed effect is to expose and eliminate whatever subjective elements find their way into scientific research by requiring the tests of criticism as well as empirical verification. These tests are passed only when consensus is achieved.[11] By submitting arguments and results to the criticism of a scientific community, scientists become certain that their individual predilections did not distort either their logical or empirical analysis.

In the methodological essays written after his breakdown, Weber continued to stress the necessity for the social scientist to see reality in relation to values. Reality presents to us "an infinite multiplicity of successively and coexistently emerging and disappearing events both 'within' and 'outside' ourselves." Consequently, "there is no absolutely 'objective' scientific analysis of culture . . . or 'social phenomena' independent of special and 'one-sided' viewpoints—expressly or tacitly, consciously or unconsciously—they are selected, analyzed and organized for expository purposes."[12] Values provide a necessary criterion by which reality can be "sorted out," by which certain aspects can be judged "relevant." But the social scientist must make other judgments as well, and if social science is to be a valid enterprise, these must ultimately be guided by the systematic presentation of evidence. Weber attempted to come to grips with the problem of "objectivity" by distinguishing among four (really three) types of decisions that the investigator must make: value-judgment, value-relevance, objective-possibility, and causal-adequacy.

"Value-judgment" is "subjective"; its importance is that the investigator must have "values" before determining which aspects of reality are relevant to the investigation. But "value-relevance" requires an additional decision. The investigator still must decide what is or could be relevant to the frustration or achievement of whatever is of value to him or her. Value-relevance is a judgment, then, of "objective-possibility," or, in more contemporary style, it is a hypothesis, just as assumptions of cause and effect, until affirmed by systematic observation, are judgments of *possibility*. Judgments of objective-possibility, however, are not the goal of social science. To explain an event or process scientifically is to test one's hypotheses against the available data. The final judgment is of "causal-adequacy," whereby an investigator decides whether the data can sufficiently discern which, if any, of the various "objective-possibilities" actually apply to the case in question. Weber's argument for the objectivity of the social sciences seems to reduce itself to two assertions: that judgments of value are different from judgments of value-relevance and that judgments of objective-possibility (including those of value-relevance) are different from judgments of causal-adequacy.[13] Since judgments of causal-adequacy are made on the basis of empirical evidence, intersubjectivity is possible for all those who can at least "understand" the values that led to the investigation initially, even if they are not their values. If they are not, one may find the study "meaningless" or "worthless" from the standpoint of his or her own interests, but not on that account subjective.[14]

If this were the extent of Weber's analysis, his defense of objectivity in social science would be inadequate. For even if scientific procedure can be analytically decomposed into three or four very different decisions, it is not obvious that different criteria must be relied upon to make each type of decision. Even if we grant that decisions of value-judgment and objective-possibility are logically distinct, we are still faced with the problem of deciding which of our objective-possibilities has sufficient evidence to be accepted or rejected. What criteria does one use to determine when the evidence is "sufficient"? In other words, evidence alone cannot make the decision of "causal-adequacy," because the investigator must always decide on the sufficiency of this evidence in terms of both quality and quantity. An experienced scientist in any field knows that one's evidence is never "a hundred percent"; how does one "objectively" decide what deviance should be attributed to "measurement error" or to "uncontrolled conditions"?[15] How does one decide whether his or her "operational definitions" are "valid," whether they measure what they are thought to measure, given the well-known fact that consistency in use ("reliability") cannot logically prove validity?[16]

What *criteria* other than values, which according to the doctrine of the fact-value dichotomy are inherently "subjective," can be used to decide these questions? A judgment cannot be made without a criterion, and "value" seems to be the only candidate.[17] In what sense can science claim to be "objective" when the criteria for the adequacy of a conclusion are as arbitrary as those that define a "worthwhile" topic? Intersubjectivity, or consensus, on such questions as those of the preceding paragraph does not change the nature of the problem, since science takes place within a context of cultural values, and the mere fact of being shared would not seem to render values any less subjective.[18]

Intersubjectivity cannot, by itself, confine values solely to the function of selection. If Weber's methodological essays merely elaborated and extended his earlier viewpoint, which implicitly accepts the fact-value dichotomy, they would present an inconclusive justification for the objectivity of social science. Weber certainly continued to believe in the meaningfulness of empirical analysis, but he recognized that such work was necessarily inconclusive. This inconclusiveness is extremely important for understanding the logical necessity of a certain sort of personal orientation for social science, what I have here called the "scientific personality."

Weber's perspective on the role of values in social science actually changed radically after his breakdown. Although he is often assumed to be a forceful proponent of the fact-value dichotomy, his new position is diametrically opposed to this doctrine. A close reading of his methodological essays discloses that Weber never asserted that values lack cognitive status.[19] In fact, he assumed that a change in our fundamental conceptions of social reality is always associated with changes in our normative orientations.[20] One should not, however, conclude that Weber was a "pragmatist" in the sense of believing that all concepts, being only instruments of whatever felt needs move us, naturally would change with the values that make them "useful." One who could find metaphysics cognitively meaningful is not likely to view all concepts as mere tools, and as Weber put it, he "was completely free of the prejudice which asserts that reflections . . . which go beyond the analysis of empirical data in order to interpret the world metaphysically can, because of their metaphysical character, fulfill no useful cognitive tasks."[21] Weber explicitly asserted that we all believe in the "metaempirical validity of ultimate and final values, in which the meaning of our existence is rooted,"[22] and that we regard these values "as objectively valuable."[23] They are in some way connected with one's cognitive view, his *Weltanschauung*.[24]

Most of Weber's commentators have assumed his advocacy of the fact-value dichotomy, despite his explicit and implicit assertions to the contrary, because of his numerous statements denying the ability of science to refute any normative position or to help one choose among contending normative orientations.[25] Although such statements are certainly compatible with the fact-value dichotomy, they do not necessarily commit one to it. Weber could assert such limitations upon science without committing himself to this doctrine, because for him "thought is not limited to science."[26] In Weber's view, science could not claim a monopoly of knowledge. In fact, scientific knowledge is relatively recent in origin and, more important, inherently limited to only a portion of what any human being believes to be true.

Science "is a fraction," although the "most important fraction," of the rationalization of Western culture, the analysis of which provides a unifying theme for the seemingly diverse topics of Weber's work. "Rationalization" is the effort to achieve security and efficiency through calculation, by reducing things down to calculable elements by which they can be rationally (intellectually) ordered and manipulated.[27] The calculable elements that define science are empirical observations systematized through formal conceptualization: in a word, *data*. As such, science is an attempt to achieve reliability by abstracting, according to formal rules, from the infinite possibilities given by sense experience those aspects that are of interest to us and to discern their consistent interrelationships with one another. This reliability, of course, is manifested as intersubjectivity.

Rationalization requires systematization, systematization requires formalism, and formalism in science leads to something of a paradox. That which makes science useful, its intersubjectivity (reliability), renders it less able to tell us anything about reality, which is what makes science meaningful for anyone who takes the problem of objectivity seriously. Science strives for intersubjectivity through rational demonstration, but the methods required to attain this goal insure that the closer one approaches it, the narrower must one's vision contract. The two goals of science, impersonal demonstration (reliability) and comprehension, are in constant tension with one another.

The problem is one of conceptualization. Reality is "constituted only by the concrete and particular," in the sense that we apprehend it only through preconceptual qualitative distinctions that we attempt to capture and communicate through conceptualization.[28] The preconceptual apprehension is the "meaning" of the concept. Concepts attempt to communicate by drawing attention to attributes of the meaning that experience has indicated already possess a sufficient degree of intersubjectivity, and the attributes that insure the highest degree of intersubjectivity, which are most easily communicated, tend to be those that lend themselves to manipulation and calculation. But by reducing the qualitative, preconceptual apprehension to a set of typical attributes, formal conceptualization necessarily involves a "loss" of meaning.[29]

Any science must, however, rely upon formal conceptualization because empirical testing presupposes that observation has been systematized. Indeed, it is this systematization according to formal rules that distinguishes between scientific data and the informed observation typical of historians, journalists, biographers, and perhaps novelists. On the other hand, even the natural sciences that attempt to maximize this systematization in order to maximize reliability, that take mechanics as their model,[30] cannot dispense completely with the qualitative distinctions that give them their initial orientations and tie them, so to speak, to reality. As these sciences progress, they tell us less and less about the "concrete reality" of experience. Questions about the "nature" of the distinctions necessarily presupposed are rejected as "metaphysical" and thereafter ignored.[31]

Obviously, a science of meaning itself, a "cultural science," cannot similarly ignore this type of question. According to Weber, such a science must take a different approach to conceptualization. Instead of increasingly constricting the unique meaning of its concepts by reducing them to manipulable properties, social science attempts to "understand" increasingly the meaning of its concepts by illustrating their manifold implications and relationships for one another. In other words, cultural science seeks to "understand" meanings by looking at them from a variety of directions.[32] But cultural science is still science, and it seeks to do more than just understand meanings; in fact, as empirical science, it strives to understand meaning only because it wishes to isolate causal connections that can be empirically demonstrated. In order to do this, cultural science must, just as natural science, formalize its concepts. It does this usually be viewing human action as goal-maximizing behavior, employing the most rational (efficient) means known to the subjects in question—another function of "ideal types."[33]

One cannot understand why some things are goals without understanding the meanings with which, as we have seen, Weber believed values to be linked. Although science can contribute to the clarification of meaning by illustrating the various functional relationships among conceptual entities, the task is largely one of "interpretation."[34] The nature of conceptual entities is a metaphysical problem that cannot be resolved by an empirical science. Science cannot decide among contending values because science cannot affirm or deny the various "world views" from which they, in some way, derive. Science only attempts either, as in the natural sciences, to formulate a systematic structure that expresses the consistent relationships among components of an extremely limited aspect of a world view or, as in the cultural sciences, to explain concrete phenomena or events in terms of a world view.

Certainly, the foregoing analysis has not solved the problem of the validity of social science. In fact, it has considerably complicated it. The problem is no longer one of the role of "emotion," "values," or "will" and how to keep such "subjective" elements in their proper place. Now the problem becomes how empirical evidence could lead to a rejection of an "objective-possibility," given that both decisions of objective-possibility and evaluations of evidence derive from the scientist's fundamental view of reality. Weber seems to be caught in a circular trap, where everything is "subjective," where one conception of reality is as valid as any other as long as all are internally consistent. But it is absurd, self-contradictory, to assert that all internally consistent conceptions of reality are equally congruent with reality. A solution to the problem of objectivity would necessarily consist of an explanation of how empirical evidence could at least call into question an incorrect view of reality.

It is possible, of course, that the riddle of objectivity cannot be solved. If so, the result is pragmatism, the belief that the aim of science can only be increased control of our environment and increased ability to solve our problems. For pragmatists, the quest for objectivity is replaced by the quest for effectiveness. Since effectiveness is ultimately the degree to which values are satisfied, the circular position that follows from the necessity of using values to evaluate evidence presents no problem for the pragmatic position.

Weber could not have accepted a pragmatic conception of social science. Such an approach blurs the distinction between scientific and political activity, and his methodological essays were attempts to understand his inability to engage in the latter. Had he concluded the pragmatic premise, he would have been forced to shun science as well as politics. Yet the evidence indicates that he sharply distinguished between the two types of activity. In fact, he apparently distinguished among the various judgments necessarily made by the social scientist in order to emphasize that practical evaluation is precluded by the very idea of science.[35]

For when Weber referred to "value judgments," he always meant evaluations of practical affairs. Value judgments, in other words, are always related to judgments of specific circumstances in relation to specific goals.[36] When he asserted the necessity of a value-free social science, he meant only that social scientists must refrain from evaluating the specific situations that they investigate.[37] To see the necessity of this, we must refer to Weber's analysis of collective concepts discussed in the previous chapter.

79

These concepts are intellectual constructions formulated to focus attention on patterns of action considered relevant to values. In the natural sciences, it is at least possible for the scientist to dispense with personal or cultural values once the problem has been defined. The scientist can be "objective" because his or her concepts are intended to correspond to objects that have persistent perceptual effects, regardless of how the scientist attempts to define them. Objectivity is possible because theoretical concepts describe or correspond to real entities with definite, lawlike properties.[38] Since the collective entities of the social scientist are always to some degree fictional, *this* sort of objectivity is impossible. In the explanation of action, it is, of course, essential to understand correctly the cultural and personal values of the actors, as well as their ideas and perceptions. But the process by which such knowledge is attained is interpretative rather than scientific, and the terms used to express it are not social concepts because they do not refer to behavior. They refer to mental phenomena that may or may not result in action.[39] The collective concepts of social science, being ideal-types, do not correspond to, or describe real objects. Consequently, social knowledge cannot be knowledge of their properties and interactions.

The only question about these ideal-types that can be answered objectively, through systematic observations, is the degree to which social reality approximates or diverges from them. Indeed, they make systematic observation possible by providing a standard with which reality can be compared. In Weber's words, the ideal-type is a "purely limiting concept with which the real situation or action is *compared* and surveyed for the explication of certain of its significant components."[40] It is not a hypothesis or an assertion about reality that may be true or false but a means by which "the adequacy of our imagination, oriented and disciplined by reality, is judged."[41] Social knowledge is not, strictly speaking, knowledge of social reality, since social reality is nothing more than a maze of individual acts that cannot be subsumed under generic concepts or universal relationships, but it is knowledge of the extent to which this reality conforms to our contrived concepts. These concepts are inevitably normative, but the question of the extent to which reality conforms to them is empirical. Objectivity in social science is simply the *ability* to recognize unpleasant facts, the degree to which reality does not conform to our (ultimately) normative concepts.[42]

Since the basis of objectivity in social science is the ability to recognize divergence of reality from ideal-type, a political or psychological need to affirm or criticize that reality is obviously incompatible with scientific work. Evaluation assumes congruence or incongruence between reality and values and therefore precludes by assumption the only question that can be answered empirically. The question of objectivity eventually becomes, how is it possible to refrain from evaluating a situation seen from a value perspective? In other words, how could one keep separate value-laden beliefs about the fundamental nature of reality from one's analysis of a specific situation? For given the necessity of evaluating empirical evidence, and the lack of an "objective" criterion to do so, the possibility of freeing social science from practical evaluations might appear to be questionable.

It is, however, possible. Even if one must, given the nature of collective concepts, view a particular social situation from a value perspective, it does not follow that one's response to that situation is dictated solely by one's values. Insofar as the individual is aware of his or her values, he or she can be expected to act consistently with them. But there are, as mentioned earlier, different ways to render behavior consistent with values, each just as "rational" as another. Any substantive value can result in a number of formal "ethics." Since each type of ethic is a distinct way by which individuals orient their behavior around their values, each can be the basis for a distinct type of "personality."

Objectivity in social science requires some sort of ethic, an identity, that does not require the evaluation of specific circumstances.

Although Weber's discussion of this scientific identity was far from ostensive, he explicitly developed the basis for it in his analysis of the ethical demands of politics. Here he unambiguously asserts the cleavage between substantive value and formal ethic.[43] Any substantive ideal implies an ethic, or way of acting, that is often transgressed in the name of the ideal that legitimizes it. Individuals must choose whether they are to "live" their values, irrespective of the consequences, or to attempt to render reality commensurate with their values at the sacrifice of the privilege to live in strict accordance with them. Similarly, one who must act in accordance with ideals must sacrifice the possibility of legislating them for society, since any such effort would demand personal compromise. At times it may be necessary to make war or revolution in order to insure "peace," to be autocratic to establish or protect "democracy," to violate the law to save "constitutionalism," or to commit regicide to save "monarchy."

The supposed moral ambiguity of political action is in reality a tension between these two types of ethics, which Weber called the "ethic of responsibility" and the "ethic of pure intentions."[44] Although both types of ethics are modes of responsibility toward ultimate ends, they differ in what one might call the "locus" of responsibility. The ethic of pure intentions is the responsibility for the consistency *of one's own behavior* toward an ultimate value, while political ethics is the responsibility for the consistency *of the consequences* of one's action to such a value. These two types of responsibility are mutually exclusive. Politics assumes conflict, the struggle of human against human; although the ethic of pure intentions may lead to inner turmoil, external struggle is essentially irrelevant.[45] Since both are forms of obligation, both require personal sacrifice, but the sacrifices demanded by each differ radically. As mentioned in the preceding paragraph, each must give up the benefits of the other.

I suspect that most readers find it easier to commiserate for the sacrifices of a "politician" than for those of a "saint." But Weber did not believe that one type of identity could be demonstrated to be superior to the other. Each is a distinct type of "personality" just because each is a way by which one might *logically* organize one's behavior according to one's values. One orientation is not any more "rational," or even "reasonable," than the other. Those who wish to live and propagate their truth regardless of the consequences, the "saints," could plausibly argue that those who attempt to render reality compatible with their truth must necessarily compromise not only their personal ethics but even the values that supposedly justify their action. For the "politicians," to be justified, must assume responsibility for the external consequences of their action, and since the consequences of any act can never be completely known, such a responsibility is at best always problematic. Indeed, if Tolstoy is correct, the consequences of any act never end, and it is simply absurd for a mortal to claim responsibility for them.[46] From the politician's perspective, the saint is guilty of social complacency; from the saint's perspective, the politician is necessarily guilty of personal duplicity.

From the "scientist's" perspective, both are guilty of hasty action. For the "scientist" must be defined by the constant questioning of his or her beliefs.[47] All individuals possess, and act upon, a conception of reality that they believe to be true. Given Weber's assumptions, it would be impossible for them to act if they did not.[48] The saint and the politician must not question their fundamental beliefs if their activity is to be meaningful. The scientist, on the other hand, must question his or her beliefs because there is no method that guarantees their truth; one can "prove" nothing about reality.[49] This, too, is a way in which one can logically organize one's behavior in accordance with one's values. Without such an orientation, empirical social science is senseless. For only persons who recognize the inescapable "subjectivity" of their fundamental conception of social reality, from which they draw their criteria of relevance, can feel the necessity of testing their beliefs, attempting to affirm them by illustrating their ability to account for particular events.[50]

Such an effort at justification is not an effort to convince, because the scientist is already convinced; it must be an effort to show why one must be convinced. Furthermore, if it is to be anything more than a useless game, the social scientist must be attempting to justify personal convictions to himself or herself rather than to an audience.[51] If one is committed to justifying one's convictions to an audience, he or she is in reality committed to convincing the audience, and this is a political, rather than a scientific, commitment. If one's purpose is primarily to convince others, the neglect of contradictions, either logical or empirical, may be convenient and perhaps necessary; but if one's purpose is to justify one's own convictions to oneself, then such techniques of deception are worse than useless—*they are admissions of personal failure.*[52]

Only the recognition that beliefs are never conclusively confirmed can make empirical testing meaningful. Objectivity is the result of this recognition, combined with the fear of believing incorrectly. Only this combination can insure that one will be as suspicious of "positive" as of "negative" evidence. Given the normative nature of collective concepts, the mistaken belief that empirical methods could either conclusively prove or disprove assertions about social reality inevitably leads to a tendency to automatically accept evidence confirming one's evaluation of a specific situation and to question the validity of unexpected results. Social scientists' need to be justified in their beliefs must be more compelling to them than the urge to realize the values that give focus to their investigations and form their collective concepts. They must continually test what they believe to be true, continually strive to account for negative or unexpected results, and try to remove whatever doubt they might have about positive evidence.

Because of the inconclusiveness of empirical testing, the moment at which belief will be deemed unwarranted and begin to change to doubt and confusion cannot be logically determined. It undoubtedly varies with the belief. Most individuals will probably abandon a belief about a particular situation more readily than beliefs about the defining characteristics of humanity, the nature of the psyche, or the fundamental components of reality. These latter beliefs are unavoidable metaphysical commitments but are at such a level of generality as to preclude plausible empirical testing. Furthermore, if they are, as Weber believed, the source of our normative commitments, this alone would guarantee their relative stability.[53]

Rejection of any belief, however, would be highly unlikely unless one first recognizes the tentative nature of all belief and concluded from this recognition the personal responsibility to justify personal beliefs by illustrating their ability to survive continually the systematic scrutiny of both logical and empirical analyses. While one cannot conclusively prove or disprove anything about reality, persons with a genuine need to justify their beliefs to themselves can at least call them into question. This may not satisfy those who look to science for certainty, but given the inconclusiveness of empirical evidence, it is the best that can be attained, and it is a sufficient justification of the hope that social science can contribute toward a greater comprehension of social reality.

Unfortunately, Weber never really discussed the personal attributes conducive to a scientific orientation. His renowned essay, "Science as a Vocation," is primarily devoted to the personal and practical value of science rather than to the personal requisites for its conduct. He only pointed out that scientists must, given the development of modern scientific discipline, accommodate themselves to both specialization and the likelihood that their accomplishments will become obsolete as science progresses. Neither requirement would be an obstacle to a person more concerned with being correct than with having personal appeal or professional standing.[54] Despite Weber's silence on the matter, it would appear obvious that those who felt the necessity of justifying their beliefs to themselves, and yet recognized the inconclusiveness of all such justification, would become temperamentally rather cautious, given to qualification and hesitation. All in all, a scientific personality will tend to be indecisive in one fashion or another.

Weber does not distinguish science as a distinct form of activity, or "calling," by its commitment to self-criticism. All forms of activity depend upon this meaning of "objectivity" for their effectiveness, and this is certainly true of politics.[55] For this very reason social science can be useful, indeed in some form essential, to political actors. As earlier discussed, empirical testing requires systematization, and systematization leads to intersubjectivity, which, in turn, maximizes reliability. Reliable information is an obvious condition of political effectiveness. Other essential conditions, however, are decisiveness and the confidence that makes decisiveness possible. A precondition of confidence is a firm faith in the fundamentals of one's view of human conduct and social affairs. When confronted with the ultimate "subjectivity" of their fundamental beliefs, politicians should be able to shrug their shoulders. They are not interested in justifying their general view of social reality but rather in changing or controlling a particular situation in conformity with this general view. Since the criteria for accomplishing this derive from politicians' view of social reality, they cannot question it and remain effectively partisan.

Weber argued that a political orientation requires three personal characteristics. Above all, it requires a willingness to take responsibility for the consequences of one's action. Second, it requires the possession of a "sense of proportion," essential to those who must risk compromise, who cannot follow a direct course in order to maximize a goal. Finally, and for present purposes most important, politicians must have "passion," in the sense of partisanship to a cause.[56] Only partisanship can provide them with motivation in the face of seemingly insurmountable obstacles and, especially, give them a fixed criterion by which they can both guide their action to eventual success and justify their necessary compromises to the ultimate goal. Although politicians must be self-critical, they cannot be plagued by self-doubt.

Science is distinguished as a "calling" by a commitment to justify one's view of reality to one's self. It requires a sort of humility that politicians cannot afford, a personal admission that they may be wrong in their fundamental beliefs. The cost of this humility, which may be more than it is worth, is the confidence required to realize values socially through direct action. Although it is perhaps too melodramatic, we might say that Weber viewed the social scientist as a person who is haunted by the fear of having false fundamental conceptions, and as a consequence, the only way the social scientist can behave on the basis of personal convictions is to strive to justify them by means of logical analysis and empirical testing of the expectations derived from them.

Social scientific and political activity cannot be pursued simultaneously because each is a quite distinct way of acting in conformity with one's basic beliefs or values. Although the values may be the same, their realization is much different. So much so, we can say that the same ultimate values can lead to different ultimate ends. Furthermore, each type of activity is likely to be associated with different traits of character, although at this stage of the analysis there would seem to be nothing absolutely precluding sufficient personal flexibility to alternate between these two types of responsible action. For the present, it is important to understand not only that they are distinct types of activity but also that each is inimical to the other. Anyone incapable of at least suspending his or her commitment to changing or preserving his or her social environment cannot genuinely engage in social scientific work. This much can be derived from Weber's own analysis. The next chapter is devoted to extending this analysis in such a manner as to explain why an individual is unlikely to have the flexibility to alternate between these two endeavors. It will explain, to use Weber's terminology, why each really does involve a distinct "personality."

CHAPTER FIVE

Personal Identity and Social Theory

I have come about as far as Weber's own analysis can take me toward the substantiation of my thesis that politics and social science require incompatible sets of personal characteristics and that any effort to engage seriously in both types of activity will inevitably vitiate at least one if not both. As indicated at the conclusion of the preceding chapter, Weber presents no compelling reason as to why an individual might not be able to compartmentalize these two incompatible types of activity, assuming temporarily the appropriate personal orientation for each. On the origin of the manner in which one attempted to render behavior compatible with values, he remained silent, only stating at one point that one must simply "find and obey the demon who holds the threads of his life." Weber found his demon in science. He could not, apparently, explain why it was such a jealous demon.

The limitations of Weber's analysis stem from his mistaken belief that "personality," in his sense of the organization of action around values, was a cultural product rather than a necessary requisite for agency itself. From his perspective, one only needed to be "self-disciplined" in this manner if one needed to know

oneself, and originally this self-knowledge was important culturally because of the rise of a certain view of the nature of salvation.
In this chapter, I intend to demonstrate that all agents must have
a personal identity that corresponds fairly well to Weber's notion
of personality. In the process, the extreme difficulty of attempting
to consciously compartmentalize social scientific and political
endeavor will become apparent.

Although the argument of the present chapter does not rest
directly upon Weber's work, once again his example will prove
instructive. After painful experience, Weber came to recognize
his own proclivities and the apparent futility of attempting to
escape them. He accepted himself for what he had to be and for
the next decade devoted himself primarily to scholarship. During
this decade he formulated all the ideas for which he later became
famous and completed at least preliminary drafts of the works in
which these ideas were expressed. Having learned from both experience and reflection the incompatibility between scientific and
political activity, he gave up all hope for a life *primarily* devoted
to public affairs.

But he could not entirely escape the lure of politics, and for this
reason his recovery was only partial. Throughout this decade he
continued to take periodic trips abroad, and his wife leaves no
doubt that they were a therapeutic necessity in the initial years.[1]
At first Weber traveled to places he had never visited before: Si-
cily in 1906, Lake Como in 1907, and the coast of Provence in
1908 (in addition to returning to Florence). From 1910 to 1914,
he returned to familiar scenes, although he added Paris in 1911.
This change is highly significant if one recalls that the therapeutic
function of travel was achieved through distraction. For in the
later years of this period his trips obviously were intended to be
"vacations," to be relaxing rather than distracting.[2]

In fact, for Weber the decade was divided into two distinct

parts. During the first, from 1904 to mid-1909, he continued to suffer from sleeplessness, exhaustion, and excitability to the point that he was occasionally unable to work.[3] In the second, from mid-1909 to 1914, his ability to work was largely unimpaired, although he was still subject to exhaustion and overexcitation.[4] Commenting upon this later period, Marianne Weber observed that "despite periodic exhaustion, Weber's productive power and his agility were now so steady, that only the memory of illness" kept him from being in good health.[5]

Something other than bad memories, however, prevented full recovery. As in the earlier years of his illness, its course was strongly associated with different degrees of political preoccupation. It is apparent that involvement with political affairs aroused an "urge" to engage actively in politics that Weber could neither repress nor satisfy. The psychological difference between the two periods of the pre-war decade was the result of his efforts in the first to satisfy this urge partially by indirect or vicarious political activity. In this first period, Weber had not yet learned the difficult lesson that political involvement was foreclosed to him.

Weber tried two different methods at indirect participation, both of which were psychologically unsuccessful. The first followed the example of his uncle's later life and his own years at Freiburg: he engaged in academic analysis intended to influence political sentiments. In 1905 and 1906 he became seriously involved in sorting out the consequences and implications of the 1905 revolution in Russia. Although the essays that resulted from this effort contain much solid sociological analysis,[6] Weber explicitly stated that they were without scholarly merit.[7] He became quite agitated at the slow printing of the second essay, no doubt because its purpose was to discern "the probable influence of the events in Russia upon German developments," and its late appearance would undermine its educational effect.[8] But the writing of the essays "caused him great annoyance every day."[9] So great, in fact, that he never attempted a similar venture until well after the outbreak of World War I.

Having failed to reconcile himself with academic criticism, he turned to another form of vicarious politics: he became an advisor to a politician, his old friend Friedrich Naumann. Weber became quite upset over the Moroccan Affair and the Kaiser's subsequent handling of German foreign policy. Unable to restrain himself, he wrote Naumann a lengthy letter on December 14, 1906, counseling him on political tactics. The introduction to this letter is a strained apology for writing it:

> I have neither the authority nor, usually, the slightest desire to interfere with your political decisions, and you would not stand for it if I did so. Permit me, however, to express my *opinion*. You will hear plenty of opinions from other quarters and then make your own decision.

After telling Naumann what he should do in the Reichstag, Weber concluded the letter by saying that it indicates what he would do if he were a member and asking Naumann to "forgive me for bothering you."[10] Naumann no doubt hastened to reassure and encourage his old friend, as no doubt Weber knew he would. At any rate, Weber wrote similar letters quite regularly over the next two years.

These years saw the persistence of Weber's infirmities, requiring lengthy trips in the spring of both 1907 and 1908. In the first months of 1909, Weber suffered a severe nervous crisis, forcing him to rest in seclusion at a resort in the Black Forest (it perhaps being too late for a comfortable stay farther south). By mid-summer he had recovered sufficiently to resume his work. It proved to be the last such crisis. Afterward Weber immediately undertook several research projects, thus beginning the second phase of his productive decade. This phase was marked by intensive and consistent scholarly activity as well as by the absence of direct attempts at overt political influence.[11]

Although no longer subject to crises that precluded normal activity, he was still under strain and easily exhausted. However, whether he should be considered to have been "ill" is largely a matter of definition. His "urge" to be engaged in political affairs was not an unconscious impulse, and his inability to satisfy it was not due to an unconscious defense mechanism. I believe that Weber's problem was largely intellectual in nature; he wanted to be two incompatible things. This is bound to be frustrating. But while frustration can be both exhausting and irritating, it is not in itself a symptom of illness.[12]

As I shall demonstrate in the next chapter, the "value" that gave focus to Weber's scholarly work was his concern for politics. Political action, in other words, was for Weber an "ultimate value." It gave focus to his scholarly work and meaning to his conscious behavior. But the only way that Weber could make his behavior consistent with this value was through scientific analysis. As we have seen, this was not a matter of choice but the result of habit and temperament, inculcated and developed during youth. It is probably not unusual for individuals to value political activity as a greater good than any of its goals. Machiavelli comes readily to mind. But to esteem two types of activity can create tensions if the two are mutually exclusive. This is especially so if, as Weber believed of science and politics, these two types of activity are among a limited number of ways by which one can be ethical, orienting action in accordance with ultimate values. Of course, tension produced by enjoyment of such divergent activities as sports and quiet conversation can be negated simply by budgeting one's time. The certain tension created by commitment to two different ethics by which one gives oneself identity and meaning cannot, as will be seen, be avoided so easily.

In fact, if the argument presented in this chapter is correct, consciousness of such a dual commitment would be completely debilitating. Weber was able to incorporate both commitments into his self-concept only by seeing politics as an objective social phenomenon, rather than a personal option. He was a scientist of politics, as will be seen in the following chapter. When he forgot this and attempted to engage even indirectly in political life, he suffered the effects of a partial loss of identity.

If Weber's problem was intellectual in character, why could he not simply have given up political interests altogether? Or, if politics was too great a value to be given up, why couldn't he have decided to be as good a politician as possible, hoping to develop the necessary attributes for effective political action? Why couldn't Weber make a choice between these two ethics?[13]

He couldn't because they were both components of his identity, and identity is not a matter of choice. I want to establish in this chapter that identity is a precondition of choice in that choosing would be logically impossible without a self-conception. Furthermore, an individual has no choice but to be normatively committed to his or her self-conception. Politics was an ultimate value for Weber because it was a central component of his identity, and science necessarily was elevated to the same status once he accepted the fact that he was a scientist. Politics remained a central component of his identity because it was an important aspect of his social thought, and as we shall see, personal identity is to a great extent dictated by social belief.

Both a philosophical advocate of the fact-value dichotomy and an advocate of orthodox psychoanalytical theory would be quick to reject these assertions. For the latter, the inability to choose would mean the breakdown of the ego, the agency that develops within the psyche in order to cope with reality. If Weber could not consciously reject either politics or science, then it must have been due to some factor, necessarily unconscious, beyond the ego's control. For advocates of the fact-value dichotomy, a value might be causally or psychologically necessary, but it could never be logically entailed in beliefs about reality, including beliefs about oneself. Just because Weber believed himself to be a scientist would not logically entail that he become committed to science.

Weber, too, might have objected to the view of the nature and necessity of personal identity to be developed in the following pages. Rather than believe that values derive from identity, he believed that identity derives from values. We achieve, according to his analysis, "personality" by rendering our behavior consistent in some way with our ultimate commitments. These commitments, in turn, are entailed in some unknown manner in our most general and, therefore, metaphysical views of reality. Furthermore, as previously mentioned, Weber seemed to assert that the need for identity was historical rather than universal.

As will be seen, Weber's views on the nature of "personality" and the origin of commitment are easily reconcilable with the view presented here. He was mistaken, however, in believing that individuals of any historical era could be free of the need to maintain a personal identity. The very idea of action, so crucial in Weber's social science, is inconceivable without reference to an agent.[14] To see our own behavior as action, quite obviously we must refer to ourselves as agents. In doing this, we clearly are objectifying ourselves, formulating a "self-conception." Self-conception, however, is required for much more than merely designating some behavior as action. It would be impossible for one to even be an agent without being in the most literal sense self-conscious. For self-conception plays a necessary role in an individual's ability to cope with reality.

Empirical support for this assertion has been provided even from some psychoanalysts. Psychoanalytical theory, of course, attributes the reality coping function to the "ego." Actually the ego is defined as "that part of the id [mind] which has been modified by the direct influence of the external world" and "seeks to bring the influence of the external world to bear upon the id [mind]."[15] Regardless of what it is called, there must be some "goal-seeking mechanism"[16] or "inner institution"[17] capable of ordering wishes in accordance with their priority or possibility of attainment and of screening sensations for relevant information. However, to order wishes and determine relevance requires the ego to repress distracting wishes and sensations.[18] Since repression is a process of keeping something from consciousness, the process itself must be unconscious. An unconscious process can only be set in motion automatically, "like a conditioned reflex" rather than a deliberate judgment.[19] It is generally accepted that "anxiety" activates repression, but there is some question as to what triggers, so to speak, anxiety.[20] Noting that anxiety makes its appearance only with the development of a stable "self system," more than one psychiatrist has answered that anxiety is aroused by anything that is incompatible with the individual's self-concept.[21]

Yet I suspect that most psychoanalysts would claim that other factors, such as the "superego" or a past traumatic event, are more important in arousing anxiety. Additional empirical support for the prominence of self-conception, however, is to be found in entirely different approaches to psychology. A case in point is Piaget's analysis of the relationship between the development of a self-concept and the ability to cooperate as an autonomous member of a group. Piaget's research convinced him that the individual in early childhood does not differentiate between the self and the external world. The paradoxical consequence is that very young children are egocentric, in the sense that all attention is centered on their own activity and they lack perspective on their abilities, but they are not self-conscious because they do not distinguish themselves from anything "external." Only as children construct an objective external world through experience do they begin to conceive of themselves as distinct entities, and only then will they be capable of the reciprocity that assures both personal autonomy and group cohesion. Autonomy results because of increased perspective, or objectivity, and group cohesion is made possible because "the self . . . takes its stand on the norms of reciprocity and objective discussion, and knows how to submit to these in order to make itself respected."[22]

Although empirically oriented studies have presented substantial evidence for the close relationship between goal directed behavior and self-conception, empirical evidence is always inconclusive.[23] I want to establish that action necessarily presupposes self-conception, that we must assume all mentally competent persons to possess a self-concept. Only then can I explain the reason Weber was unable either to deny or to gratify his urge to engage in politics and substantiate his conclusion that one cannot be both politician and scientist. For this purpose, only an argument based on logical considerations will suffice. One such argument could be based upon the nature of memory. Although, strictly speaking, memory is conceivable without self-reference, self-reference is an obvious requirement for memory to possess continuity, to be anything more than a random series of mental pictures.[24] Self-reference implies self-awareness, and to the extent that a coherent memory is necessary for effective interaction with one's environment, so is an awareness of self.

A more telling and, in the present context, a more useful argument can be developed from George Herbert Mead's analysis of language and thought. Communication through language requires that individuals be able to imagine themselves in the place of others in order to assess the impact of their words. The only way individuals can be assured that their symbols arouse the same response in the others that would be aroused in themselves is to take the perspective of the others toward their own verbal and physical gestures. Otherwise, one would be reduced merely to giving stimuli to the other in the form of verbal cries or threatening behavior, usually sufficient for the needs of lower animals but hardly adequate for intelligent conversation. A bird that signals a flock with a cry when startled is not uttering a warning. The cry is still given if the bird is alone.[25] Since the taking of the other's perspective to one's own verbal and physical gestures necessarily involves a degree of self-awareness, it can be argued from the analysis of linguistic communication alone that self-conception is a necessity.[26]

But the point is made more forcefully when this analysis is extended to the process of thinking or deliberation. Deliberation is a weighing of alternatives and, therefore, "simply an internalized or implicit conversation of the individual with himself,"[27] or as Piaget puts it, "internal deliberation" is a "discussion which is conducted with oneself just as it might be conducted with real interlocutors or opponents."[28] For action to be deliberate, at least one alternative course, inaction, must have been considered and rejected. Every deliberate action, in other words, must entail some deliberation. If deliberation is a conversation with oneself, then consciously motivated action would be impossible without a self-concept. For not only must one assume the perspective of the other, one must be the other. If one must be the other to oneself, then surely one must possess a self-concept. And if a self-concept is necessary for deliberation, it seems reasonable to conclude that personal identity is a "basic need" for any creature not instinctually adapted to its environment. It certainly must be presumed for that type of behavior that involves normative commitment.

Indispensability, however, does not necessarily make something obligatory in a normative sense. Many indispensable needs, such as oxygen and water, are not bestowed with moral significance. Since I have asserted that Weber's *commitments* to both science and politics were logically entailed in his self-concept, I must now demonstrate how self-conception necessarily leads to commitment.

Most of the rules that guide our behavior are derived in some way from our social and cultural context. Some we follow because it is expedient, or at least prudent, to conform to the expectations of our fellows. Others we may follow habitually, mechanically, without reflection.[29] Neither case involves normative considerations. Only internalized standards, consciously applied by the actor, can be considered moral rules and relevant to the problem at hand. To say that these rules are derived from the social context through a process of socialization might be true in most cases, but it is not very enlightening. It does not explain how the rules become internalized or why they are obligatory.

A prominent explanation is offered in the psychoanalytical analysis of the creation of the superego through infantile (and therefore unconscious) identification with authority figures upon whom the infant is dependent. Self-esteem is closely associated with guilt, which is the anxiety felt by the ego toward the superego.[30] As an empirical explanation of the origin of moral rules, this analysis is compatible with the fact-value dichotomy. Up to a certain point, it is also compatible with the argument being developed here, because to identify with something is to incorporate it into one's self-concept. On the other hand, psychoanalytical theorists typically assume that the superego is effective because the identifications that form it are unconscious and beyond control by the conscious "ego."[31] I wish to demonstrate that conscious identity is also a source of moral rules, and probably the more important source.

This can be accomplished by a brief analysis of the necessary characteristics of deliberate action. By definition, deliberate action is planned behavior. The actor chooses the most appropriate means available and decides whether to employ them (to engage in action). Evaluation assumes choice, and it is this element that makes deliberate action particularly relevant to the question of normative commitment. For the question is pointless without the assumption that normative commitments will provide criteria to make choices resulting in deliberate action. Meaningful choice presumes alternatives, the most important in the present context being action and inaction. To choose between these two alternatives, the individual is required to "project" the completed act mentally so that the effects and costs of each alternative can be estimated. To make this estimate and to assess the chances for a successful completion of the act, the actor must project not only the desired end state of affairs but also (in some degree of detail) the course of action leading to this end.[32] This "course of action" is the actor's own behavior, the actor doing what is required to achieve the end, applying the necessary means. Therefore, the actor must project at least a self-image. Consequently, it does not make sense to speak of deliberate action without a projected act or to speak of a projected act without a self-conceptualization.[33] When one engages in deliberate action, one necessarily conceptualizes himself or herself, for self-conceptualization is a precondition for such action.

Action is not, of course, always "self-conscious" in the colloquial sense of the phrase. This fact does not present an insuperable difficulty. For as Alfred Schutz's analysis of action indicates, a complex act will require the subject to concentrate on its various steps or stages in the manipulation of means, the completion of each being a condition for those that follow. Each of these stages can be considered an act in itself, acts that are given a unity and an overriding motive through being part of a single projected act, with an end state of affairs toward which all the stages are directed. It must be assumed that, even though the end state of affairs cannot completely dominate consciousness, the subject can be *immediately* aware of the entire projected act. Otherwise, a person could not effectively direct the various "sub-acts" necessary in applying the means toward the projected end state of affairs.[34] The structure of the human thought process must be assumed to be able to "hold" an intention just as it "holds" a fact or concept in memory. This holding sets the framework for action inasmuch as a projected act can become immediately conscious to the subject so that he or she can direct action and take into account information relevant to the completion of the act. In other words, one is not always conscious of either the end or all the means of a projected act at any given instance, but it must be assumed that the projected act can be immediately given to consciousness so that it can serve as a sort of "map" by which the subject directs his or her action.[35]

At first sight, this analysis may appear to repeat, from a slightly different perspective, the arguments of Mead. There is a crucial difference. One can accept the conclusions of Piaget and the logic of Mead, admit that a self-concept is necessary, and yet be dissatisfied with it. Far from being committed to it, one could be committed to changing it. We now see that anyone engaged in deliberate action is committed to the self-concept, for a self-concept is a condition for deliberate action. One may have other commitments and desires, but to pursue them consciously one must also be committed to one's self-concept.

To see the importance of this commitment, it must be realized that a self-concept cannot be viewed as merely an essential tool, requiring nothing beyond its use. For we cannot assume that the "self" will simply be "there" without effort. Self-conception is always hypothetical because of the impossibility of objectifying subjectivity. Self-identity is achieved when a subjective "I" conceives an objective "me."[36] But conceiving is a relationship between the perceiver and the perceived; if the perceiver is to be the perceived, how can a single entity relate to itself? Does not a relationship require two entities? Does not the "I," as it contemplates the "me," stand apart from it?

Various formulas have been offered either to resolve or to avoid this paradox. It has led many to question the viability of the concept of "self," denying the existence of such an entity.[37] Regardless of the ontological status of its referent, however, we have seen that self-conception is indispensable. It is immaterial whether we have something in us corresponding to "self" or "soul." Given the fact of intersubjectivity, self-conception must be a "construct which the individual forms in order to render interaction predictable and manageable."[38] A person's conception of himself must be a projection, an image, which he may or may not "live up to."

Regardless of a person's success in the effort, one has no choice but to attempt actively and continually to maintain the plausibility of one's self-concept. Even the quest to satisfy physiological needs must be guided or constrained by the individual's self-concept. For instance, neither a self-conceived "playboy" nor a self-conceived "family man" could allow himself to satisfy his desire for sex solely on the basis of opportunity, at least not without accompanying feelings of shame or guilt. In our culture, the "playboy" would confine his sexual adventures to women "worth" seducing, while the "family man" would feel obliged to confine his sexual activity to his spouse. Every genuine identity (as opposed to the mere presentation of a social "front") will entail its own ethos. One's code of behavior will be based upon logical compatibility with his or her self-concept.

But is this code of behavior necessarily moral? A critic could object that it has only been demonstrated that one is necessarily committed to one's self-concept because of its crucial function, not that one's self-concept is normatively obligatory. Why must one believe one's self-concept to be intrinsically good? Could I not believe another person intrinsically or morally better than I, even though I realize that I must live up to what I am?

One cannot consciously strive for something that is recognized as incompatible with one's self-concept. More than this, one could not even *want* to strive for something incompatible with one's self-concept. The argument presented here applies to judging as much as it does to striving. Deliberation and choice are as essential to one as to the other. Deliberation is an internal conversation with oneself. It is impossible for one of the parties in this conversation consciously to judge the other morally deficient; they are, after all, identical. One can certainly be embarrassed or feel guilty because of failure, intentional or not, to live up to what one believes oneself to truly be. But only in this sense is it legitimate to speak of "self-esteem."[39] For the individual cannot have the ability to evaluate himself or herself by a standard incompatible with his or her self-conception, since commitment to self-conception is necessary for the occurrence of evaluation. If one possessed such a standard, in memory, the "superego," or whatever, it could not be used to evaluate oneself *consciously.* To believe otherwise is to believe that it is possible to confirm and condemn the same thing at the same time.

This certainly does not mean that self-conceptions are not subject to change. Indeed, Weber changed from "politician" to "scientist" rather abruptly. But he did not "will" this change, and he surely did not choose it. It was apparently brought on by his perception of his failure to live up to what he thought he was and his belated recognition of his real proclivities.

All changes in self-conception must happen through the process of "recognition." There is an inevitable logic in the colloquial phrase "to find oneself," in that one must have a self-concept before being able to embark upon a search. This search can only be an attempt to clarify an image already seen, however dimly. Most individuals at most times in their lives are sufficiently secure to avoid this search. Yet experiences of age, failure, or even success can call into question aspects of self-conception. Everyone is occasionally forced into a degree of self-doubt that requires the effort to recognize unclear aspects of themselves.[40] What makes this search possible is that only aspects of a fairly unified self-concept are considered problematic. To the extent that a significant part of the self-concept is in doubt, an individual could not engage in any sort of sustained, deliberate inquiry.

Of course, there are, as Mead pointed out, "all sorts of different selves answering to all sorts of different social relations." A person is usually one thing to a spouse and another to a boss. Yet Mead recognized that it must be a "unified self" that is adapted to different situations.[41] If one possessed several completely unrelated identities, one would probably have several memories and several unrelated, and perhaps conflicting, patterns of behavior. To put experience in perspective and entertain alternatives requires a secure self-concept. To integrate these experiences and cope with diverse demands imposed by one's environment, one must possess a unified self-concept.[42]

Unity is a matter of degree and can be expected to vary with complexity. The more a person's self-concept is composed of varied aspects, the less likely that all of them will be closely linked with one another. As long as the more isolated elements are not the central aspects of identity, they will probably result in no more than harmless idiosyncrasies. But when pivotal ideas about oneself are in conflict, the result will tend to be contradictory, self-defeating behavior. At a minimum, such an individual will suffer a great deal of mental anguish and self-doubt.[43] One cannot compartmentalize central aspects of one's self-concept because this conscious activity would require another, "higher" self-concept. Now, if social science and politics are each seen as fundamental ways by which behavior can be consistent with "values," then they will almost inevitably be among the central components of personal identity for those who see themselves as one or the other.

Consequently, the question with which I began this chapter, that is, why one could not compartmentalize commitments to both science and politics, needs to be displaced by one that comes close to being its opposite. It now needs to be understood how Weber could eventually achieve a degree of personal stability despite being committed in some way to both types of activity. We must understand how "politics" could continue to be an element of his self-concept even after he had come to see himself as a "scientist." To understand this, we must determine the nature of a self-concept, which I believe is necessarily composed of two distinct types of elements.

Given the function of self-conception in deliberate action, one must conceive of oneself as an agent. To project oneself engaged in purposeful behavior is by definition to see oneself as an agent. To be an agent is to be capable of something. At a minimum, this capability assumes the existence of a body, and we can say that one's image of one's body is a necessary component of one's self-concept.[44] Obviously, a belief in one's own body is a cognitive belief.[45] Similarly, one's assessment of all his or her capabilities, physical, mental, or temperamental, is cognitive because it is a belief about reality. The self-concept may be mentally projected in deliberate action, but projection cannot be mere fantasy if the individual is to remain "in touch" with reality.[46]

A self-conception could not, however, be completely composed of supposed capabilities. A capability is always the capability to do something; it does not exist in the abstract. One's identity as an agent, therefore, involves at least one additional type of component: something to be accomplished as well as the capability to accomplish it. In other words, "function" is a necessary type of component of self-conception, regardless of whether it involves a certain pattern of behavior or the achievement of a certain type of goal. Since self-conception is necessary for choice, it is impossible to choose the functions by which one defines oneself. Consequently, the functions constituting any particular self-concept must be a consequence of the individual's experience. To some extent, no doubt, the individual's eventual assessment of his or her capabilities after experiences of success and frustration will determine which functions come to dominate his or her self-concept.

More decisive, however, will be the inventory of functions available to the individual. This inventory will develop concomitantly with the individual's beliefs about the nature and structure of social reality. One's self-concept is largely dictated by what one sees as his or her "place" in his or her social context. As Piaget points out, children must "liberate" themselves from "the thought and will of others," especially the parents, before they can become conscious of themselves as distinct entities.[47] The consequence is that one initially comes to see oneself in contrast and, therefore, in relation to others. Likewise, Mead argues that a "self" could originate only in social interaction because symbolic communication is the only process through which one is forced to take an objective attitude toward oneself.[48]

Mature adults, of course, are not nearly as dependent as children upon specific interpersonal relationships to maintain their sense of personal identity. As one grows older, some "significant others" become "generalized."[49] Most identify with at least one communal group, using its associated behavioral conventions to provide functional focus to their self-conceptions. Almost everyone also incorporates a number of social roles into their self-concepts, those relating to occupation often being of central importance.[50] These sources of functional identity free the individual to some extent from dependence upon authority figures, allowing much greater flexibility in interpersonal relations than in childhood. But they simultaneously render the adult more dependent upon the social and cultural context in which particular groups and roles are relevant, as well as the explicit and implicit ideas, ideology, or theology that rationalizes them.

This dependence is not a universal necessity; it is simply the result of the manner in which most people "find" their identity. Although a self-conception can arise only in a social context, once one exists it is at least possible for it to change through the impact of new ideas concerning social roles or the nature of community that may go "against the whole world."[51] Weber's experience is a case in point. As a young man, he believed he was to play some sort of political role in the service of the German nation. After his breakdown he was forced to recognize himself as a scientist in the service of politics.

In Weber's sense, to be a scientist is not simply to perform a social role. It is one of a limited number of ways by which one can act "ethically," in accordance with ultimate values. These types of ethical behavior, and the identities they confer, transcend social context because they are purely formal; regardless of a particular individual's or society's ultimate values, from a strictly logical perspective, they can be pursued only in these ways.

Very few individuals take a strictly logical perspective. Most simply accept, without much reflection, the roles made available by circumstance and justified in terms of social functionality and cultural values. To some extent, the various roles and communal attachments that formulate the typical self-concept must be ordered into a hierarchy, since the self-concept must display some unity if the individual is to cope with the environment.[52] But very few individuals are completely conscious of the ultimate values or ideas that rationalize and legitimate the various aspects of their identities, let alone attempt to order them into a rational hierarchy. Typically, identities are sufficiently secure to allow the conduct of daily affairs without continual concern for them.[53] This no doubt allows a good deal of behavior incommensurate with one's self-concept and even incompatible elements within the same self-conception. Since we must constantly refer to ourselves, it cannot be said that we lack awareness of self, but we normally are not "self-conscious" unless we are for some reason "called into question." For most, self-conception is, in Rokeach's words, a "primitive belief" in the sense that it is simply taken for granted.[54]

At one time or another, however, everyone is called into question and experiences a painful modification of self-conception. A common source of this personal instability is tension between the functional and capability aspects of identity. For example, those who identify significantly with a competitive sport at which they cannot excel will eventually have to adapt their functional identity to reality or suffer persistent self-doubt.[55] Weber's problem was similar, except that his chances for adaptation were largely foreclosed. He had made politics a pivotal aspect of his self-concept, and it remained so even after he came to accept his inability to be a politician. As we have seen, politics and science are incompatible ways by which behavior can be rendered consistent with ultimate values. The most significant capabilities incorporated into Weber's self-concept were those appropriate to science, but the value that gave focus to his scientific activity, and therefore the most important functional aspect of his identity, was politics. In other words, Weber was committed to a type of activity in which he could not be active.

This was bound to be frustrating, but more so to Weber than to an ordinary individual. For he saw his inability not as a mere physical or even psychological handicap that might somehow be overcome but as a permanent, logical necessity. Furthermore, Weber could not embark upon a "search" for his "true identity," since his paradoxical view of himself was the result of a great deal of reflection and "soul searching." Unlike most, Weber could not take advantage of an unarticulated self-concept that could be altered through "recognition." Weber was already fully "recognized." In his own words, he was of necessity a "virtuoso," forced by his shattering experience to demand complete consistency between belief and life. For the scientist who emerged from this experience, persistent self-deception, or any kind of dissembling, was an impossibility. He simply had to live with his tension.[56]

If Weber could have seen himself primarily as a "German," a liberal "individualist," or an "educator" (all of which are implied by the ultimate values that various commentators have mistakenly ascribed to him), life would have been much easier. But despite considerable psychological pressure to emphasize other aspects and a number of seemingly available alternatives, politics was the functional focus of Weber's identity. As seen in Chapter Two, Weber devoted himself to politics at an early age. But the way in which politics was incorporated into his self-concept changed drastically. The primary capability aspect of his identity changed from politician to scientist. Politics then became the most important functional aspect of his identity. But perhaps it always had been. Perhaps his long period of "preparing for politics" required that politics be seen as more important even than its chief object, the German nation. As will be seen presently, Weber's later nationalism was the result of a need for a communal context for politics, rather than of a love of things German. Perhaps this was unconsciously so even at the time he gave his Freiburg address.

We will never know; the necessary evidence is gone forever. More important, however, is the reason politics inevitably came to displace nation as the primary functional aspect of Weber's conscious identity. It was, despite the doctrine of the fact-value dichotomy, a logical consequence of his social thought. Weber was not entirely incorrect in believing that general views of reality determine ultimate values, which, in turn, allow the formation of "personality." He only had the sequence and a few of the details wrong. General views of social reality provide the functional aspects of identity, which, in turn, determine the ultimate commitments by which individuals try to guide their behavior.

Strictly speaking, this assertion does not necessarily contradict the doctrine of the fact-value dichotomy, but rather renders it irrelevant to the understanding of human affairs. Whether value statements can be deduced from fact statements is perhaps an interesting puzzle. It is relevant to social science, however, only if it is concluded that cognitive beliefs cannot logically require normative commitments. If identity is derived from cognitive beliefs, then cognitive beliefs do logically entail normative commitments. For self-conception is a prerequisite for evaluation and choice, and the individual has no choice but to be committed to his or her self-concept. This self-concept cannot itself be a matter of choice. Consequently, its components are valued because they are incorporated into self-conception, not incorporated into self-conception because they are valued.

Self-concepts are indeed composed of cognitive beliefs. As previously discussed, a self-concept must refer to an agent. As such, it must be analytically composed of both capability and functional aspects, even though these two types of components may be fused into an undifferentiated "image" in the mind of an individual.[57] Assessments of capability are by definition judgments of fact. The social roles and communal groups that provide the functional aspects of identity are also cognitive beliefs since they refer to the things, processes, or forces that are believed to make up social reality. In the broadest sense of the term, they constitute social theory, unarticulated as it may be for most. Yet even those whose preoccupations are with day to day living and year to year planning, with the particularities of a culture they neither articulate nor question, must presume meanings for such notions as "society," "government," "nation," and "human being."

Of course, the social conceptions assumed by the typical person are largely received from the cultural context, inculcated by a process of "socialization" and conditioned by a variety of historical and psychological factors. Certainly in this respect Weber was not the typical person. He was quite conscious of his most fundamental concepts. Far from received knowledge, his social thought was an intricate and in many respects innovative effort to make sense of his social context and personal experience. We have already seen how he isolated the most significant capability and functional aspects of his identity by formulating a theory of "personality," which posits a finite set of personality types found in varying degrees in all social contexts. Although his aptitude for science was developed in youth as a response to definite needs, his commitment to politics was a *logical* consequence of his social thought. The following chapter will detail the role that Weber believed politics to play in the development and maintenance of civilization. But more decisive for his identification with and evaluation of political activity was that he considered it the defining characteristic of humanity.

Weber did not attempt to explicate his conception of human nature. We can assume he had one, however, because everyone must. Anyone, that is, who considers himself human. For such a presumption only makes sense given the possibility of distinguishing between human and non-human. In other words, anyone who considers himself a human being presupposes a defining characteristic, irrespective of his ability to articulate it. Similarly, any *comprehensive* social theory must contain at least an implicit conception of human nature insomuch as the very idea of the "social" depends upon the collective behavior of individuals. Even theories that hold that social events are largely unaffected by will and purpose must recognize the existence of individuals and at least implicitly indicate their nature.[58]

All defensible conceptions of human nature define it in terms of an ability or a propensity to use an ability in a certain manner.

For example, a historically frequent defining characteristic is "rationality," although teleological definitions require that this ability be used to understand a natural or divine order. Rather than "ability," theories that postulate a mechanistic model of human nature might more appropriately refer to a mode of "interaction," but regardless of terminology, it is difficult to see how humanity could be defined other than "functionally."[59] Descriptive definitions, those that do no more than focus upon a set of physical features, do not tell us what we are but only attempt to find attributes that we all supposedly share. This exercise presupposes that the set of subjects sharing these attributes has already been identified by some other, unspecified criterion. Consequently, empirical analysis can only discern the extent to which a specified set of subjects displays the defining characteristic. In other words, empirical analysis can only provide evidence of whether, or to what extent, a given group or individual can be considered human. The criterion itself has to be a presupposition of empirical research, not its result. It is a metaphysical assumption necessary for social thought.[60]

Weber conceived of human nature as the ability to engage in politics. This assertion will be substantiated and developed in the next chapter. My purpose at this juncture is simply to point out the necessary relation between social theory and identity and, therefore, between such theory and commitment. Given the previous analysis of the relationship between self-conception and commitment, this can be done rather concisely. Every comprehensive social theory at least implies a conception of human nature. As a result, self-maintenance for a person conscious of his or her most general assumptions about the nature of society necessarily entails the furthering of the conditions conducive to humanity. For every comprehensive social theory defines to some extent its advocate, at least to the extent that one considers oneself human.

Assuming consciousness of fundamental assumptions, the logical relationship between self-conception and commitment would seem to require that scholarly activity will be focused upon topics believed to affect the possibilities for human expression and development. This was clearly the case for Weber. Although his initial studies in the post-breakdown period were focused upon the social factors that conditioned the occurrence of "personality," his later work was almost exclusively, albeit often indirectly, concerned with the possibilities for meaningful political action in modern society. Unlike in his pre-breakdown period, he no longer considered himself occupied with political problems but rather with the problem of politics itself. Given the paradox within his self-concept, it is not surprising that part of this problem concerned the political possibilities of an organized social science, conscious of its own needs and limitations.

CHAPTER SIX

The Political Function of Social Science

Despite the inability of a genuinely committed social scientist to engage in serious political activity, organized social science is a significant social phenomenon with potentially important political implications. Weber was not oblivious to these implications. In fact, he believed that organized social science could contribute to conditions encouraging a high degree of meaningful political action and rational public policy. In this chapter, I am ultimately concerned with the reasons Weber felt social science was crucial to meaningful politics, as well as the organizational principles that would allow it to perform its political function without undermining the integrity of social scientific endeavor. It is first necessary, however, to understand what Weber meant by meaningful politics. In the process of making this clear, I hope also to clarify the unifying relationship that his concern with politics had for the seemingly diverse topics of his mature scholarship.

There has been some confusion over Weber's notion of politics. It is frequently asserted that he used the term to describe any behavior that employs or at least tacitly threatens physical coercion.[1] Actually, Weber used this criterion only to distinguish between political and nonpolitical *organizations*.[2] Given his view of the nature of collective concepts, the grounds for characterizing an organization would have to be pragmatic, and therefore provisional. Collective concepts are ideal-types, intellectual constructions formulated to highlight relevant behavior rather than refer to real entities. As noted previously, Weber defined politics in terms of action. Obviously, he believed that those collective endeavors in which physical force tends to be employed have especially important consequences for political action; otherwise he would not have called them "political organizations." However, there is absolutely no evidence that he attempted to characterize as "political" all action in which force is used. Since collective concepts are themselves defined in terms of action, it would have been rather odd for Weber to have defined a type of action as an attribute of a collective concept.

He defined politics quite explicitly as "any kind of *independent* leadership in action."[3] Because concepts referring to individual action are not ideal-typical, at least not in the same sense as collective concepts, "leadership in action" must refer to individual initiative, and a political act must be an individual initiative to achieve a social goal. In a certain sense, of course, all action by definition entails individual initiative. Yet there is clearly a distinction between adapting to circumstances or conforming to expectation and trying to defend or change circumstances and expectations. The latter type of activity involves a higher degree of risk and a different kind of initiative. It requires the readiness to accept responsibility for the consequences of one's action. This responsibility, we have seen, is the basis for a distinctively political ethic, and a distinctively political personality.

We have also seen that personality, or identity, is ideal-typical. Like collective concepts, personal identities are always intellectual constructions or projections that are never completely descriptive of real behavior or propensities. Political action itself, however, is a ubiquitous aspect of social experience. It is so because of the ubiquity of conflict in social life. The perfect adaptation of all social phenomena, or the complete conformity of all behavior to universally shared expectations would eliminate any need or occasion for political action. But conflict cannot be excluded from social life. It can change its form, its means, or its context, but it cannot be eliminated. " 'Peace' is nothing more than a change in the form of the conflict or in the antagonists or in the objects of the conflict, or *finally* in the chances of selection."[4] Conflict means struggle, and struggle requires the antagonists to recruit followers, forge compromises, and accept the kind of risk that defines their action as political.[5]

Although politics is a ubiquitous aspect of social life, the extent to which different individuals engage in it varies considerably. Political action is a matter of degree, in both frequency and scope. As far as the latter is concerned, it is obvious that many confine their politics, as defined by Weber, to the workplace or perhaps the family, accepting the broader structures of authority as unalterable givens of social reality. In modern society, characterized by mass populations and dominated by impersonal organizations, almost all are forced to accept restraints upon the scope of their political activity. Few are so situated as to realistically hope to exercise any significant measure of social control.

Even those so situated are quite often incapable of exercising or really even accepting this responsibility. According to Weber, for instance, the fundamental political problem facing Germany before the World War I was the rule of a political dilettante in the person of the Kaiser, aided by bureaucratic executives pretending to be political leaders.[6] For Weber argued that bureaucratic organizations require their functionaries to develop capabilities fundamentally incompatible with those required by politics.[7] Political office holders in Germany were not political leaders because they lacked those personal characteristics, discussed in an earlier chapter, conducive to political action.[8] In the following pages, I will discuss Weber's analysis of the impediments placed upon the development of political attributes by the growth of bureaucratic organization. For the moment, I want only to emphasize that despite the ubiquity of politics, both the chances for political action in any given context and the personal aptitude for such activity are matters of degree and, therefore, susceptible to maximization.

Weber wanted to see political capabilities maximized even though precluded from engaging in politics himself. He wanted this because politics was his ultimate "value." In Wolfgang Mommsen's words, the image of the politician, especially the democratic politician, presents "the features . . . of his own ideal personality."[9] But it could not have been his image of himself, only of what he thought individuals must be if they are to be fully human. In other words, Weber believed that the ability to engage in politics is the defining characteristic of humanity. Textual evidence for this assertion is far from abundant. In fact, I can find only two explicit expressions of Weber's conception of humanity. Neither directly points to politics as the defining characteristic, although one, that "nothing is worthwhile for men as men which *cannot be done with passion*," does refer to one of the three attributes of the political personality.[10]

The other, that "we are cultural beings, endowed with the capacity and the will to take a deliberate attitude towards the world and to lend it significance," refers even less directly to politics.[11] It merely states that we have the ability to value, to find significance in things. Given the nature of personal identity we have no choice but to exercise this ability, as Weber knew.[12] Yet this second statement does indicate the reason we should not expect to find an *explicit* conception of human nature in Weber's writings.

Thinking that values were the basis of identity, or "personality," he was forced to conclude that his preference for the political personality was the result of blind will. Any other logical orientation to behavior would be just as reasonable, just as valid.[13] Although he saw that values were derived in some way from general conceptions of reality, he did not realize that this is because such conceptions determine to some extent personal identities. And he apparently did not consider the possibility that a conception of humanity was one of those metaphysical beliefs that he knew were unavoidable.

As discussed near the conclusion of the preceding chapter, a conception of human nature is unavoidable, and Weber's is clear even if implicit. It can be seen in his respective attitudes toward the three types of personality that he isolated. He seems, at times, to be discouraging those tempted by the two alternatives to the "politician." Those who chose the role of "saint," he argued, must acknowledge their own social irrelevance if they are to avoid inconsistency and "sentimental fraud."[14] And only a person ready to put on "blinders," thinking that the "fate of his soul depends upon whether or not he makes the correct conjecture at this passage of this manuscript," is fit for science.[15] On the other hand, Weber emphasized the meaningfulness of politics:

> The career of politics grants a feeling of power. The knowledge of influencing men, of participating in power over them, and *above all,* the feeling of holding in one's hands a nerve fiber of historically important events can elevate the professional politician above everyday routine even when he is placed in formally modest positions.[16]

Although he did not fail to point out the difficulties of fulfilling a commitment to a life of politics, he certainly did not discourage those who might be able to make such a commitment.[17] It is not surprising that of his three types of personality, he delineated the distinctive personal attributes only of the politician.[18]

By far the most decisive grounds, however, for attributing a political conception of human nature to Weber is that a concern for politics provided the basic "value" that unified the seemingly diverse topics of his mature work by providing the rationale for his collective concepts. As discussed in the preceding chapter, every comprehensive social theory must entail a conception of humanity and, therefore, must define the theory's advocate, at least to the extent that he is aware of his theoretical assumptions. Given the logical relationships between self-identity and commitment, the theoretically self-conscious scholar necessarily focuses upon topics and formulates collective concepts that he hopes will reveal the dimensions and problems of being human.

Weber could not be an exception to this logical necessity. In the pages immediately following, I will demonstrate that a concern for politics does play a pivotal, unifying role in Weber's social thought.[19] This demonstration will not only illustrate the manner in which all social theory is "normative" but also serve to highlight the dangers and possibilities of political life in the modern world. An understanding of these dangers is essential for understanding the political function that an organized social science can fulfill. For while Weber argued that active political partisanship was fundamentally incompatible with scientific objectivity, he also believed that social science had to perform a political function in order for meaningful politics to flourish in modern society. In reconciling these two beliefs, he formulated institutional principles for social science compatible with both the personal requisites of social science and his commitment to politics.

To this point, I have attempted to present the logic of Weber's analysis, not hesitating to supplement his arguments when appropriate. Now, however, his argument appears to rest upon empirical theses concerning conditions in modern society and their implications for political life. Consequently, it may appear to be beyond the scope of this study to establish the validity of his institutional principles for social science. This is only partly the case. For Weber's conceptualizations are ideal-types. If his logic is sound and if one accepts his most fundamental definitions, the ideal-typical processes that he analyzed are logical possibilities. This much cannot be denied. But the extent to which a given context approximates these possibilities is indeed an empirical question, which I cannot answer here. Weber believed that his ideal-typical processes were relevant, or "real," possibilities because they expressed the probable consequences of a continued rationalization of Western culture. This process, mentioned in Chapter Four, is a collective concept itself. Weber's historical investigations have convinced many of their empirical validity, but it should be recognized that such validity is simply assumed here.

Rationalization is the ordering of experience by reducing it to calculable elements. Calculation allows predictability, if not control, and perhaps an increased measure of security and efficiency, which are its primary benefits.[20] *Cultural* rationalization is simply the increasing propensity to rationalize the various aspects of life. Weber discerned this cultural phenomenon while attempting to come to an understanding of his personal malaise. The concept first appeared in his famous study, *The Protestant Ethic and the Spirit of Capitalism,* in which he was trying to do more than discover the origins of the mentality conducive for a high degree of capital accumulation. He was also, and more important for him, trying to understand the need of modern individuals for a "calling": a purpose in life that defines them as "personalities."[21]

There is some evidence that Weber realized, even at this early date, the threat to politics potentially posed by cultural rationalization.[22] In any case, it became his overriding concern in the following years. Many of the topics of Weber's somewhat fragmentary work only occasionally deal explicitly with political matters, and some scholars would disagree with this assertion.

Most notably, Wolfgang Schluchter and Juergen Habermas have concluded that it is the multiform rationalization of Western society itself that provides the unifying theme. Certainly the diverse topics covered in his most comprehensive work, *Economy and Society*, are linked to this theme, but the obvious question raised from Weber's methodological perspective concerns the reason he saw this as a meaningful focal point. Schluchter and Habermas do not dwell on the issue because they reject this methodological perspective. They are concerned with the process of rationalization because they believe its analysis provides the conceptual equipment allowing for the objective, universal history that Weber thought impossible.[23] Consequently, whatever the ultimate validity of their endeavor, one cannot hold that rationalization itself was Weber's unifying theme unless one maintains that he valued it for itself. Since this is manifestly incorrect, it must be assumed that Weber's explicit ideal-types, including that of rationalization, were formulated with regard to some other value.

Other scholars, most notably Wolfgang J. Mommsen, have mistakenly believed Weber's ultimate political value to have been nationalism rather than politics itself. This misperception is certainly not the result of careless reading, for Weber on numerous occasions confirmed his commitment to the interests of the German nation.[24] What has been overlooked even by such an eminent and well-informed scholar as Professor Mommsen is the possibility that nationalism was of instrumental value to Weber, rather than something meaningful in and of itself.[25] In an explicit effort to avoid attaching any "mystical" connotation to the term, he defined the *nation-state* simply as the "secular power organization of the nation."[26] A person of Weber's temperament and intellectual sophistication is not likely to become too emotional over a power organization. He reportedly expressed amazement that anyone could be expected to "love the monster."[27] Lest one think that he mindlessly glorified the German "nation," of which the nation-state is only the organizational expression, his numerous uncomplimentary remarks concerning German character, especially when made in comparison to Latin and English character, ought to be kept in mind.[28]

Actually he had no choice; he had to be a nationalist. Not because such an orientation had been inculcated at an early age or because of some deep unconscious need, but simply because for the foreseeable future the nation will be the basis for political community in the modern world.[29] Meaningful politics can only occur within a communal context. Any meaningful action, action that affirms one's sense of identity, involves both commitment and a sense of responsibility. The nature of personal identity requires this. Consequently, to be meaningful, political action requires a social commitment:

> The mere "power politician" may get strong effects, but actually his work leads nowhere and is senseless. . . . It is a product of a shoddy and superficially blasé attitude towards the meaning of human conduct; and it has no relation whatsoever to the knowledge of tragedy with which all action, but especially political action, is truly interwoven. The final result of political action often, no, even regularly, stands in completely inadequate and often paradoxical relation to its original meaning. This is fundamental to all history. . . . But because of this fact, the serving of a cause must not be absent if action is to have inner strength.[30]

To repeat an earlier quotation, the feeling of meaningfulness that politics can give is due to "the feeling of holding in one's hands a nerve fiber of historically important events." In the broadest view, politics is the effort to control history, to take at least partial responsibility for the development of one's species. This is so because meaningful politics requires not just a personal commitment but also a community that can potentially appreciate and realize that commitment. To attempt to control one's "history" assumes that one is a part of either an actual or a potential community, for only community provides the individual with a link to the future. Only given some form of communal identification could one's values find realization through "descendents."[31]

In the modern world the nation provides this bridge to the future. At least this is the way Weber saw it: "The fatherland does not lie as a mummy in the grave of our ancestors, but it should live as the land of our descendents."[32] He left little doubt that he wanted the descendents of contemporary Germans to be politically mature, as indicated by the following passage, written in the midst of what was then considered total war:

> The "will to impotence" domestically, . . . is incompatible with the "will to power" internationally. . . . If the nation refuses to risk one, then may it also deny to itself the other. For it would lead to nothing politically. Then, in fact, this war, a battle for the participation of our nation in the responsibility for the future of the earth, would be "meaningless" and a naked slaughter.[33]

For a number of social and historical reasons peculiar to Germany, he felt that the German people had far to go before learning to cope with political responsibility.[34] Indeed, most of the institutional prescriptions he offered for post-war Germany were intended to increase the political maturity of the populace in general, and thereby encourage the development of genuinely political leaders.

Before these institutional prescriptions can be understood, especially those for social science, the problem they were to alleviate must be grasped. As indicated previously, the problem for meaningful politics followed in the train of cultural rationalization. This process is almost inevitable, or as inevitable as anything can be in social life.[35] An uncertain, competitive environment is bound to create an almost irresistible incentive to maximize reliability, and this is exactly the motive behind the rationalization of experience. For rationalization by definition results in a degree of calculation, which, in turn, allows the weighing of immediate benefits, the assessment of relative advantage, and, most important, relatively predictable results. Weber argued that cultural rationalization tended to create an environment hostile to communal values, including even nationalism.[36] Since meaningful politics can take place only within a communal context, cultural rationalization threatened one of its prerequisites, and therefore humanity itself.

To comprehend the process by which cultural rationalization threatens communal commitment and to see how Weber's most important collective concepts are a response to this perceived threat, it is necessary to begin with the first of his two levels of conceptualization: that referring to individual action. His distinction between two type of conscious action is quite familiar. Briefly, *value-rational* action is a direct attempt to achieve something valued for itself, while *goal-rational* action attempts to achieve something instrumental to some higher value.[37]

"Social action" is either goal- or value-rational action that "takes account of the behavior of others and is thereby oriented in its course."[38] Action can be oriented socially in two distinct ways, each of which results in a distinct type of social relationship: either "communal" or "associative." This distinction was almost as commonplace in social thought for Weber's generation as it is for ours; Weber's contribution was only to have defined it in terms of his two types of individual action. "Community," cooperation through value-rational action because the social relationship is valued for itself, rests upon shared values. These values may range from the belief in a natural order reflected in the stratification of social status to a simple sense of identity or "belongingness." "Association," cooperation through goal-rational action because the social relationship is instrumental to some individual value, rests upon the complementary values of the participants. In an association, each intends to maximize his particular interest.[39]

Political action, in Weber's sense, may be either goal-rational or value-rational, but it is always oriented and justified by communal relationships. Indeed, such activity is by definition intended to legislate or protect the values that sustain a community. In itself, rationalization threatens neither communal commitment nor meaningful politics:

> [It] can proceed in a variety of . . . directions; *positively* in that of a deliberate formulation of ultimate values; or negatively, at the expense of emotional values; and finally, in favor of a lapse of belief in values, a pure goal-rationalism, at the expense of value-rational action.[40]

The last alternative would result, of course, in the destruction of communal values and the end of meaningful politics. Weber feared that this was the direction in which cultural rationalization was turning. With the concept of "bureaucracy," he believed he had isolated the chief impetus pushing the process of rationalization in this negative direction. Since organization by definition involves a division of labor instrumental to some overall end, it is always to some degree associational.[41] "Bureaucracy," simply put, is completely rationalized organization that, under ideal conditions, maximizes reliability. As such, it is characterized by specialization and training, clear responsibility, and a hierarchical chain of command. A bureaucracy is a "living machine," where routine and impersonal expertise dominates subjective evaluation and socially sanctioned patterns of deference.[42]

No one has ever worked in such a robot-like environment. "Bureaucracy" is a collective concept, a mental construction used to direct attention to patterns of behavior "relevant" to a problem. The collective concepts used by Weber had their source in his commitment to meaningful politics. Failure to understand this has resulted in a number of misconceived criticisms of Weber's approach to bureaucracy. He is typically taken to task for one or both of two reasons. First, it is often assumed that he defined the elements of bureaucracy by the "extent that they contribute to administrative efficiency."[43] His "model" is then criticized as an inadequate guide for maximizing administrative goals. Such criticism misses the mark because it ignores the purpose of Weber's concept, which is to isolate those patterns of action that lead to a certain kind of cultural rationalization. Although his discussion of the benefits of bureaucratic organization do indicate that efficiency might be among them, the primary benefit attained by increasing bureaucratization is *reliability*, achieved through predictability and calculation.[44]

Weber's ideal-type of bureaucracy is also often criticized for supposed descriptive inadequacies. It is frequently charged that it blinded him to some important problem of organization.[45] It would not serve my purpose to discuss whether Weber's ideal-type necessarily precludes consideration of certain problems. It is sufficient to note that these critics either err in assuming that Weber intended his ideal-type to describe some sort of ontologically independent entity or simply accept as axiomatic that their particular problem is normatively more crucial than Weber's. He was concerned with the obstacles and prospects for meaningful politics. His conception of bureaucratic organization enabled him to analyze the chief threat to such activity. This analysis, in turn, enabled him to propose a partial defense against this threat.

The basic tenet of Weber's analysis is the general bifurcation of organizational goals and the individual goals of organizational workers in a bureaucracy. The organizational goal is imposed upon the bureaucracy from "without," justifying the organization to its membership. But the individual bureaucrat views the organization from "within"—as an organization that is a system of roles and status. In other words, the organization is instrumental to the bureaucrat's own personal career goals. Consequently, the organization has an instrumental value by itself, quite apart from its ability to accomplish organizational goals.[46] The important point is that the bifurcation of organizational and individual goals is not necessarily due to corruption on the part of the bureaucrat but rather is presumed by the very idea of bureaucracy. The bureaucrat is a specialist; the bureaucrat is not supposed to be concerned with the larger goals of the organization but is supposed to do the job for which he or she is trained and held responsible. It is the bureaucrat's "honor" to be self-disciplined to submit to the will of superiors even when he or she believes their orders to be ill advised or morally reprehensible. Without such discipline, rational, efficient organization would be impossible.[47]

Such is the ethos of bureaucracy. Specialization and careerism lead to professionalism, buttressed by an elaborate system of material rewards and, more important, status. The self-esteem, as well as career, of bureaucrats is bound up in this ethos.[48] But what criterion will they use to assess the adequacy of their own performance and that of their subordinates? They will certainly not refer to the abstract, legitimizing goal of the organization, since they are trained and disciplined to avoid assuming this responsibility. It is likely that they will engage in what in modern jargon is called "satisficing." The bureaucrats will attempt to accomplish their specialized task in such a way that all interested parties have their "short-term" interests sufficiently satisfied to prevent them from complaining.[49] And who is to complain or even notice if most organizational activity has little relevance to organizational goals? Certainly not those interested parties who tend to have their needs protected. Rarely, if ever, the "public," which is largely unorganized and always uninformed except in regard to immediate needs for material comfort and personal security;[50] it is just these latter interests with which the bureaucracy is primarily concerned, because they provide convenient measures of personal adequacy while being compatible with bureaucratic "honor."

Indeed, as society becomes increasingly bureaucratized, the citizens become increasingly dependent upon bureaucracy for even the essentials of life. Increasing dependence upon bureaucracy means that social life becomes increasingly goal-rational as citizens approach bureaucracy out of a sense of self-interest. Bureaucracy tends to deal with immediate needs, needs that are to some degree hedonistic in that they serve the individual's self-interest.[51] This tendency toward a goal-rational social orientation will increase as a greater proportion of the population becomes employed in bureaucratic institutions and is inculcated with the bureaucratic ethos, including its bifurcation of social and individual goals.[52]

Both directly and indirectly the bureaucratization of modern society tends to destroy the opportunities for meaningful political action. It does so directly by making it extremely difficult for the non-bureaucrat to participate in public life, denying this person the opportunities to develop the knowledge, skills, and aptitudes necessary for effective political action. Citizens tend to become dependent upon the state bureaucracy to make the crucial decisions concerning general social policy. They never develop a political "sense of proportion" because they are never called upon to weigh alternatives, to consider great risks.[53] The indirect threat, and the more dangerous, is the creation of a hostile environment for communal values. To the extent that citizens become preoccupied with individual concerns, they lose any sense of social responsibility, and their activity is increasingly goal-rational. Weber even hinted that cultural rationalization, given irresistible force by the technical superiority of bureaucracy, could destroy the capacity for meaningful politics.[54]

A lifeless machine is *congealed genius* [geronnener Geist]. Only this gives it the power to force men into its service and determine daily their working lives so completely as is the case in the factory. *Congealed genius* is also this living machine, bureaucratic organization, with its specialization and training, its division of jurisdiction, its rules and hierarchical relations of authority. In union with the dead machine it is at work manufacturing the shell of bondage which men will be forced to inhabit some day, as powerless as the Fellahs of ancient Egypt, if a technically superior administration were to be the ultimate and sole value in the ordering of their affairs.[55]

But despite his often discussed heroic pessimism, Weber did not think that this state of affairs was inevitable. In addition to analyzing the potential dangers to communal ideals, he also attempted to isolate the processes that could counteract these dangers, and from these possibilities he derived his political prescriptions. "Charismatic leadership" is the collective concept used to elucidate these positive possibilities. He conceived of it as an anti-bureaucratic force that might divert the course of cultural rationalization toward the positive direction of "deliberate formulation of ultimate values."

As previously noted, Weber defined politics as "any sort of leadership in action." But such leadership has nothing to do with followers, since politics is an action concept. Charismatic leadership, like bureaucracy, is quite obviously a collective concept. It refers to a pattern of activity that is never completely the case, and the activity that defines it is of followers, not leaders. For it is a form of legitimacy, a pattern of voluntary submission to another's will due to "belief in revelation and heroes."[56] Like bureaucracy, Weber's concept of charismatic leadership has occasionally been misunderstood or inappropriately criticized, usually because neither its ideal-typical character nor its function in Weber's thought is appreciated. For instance, Weber is frequently supposed to be asserting that charisma is an actual personal quality rather than only imputed.[57] Quite apart from the question of whether his words can be stretched to cover such an interpretation, it should be apparent that the actual personal qualities of a leader do not have a necessary connection with the pattern of submission;[58] a collective concept is a projected pattern of action rather than a description of the real characteristics of some phenomenon.

Weber is also taken to task because of the supposed emphasis upon the appeal of the leader's personality, as opposed to the appeal of his message. Since the effect of each of these two factors is extremely difficult to distinguish from that of the other, some believe charisma "easy to assert, but extraordinarily difficult to prove."[59] But Weber's definition of the concept includes both "heroes" and "revelation." Consequently, Carl J. Friedrich was on much firmer ground when he criticized the concept because of its inability to distinguish between religious and totalitarian leaders.[60] For despite the religious connotations the term *charisma* evokes, the "revelation" involved need not be theological, and the abilities by which the hero is characterized need not be magical. Weber explicitly stated that any shared conviction, when combined with the belief in an individual's exceptional ability, could lead to charisma in any arena of human endeavor.[61]

Friedrich's criticism is only appropriate, however, if one feels the need to characterize certain rulers as "totalitarian." This clearly could not have been Weber's intention. He was attempting to isolate tendencies encouraging meaningful politics, and he saw a partial solution to the bureaucratic threat in charismatic leadership. Given institutional arrangements that allowed some degree of hegemony over state bureaucracies by charismatic political leaders, he believed that meaningful politics could be preserved even in a highly rationalized society.

His analysis was based upon the recognition that any large

scale organization must obtain a degree of voluntary compliance from its membership because organizations demand sacrifices as well as bestow benefits. Such compliance can be given either from the individual interests of the members or from a felt obligation to obey.[62] But only so long as the membership perceives a profit in the exchange of costs for benefits can a bureaucracy dispense with legitimacy. A governmental bureaucracy which provides not only the "minimum requirements of life," but also a "battlefield for death,"[63] cannot rely upon a balance sheet. Political organization, the goals of which are rarely sufficiently specific to provide a definite calculation of advantages over disadvantages, must foster a legitimizing ideology, even if only a feeling of communal identity. In the process, it fosters a value-rational orientation toward social life. Of course, these social values are not necessarily a crucial factor in public policy, nor is it likely that the bureaucrats will take them seriously.[64] It does mean, however, that a value-rational social orientation will be kept alive and, with it, the possibility for meaningful politics.

For it is not enough for the state bureaucracy to keep alive the possibility of meaningful political experience; if it is to survive in a fluid, competitive environment, it must actually provide opportunities for the development and exercise of political qualities. Organizations need politicians in order to adapt to changing circumstances. The bureaucratic ethos, with its emphasis upon limited responsibility, impersonality, and trained expertise, is useless in a situation that cannot be subsumed under some precedent, which requires individual initiative and the willingness to assume responsibility for radical departures from established policy.[65] A politician is required for this, a fact that is at least formally recognized in all state bureaucracies.[66] Bureaucrats are naturally suspicious of novelty, both because their ethos does not prepare them to cope with it and because new policy almost inevitably entails reorganization, which, in turn, results in upsetting career patterns. Although bureaucrats and politicians need one another to accomplish their aims, they are natural enemies.[67] Powerful as bureaucracy may be, it is dependent upon those with political qualities.[68]

From Weber's perspective, history is a continual struggle between the impact of economic necessity or convenience and the effort of humans to realize their values and legislate them for posterity. Until recently, the struggle was largely between "charismatic" and "traditional" authority. Today it is between "charismatic" and the "legal" authority closely associated with bureaucratic domination.[69]

> As we have seen, bureaucratic rationalization . . . often has been a major revolutionary force with regard to tradition. But it revolutionizes with *technical means,* in principle, as does every economic reorganization, "from without": It *first* changes the material and social orders, and *through* them the people, by changing the conditions of adaptation, and perhaps the opportunities for adaptation, through a rational determination of means and ends. Charismatic belief revolutionizes men "from within" and shapes material and social conditions according to its revolutionary will.[70]

Although convenience, and certainly necessity, must be given its due, there can be no doubt of Weber's sympathies in this eternal contest.[71] They were dictated by his incentive for perceiving it. His social concepts were manifestations of his general concern for a social order attuned to his conception of humanity,[72] and his political prescriptions were specific manifestations of the same concern.

Bureaucratic dependence upon political leadership, combined with the necessity for at least the state bureaucracy to foster a communal orientation among citizens, allows for the possibility of meaningful politics even in a highly bureaucratized context. It will be possible if leaders can transform popular support into political power, thereby attaining a degree of independence and hegemony over the organizations they are supposed to lead. If so, they can be expected to appeal to the communal values shared by most citizens and seek support by claiming their unique abilities to protect or realize these values. In short, a situation that encourages or requires politicians to achieve a measure of charismatic legitimacy creates a climate in which meaningful politics is likely to flourish.

It is not surprising, therefore, that Weber encouraged the development of such a situation in his own nation. His mature polemical writings, completed after the outbreak of World War I, called for the adoption of political institutions that would: (1) encourage the control of state affairs by individuals with political qualities;[73] (2) give these individuals a popular base of power independent of the bureaucracies they head;[74] (3) develop a citizenry of sufficient political sophistication to provide and support a steady stream of gifted political leaders.[75] In general, Weber recommended a combination of parliamentary sovereignty and plebiscitary democracy to advance these goals.[76]

It would not serve my purpose to examine his reasoning in great detail. In brief, Weber believed that some form of popular legitimacy was almost required in highly industrialized nations owing to the impersonal nature of social organizations in these societies.[77] If, as in the West, this popular legitimacy is achieved through electoral institutions, mass-based party organizations will inevitably be formed to conduct electoral campaigns. Since these organizations naturally display the same tendencies as other bureaucracies, parliamentary democracy tends to result in the monopolization of office by the organizational officials of the party, who cater primarily to material interests.[78] However, if required by constitutional provision to compete for a popularly elected executive office in addition to legislative seats, these party organizations will be forced to promote and submit to leaders with popular followings.[79] A popular following is won by the art of demagoguery, and bureaucratic officials are not likely to be very adept at dramatization and personal projection.[80] It is reasonable to assume that these popular leaders would possess political attributes. Only those with political "instincts" are likely to be subject themselves to, let alone survive, the rigors of both organizational infighting and the personal conflict of this kind of electoral contest.

Although he hoped that journalistic scrutiny of open political competition would to some extent educate citizens to political realities, Weber was free of any idealistic illusions of popular sovereignty.[81] He became a democrat because he believed electoral competition for executive office was the best means of recruiting real politicians to positions of power rather than because of some attachment to the idea of popular rule or the rights of the individual. Politics is always an affair of small numbers, and in a mass state the "caesarist element is ineradicable."[82] Indeed, he even argued that the only meaningful criterion for evaluating a social order is the "opportunity which it affords to *certain types of persons* to rise to positions of superiority."

A social order cannot be evaluated as such because "empirical investigation is not really exhaustive," and the factual basis for such an evaluation simply cannot exist.[83] This assertion is clearly implied by Weber's analysis of social conceptualization. Collective concepts are "one-sided accentuations," and any given social context can be conceptually "ordered" ad infinitum. To judge a social context on the basis of any finite number of viewpoints, therefore, requires one to arbitrarily disregard the possibility that other ways of looking at the same society may disclose entirely different implications for one's values. Even if one is willing to do this, there is no point at which one can say that a sufficient degree of correspondence between ideal-type and reality exists to logically or "objectively" justify declaring a regime, for instance, to be "democratic," "dictatorial," or "totalitarian." One can usefully label aspects of social contexts with these terms, but only if these aspects cause individuals to be predisposed and objectively able to act in a "democratic," "dictatorial," or "totalitarian" manner.

For these reasons, Weber's institutional prescriptions could not have been derived from some envisioned ideal social order. They were expedients, formulated in response to a specific danger in a specific context. They were intended to enhance the probability that those who rule possess political attributes. Like all expedients, they are risky. They could never insure success, and they certainly could not guarantee that the "best" individuals (by any criterion) would prevail.[84] Consequently, Weber prescribed a number of precautionary measures, the most obvious of which is the authority of the legislature to hold the popularly elected executive "responsible."[85]

Of greater relevance to my purpose is Weber's concern for another potential danger of plebiscitary democracy. He clearly recognized that demagoguery has a negative side:

> The potential danger of mass democracy for the polity lies first of all in the possibility that emotional elements will predominate in politics. The "mass" as such (irrespective of the social strata which it comprises in any given case) thinks only in short-run terms. For it is, as every experience teaches, always exposed to direct, purely emotional and irrational influence.[86]

He hoped that a relatively small number of decision makers with clear political responsibility would work to reduce the effects of the inevitable emotional factors. More important, he hoped that an organized social science could effectively articulate social realities relevant to public policy. To the extent that political leaders generally respected the objectivity of social scientists,[87] they could be made aware of the probable long range consequences of various policy options and forced to recognize the limits of what they can do.

In other words, Weber's institutional prescriptions included a political role for social science; it was to be organized as a "policy science." This prescription raises obvious difficulties. For objectivity in the social sciences is incompatible with active partisanship. Partisanship requires not only that one view reality from a value perspective but also that one judge or evaluate a particular situation in terms of this perspective. Yet this is just what the social scientist cannot do if his or her empirical work is to mean anything scientifically. The only question that can be answered objectively is the extent to which a particular context actually conforms to ideal-typical conceptualizations. Ideal-types are in one way or another grounded in the social scientist's commitments, for one must view reality from a value perspective. But if one uses one's commitments to evaluate a specific context, as required by political partisanship, congruence or incongruence is simply assumed. All this has been discussed in Chapter Four. What is problematic at this point is how social science could be so organized as, on the one hand, to foster scientific objectivity and, on the other, to perform any kind of political function.

Despite his failure to present his solutions explicitly in a coherent form, Weber clearly gave a great deal of thought to this question. The consistency with which he approached it can be seen in his efforts to change the nature of the *Verein fuer Sozial Politik* and his attempts to influence other associations of his professional peers. This activity led to a series of conflicts with the leaders of the *Verein,* as well as with the majority of its members.[88] His famous essay, "Social Scientific 'Objectivity' and Social/Political Knowledge," can be considered his manifesto in this struggle.[89] His ideas concerning the nature of conceptualization and the role of values were first given unambiguous expression in this essay, and they often reappeared in the polemics that followed in much the same form.

The first confrontation occurred at the 1905 meeting of the *Verein*. Friedrich Naumann delivered a speech criticizing the belief that the state could be expected to initiate real social reform, since it was firmly controlled by privileged classes. The venerable chairman of the *Verein*, Gustav Schmoller, immediately criticized the speech, calling Naumann a "demagogue." This apparently struck a responsive cord among the attending membership, who heartily applauded Schmoller's comments.[90] Weber, however, was furious. He soon began a determined attack upon Schmoller's conception of the purpose of the *Verein* and the role of its chairman.[91] In general, Weber accused Schmoller, and by implication the majority of those attending the meeting, of imposing a particular political orientation or "line" upon the *Verein*.[92] Schmoller's defense was simply to point out that the *Verein* had always possessed a double nature and that in both scientific and political aspects its "leading purpose" was to educate the middle classes. The *Verein* had always been characterized by its moderately reformist position. The more extreme members were certainly free to express their opinions, whether of the left or the right, but they should not expect to set the political tone of the association.[93]

Schmoller completely missed the point of Weber's reprobation. The latter's purpose was not to influence the political stance of the *Verein*; he did not want it to have a political stance. His demand was that it be politically uncommitted, regardless of the political convictions of the majority.[94] The organizational changes he demanded were intended to insure that the association could not assume a partisan position. This would be accomplished by making it extremely difficult for organizational leaders to emerge. As he noted in another context, direction through some form of collegiality is employed chiefly "to promote objectivity and integrity and to this end to limit the power of individuals."[95] Consequently, he believed that a scientific association should have several officers, rendering it unlikely for any individual to determine its agenda or dominate its proceedings.[96] He also warned against awarding such offices as honors for notable scientific achievement, since prestige could make a position as influential as formal authority.[97] In 1905, he went so far as to ask for the abolishment of the general meeting of the *Verein,* probably to preclude potential leaders from forming a following and certainly to reduce the influence of a majority on substantive issues.

Paradoxically, the imposition of a partisan stance on policy issues would undermine not only the scientific potential of an association of social scientists but also any real contributions it might make to more effective public policy. Partisan considerations, relevant only in a context of struggle, almost necessitate conceptual rigidity. This rigidity is detrimental to both progress in cultural science and its ability to contribute to the formation of rational public policy. Both goals require the mutual criticism of diverse perspectives, and Weber believed that this should be fostered by associations of social science.[98]

Diversity is required scientifically not only because of the incompatibility of partisanship and objectivity but also because progress in cultural science cannot be assessed by the achievement of a comprehensive theory "in which reality is synthesized in some sort of *permanently* and *universally* valid classification."[99] Collective concepts are ideal-typical, formulated only to highlight "relevant" behavior. Relevance is determined in the last analysis by values derived from fundamental conceptions of reality which cannot be conclusively confirmed or disproved by empirical analysis. Since an ideal-type is a "one-sided accentuation," any particular set of collective concepts is likely to exclude potentially relevant as well as irrelevant behavior. But if the perspectives formed by different ideal-typical constructions share at least some fundamental values, mutual criticism can be conducive to the purposes of each. It can even lead to a synthesis, broadening their applicability and, especially important, allowing analysis of the relative costs that the achievement of different values are likely to entail for one another.[100]

These profitable exchanges could occur only among those who share at least some fundamental values. Common values do not, however, inevitably or even usually lead to identical goals and perspectives. Indeed, political struggle among groups with conflicting interests or ideals typically takes place within a cultural context, the validity of which all implicitly assume to some degree. As discussed in Chapter Three, cultural ideals condition all activity, but they do not determine it. Nor could they, even if the only source of ultimate value in a particular case, determine the ideal-types used to make sense of social experience. For ultimate values, derived from *comprehensive* conceptions of reality, are far too abstract to be the sole criteria for the construction of ideal-types adequate for empirical analysis.[101] The goals and interests providing the rationale for collective concepts are conditioned by specific experiences as well as abstract cultural ideals. Diversity of perspective clearly does not preclude consensus on fundamental values.

> The belief which we all have in some form or other, in the metaempirical validity of ultimate and final values, in which the meaning of our existence is rooted, is not incompatible with the incessant changefulness of the concrete viewpoints, from which empirical reality gets its significance. Both these views are, on the contrary, in harmony with each other. Life with its irrational reality and its store of possible meanings is inexhaustible. The concrete form in which value-relevance occurs remains perpetually in flux, ever subject to change in the dimly seen future of human culture. The light which emanates from those highest evaluative ideas always falls on an ever changing

finite segment of the vast chaotic stream of events which flows away through time.[102]

A consensus cannot be imposed upon an association meant to advance social science without undermining its purpose. Yet such an organization could only be formed among those who share a fundamental value orientation. Otherwise, the participants would find their various collective concepts mutually meaningless, in both senses of the term. In reality, this means that social scientific associations are likely to develop only among those within a common cultural context.[103] An individual scientist, at least insofar as he or she approached the ideal-typical scientific personality, would find such an association useful because the clash of perspectives could provide both useful suggestions to develop ideas and a forum in which the scientist could test those ideas by attempting to defend them. Given that the organization in principle would not sanction particular positions, the individual scientist need not worry about convincing critics and could afford to consider their criticisms seriously.

More germane to the present discussion is the political value of a properly organized social science. It could help turn cultural rationalization in the "positive" direction, toward the "deliberate formulation of ultimate values," and as a result encourage a measure of political objectivity.[104] As mentioned previously, the mutual criticism of perspectives informed by the same set of fundamental values will encourage the participants to rank the relative value of potentially conflicting goals explicitly. Not only will this serve to articulate the meaning and implications of cultural values in light of current political conflict, but it will also tend to highlight potential benefits and costs of various policy options in terms of these values. A properly organized social science, just because of its non-partisan stance, can rationally criticize political positions from the general perspective of cultural values.[105] As we have seen, this function is crucially important in a regime where political elites must compete for popular support. By laying bare the policy choices in all their starkness, social science can help provide political leaders with that "sense of proportion," that personal distance that even genuine political personalities may find difficult to maintain while catering to the demands of interest constellations and the emotions of mass followings.

Organization structure alone, however, would not assure the performance of this function. The receptivity of politicians, the communication of associational proceedings, and the tendency to seek approval from colleagues to advance academic careers are among the innumerable factors that could impede the effectiveness of scientific criticism of social policy, regardless of organizational structure.[106] Yet the implementation of proper organizational principles is an obvious first step. In addition to attempting to change the program and structure of the *Verein,* Weber also tried to have his ideas embodied in two other social scientific organizations. He was one of the founders of the German Sociological Association and delivered the "business report" at its first meeting in 1910. In this speech, he outlined a number of topics that he believed the association should pursue and reiterated in the strongest possible terms the non-partisan nature of the association.[107]

The second effort is more revealing of the consistency with which he approached the political function of organized social science. For rather than seeking to influence a permanent organization devoted to the advancement of social science, he was here attempting, in league with his older colleague Lujo Brentano, to organize a convocation of social scientists to consider a pressing problem of public policy (right of workers to organize and strike). The enterprise was eventually abandoned, obviously because Brentano felt that Weber's guidelines for the meeting would so dilute its political impact as to make it meaningless.

Brentano was probably correct. His purpose was to generate propaganda to support his political viewpoint, while Weber attempted to preclude this possibility. Weber could not, of course, lecture his distinguished senior on the nature and limitations of social science. The tactic he took in their private correspondence was to argue that the opinions of a small group of like-minded "radicals" would simply not have much influence. Rather than meet in a small isolated city, as Brentano at first advocated, Weber wanted to meet in Berlin, where a large number of individuals could contribute to the proceedings. In a more isolated location, only those in agreement with the organizers would attend. Weber wanted to give all interested scholars, including the leaders of the *Verein,* an opportunity to present their views.[108] According to Weber's own testimony, this was the fundamental difference dividing them.[109] But the dispute that ended any hope of compromise occurred when Brentano insisted that the assembly also consider the issue of free trade. Although there were no significant differences in the political positions of the two men, Weber argued that the inclusion of more than one topic would be divisive.[110]

These tactical arguments apparently made little impression upon Brentano. His primary purpose was probably to demonstrate that a significant number of respected academics did not endorse the views of the right. Consequently, any equivocation caused by the participation of "moderates" would be dysfunctional from his perspective. Any consensus reached by a convention of all interested parties was bound to be poor propaganda. He was clearly more concerned with the partisan implications of the endeavor than with exploring various policy options.

To produce propaganda was the last thing Weber wanted to

do.[111] He wanted to include scholars with a diversity of viewpoints in order to explore implications and consequences and, if possible, to reach at least a general consensus. Only the presence of all interested parties could insure that the purpose of the meeting was to consider implications rather than give speeches, and only this would give any consensus the authority of science. Even in his private communication with Brentano he stated that his stand against including more than one general topic was one of principle rather than merely tactical.[111] An explicit reason for his opposition to this move was that it would give the impression of a party program.[113] Another was that the antagonistic positions on the trade issue were so tied to specific interests as to be impervious to rational criticism.[114] The most decisive evidence for his non-partisan intent, however, is the fact that, in open communication addressed to potential participants, Weber explicitly and forcefully repudiated any intent to create propaganda for a partisan cause:

> It is self-evident that the participants in these discussions are not obliged by accepting our invitation to anything. The conveners intentionally neglect to develop suggestions, for they in no way wish to prejudice the meeting. Only from open expression and the suggestions of all individual participants will the material for a further advance be achieved.[115]

In his mind, this quite clearly was to be a scientific rather than a political meeting, despite its focus upon public policy.

In this instance as in others, his efforts to influence the associations of his peers were largely unsuccessful. Although he apparently forced a compromise of some sort in 1905, and in the intervening years was able to conduct an extensive research project under the auspices of the *Verein*,[116] the association decisively rejected his views on the role of values in social science after a lengthy debate in 1909 and 1910.[117] His experience with the

German Sociological Association was even more frustrating. Even though he was apparently successful at having the association officially adopt his views at its first meeting, almost no one observed his strictures concerning freedom from value-judgments. After the second meeting in 1912, he withdrew from the leadership, "sick and tired of appearing time and again as a Don Quixote of an allegedly unfeasible principle."[118]

Part of the problem was probably the difficulty of following Weber's argument. His methodological essays tend to be obscure. He invariably fails, in my opinion, to give sufficient emphasis to such important distinctions as the difference between freedom from values and freedom from value judgments. I suspect, however, that the most important factor was simply that his audience was not receptive to his message. Before his breakdown, could Weber himself have been convinced by any analysis that concluded that he had to choose between science and politics if he were to retain his personal integrity?

Rigidity of self-conception, however, is not the most serious problem that could diminish the chances for a properly organized social science capable of fulfilling its political function. Worse, by far, is the possibility that those who, at least intellectually, recognize that the right to judge reality is foreclosed to a genuine social scientist are through self-deception able to indulge in at least the outward forms of both activities. Just as Weber was a scholar pretending to be a politician before his breakdown, in the last years of his life he became a politician pretending to be a scholar. And just as his politics suffered as a result of his earlier confusion, so too did his scholarship through the latter. I do not mean that he began to produce a shoddy product but that he ceased to be genuinely engaged in a process of justifying his beliefs to himself by calling them into question.

CHAPTER SEVEN

Max Weber Becomes a Politician

Insofar as any date can signify the beginning or close of a historical era, by any criterion other than the strictly definitional August, 1914, marks the end of the nineteenth century and the beginning of the twentieth.[1] It also marks a watershed for Max Weber. For while the "Great War" ushered in an age of cultural neurosis for Germany, as perhaps for all of Western civilization, its effects upon Weber were distinctly therapeutic. The last six years of his life were undoubtedly his happiest, despite the despair of witnessing Germany's collapse and the frustration of his efforts to prevent it.

The war "cured" Weber.[2] He could now engage in all the activities previously impossible for him. Although he frequently feared the psychic consequences of attempting too much, they never appeared.[3] At the beginning of the war he accepted the strenuous responsibility for organizing and administering a number of military hospitals. As it progressed, he became increasingly involved in political activity. At its conclusion he was able to return to the classroom after a twenty year absence, accepting a temporary position at the University of Vienna in the summer of 1918 and then a permanent position at Munich the following year. The war was his great trip, serving the same therapeutic function as his earlier travels. All other problems, all other considerations paled into insignificance.[4] Although well aware of its horrors, having lost a brother, a brother-in-law, and several friends in the early months, he nevertheless on a number of occasions referred to the war as "great and wonderful."[5]

In the previous decade he had become something of a legend to the students at Heidelberg, who called him the "myth of Heidelberg," the difficult presence across the river, accessible only to a select few.[6] With his ability to speak publicly and teach restored, another legend grew, although this one is more appropriately called a myth. Like any good myth, it contains an element of tragedy—indeed, a double tragedy. The first is a tragedy for Germany. According to the myth, Weber was the great political leader who might have had the presence of mind and the ability to guide the German nation to a stable political order and a responsible role in world affairs.[7] Yet he was denied his political destiny by the foolishness of a politically naive people and the ambitions of the mediocre. The second is a tragedy for science. Free from both the burden of illness and the distractions of politics, he was now for the first time prepared to concentrate the full force of his powerful intellect upon scholarly pursuits. Before he could really begin, however, he died at the height of his powers.[8]

This myth was apparently consciously propagated by his wife and friends.[9] Their sincerity cannot be doubted, and many of those who had encountered Weber during these years were bound to find the myth plausible. Friend, foe, and even casual observer testify as to the "charismatic" impact of the man.[10] But the myth is a myth. Weber's recovery, and therefore the ability to project himself forcefully, was the result of the great distraction of war. Unlike the earlier distraction through travel, which allowed him to gain a perspective on himself, the preoccupation with war owed its therapeutic value to a loss of perspective. Given the logical incompatibility of political and scientific action, to engage in both requires such a loss. Initially, the war justified a political interlude, even for one who considered himself a political eunuch. By its end, when Weber once again affirmed his commitment to scholarship and the requisite disavowal of politics, he was capable of an insidious self-deception, which undermined the genuineness of his commitment to either type of action. His premature death was no more than a personal tragedy, for he had little of significance to offer either his nation or his science.

He convinced himself that he was devoting his energies to science while actually engaged in a truncated form of politics. Since his views concerning the absolute disparity of scientific and political action did not change, he must have been unconscious of the political nature of his activity. Consequently, the role he was actually playing and the false assumptions that made it possible can be discerned only through an analysis of his activity, not his thought. My next step will be to describe the political aspects of the role he came to play. I will then explain, relying upon Weber's own analysis of progress in social science, why his scientific work of this period was necessarily less significant than that of the previous decade. For Weber did provide the conceptual tools by which the potential significance of his or anyone else's social scientific activity can be assessed. I will then describe the false assumptions that enabled Weber to reconcile his contradictory behavior at least psychologically. I will conclude with a discussion of the ever present danger that these typically unconscious assumptions pose for the integrity of social scientific endeavor.

With the outbreak of war, Weber immediately set aside all scholarly activity in order to make himself useful to the great collective effort. He regretted that he was too old to play a military role and believed that he was obliged to devote whatever talents he possessed to the support of those at the front.[11] Self-sacrifice was the order of the day, and one did what one could, irrespective of the personal consequences. In the first year of the war, he devoted all his energy to the military hospitals that he had organized. Since he was only a reserve officer, however, the law required that he be replaced when regular military personnel were available. As soon as he learned that his military superiors intended to keep him on in some capacity just to "take care of him," he resigned in order to find a more meaningful function in the war effort.[12]

His search took him first to Belgium, where he hoped to take part in an official study of the difficulties to be encountered before that country's economic and administrative processes could be integrated into Germany's.[13] Because this prospect did not lead to anything, Weber went to Berlin to seek adequate employment for his talents. There he remained for several months, trying to convince governmental authorities to give him a position in which he could use his expertise in Eastern affairs to plan for an independent Poland under German influence.[14] He even studied the Polish language in preparation for this task. But the authorities were not receptive. The only organization wanting to use his abilities was that formed by Naumann to advance his vision of an economic union of Germany and the Austro-Hungarian Empire. Although Weber did travel to Vienna to explore interest in such a venture among political and economic elites, he correctly believed that the idea had little chance of success and was, in any case, not very important.[15]

Without an official position with specific duties, a well-known and respected scholar could make only one contribution to the war effort, and that was occasional advice and criticism on social and political matters. Apparently Weber felt compelled to do this if more direct involvement were foreclosed.[16] For instance, in March, 1916, he sent a memorandum to the foreign secretary on the serious political risks entailed in an increase of submarine warfare.[17] Even before this incident, however, Weber became involved in the public debate on the nature of Germany's war aims.

From the beginning he had definite ideas concerning the goals that Germany should pursue in the East. In this, he was far ahead of most of his fellow citizens. At the outbreak of the war very few Germans had definite notions on what should be gained from the conflict. Initially, most governmental officials and certainly the populace viewed the war as a defensive struggle for survival.[18] Once they were engaged and enjoying a measure of success, however, the question of what would constitute a satisfactory peace inevitably became more complex. It also inevitably became politicized, for the question involved constitutional considerations as well as national defense. The only influential group with well-defined war aims was the Pan German League, closely linked to the political right. Imperial expansion was viewed by the group as necessary if pressure for democratization and parliamentary government were to be resisted.[19]

As mentioned in the preceding chapter, Weber believed that some form of democratization was necessary. He also saw that demands for territorial annexations could only prolong the war, decreasing the likelihood of a satisfactory outcome for Germany. Even while submerged in his work with the hospitals he was drawn into the debate. In July, 1915, he signed a petition of leading academics opposing radical annexations.[20] At about the same time he invited a number of leading parliamentarians to Heidelberg to organize an opposition to the annexation of Belgium, although apparently the meeting was never held.[21] At the end of the year he wrote a letter to the *Frankfurt Times,* explaining his position and stating at its conclusion that this would be the last of his polemics against opposing positions.[22] But this was an unfulfilled promise. On August 1, 1916, he delivered a highly polemical address to the German National Committee, a semi-official group encouraged by the prime minister to help combat the propaganda of the Pan German League. Weber re-fused to join officially because he wanted to attack the League explicitly, and the Committee imposed a policy of circumspec-tion upon its members.[23] Later in the month he sent an even sharper attack on the right to the *Frankfurt Times*, and in Oc-tober he delivered a similar talk to the Progressive People's Party.[24]

As early as the summer of 1916, Weber obviously saw himself as a combatant in an all-out battle with the Pan German League.[25] By the beginning of 1917, he was actively agitating for constitu-tional reform, writing several polemical essays on the subject for the *Frankfurt Times*.[26] One of these essays so enraged the au-thorities that they henceforth subjected the paper to censorship. The depth of his political involvement is indicated by his pleasure at learning that one of his articles played a role in a governmental crisis of the summer of 1917, as well as his readiness at one point to underwrite financially a private peace initiative.[27]

This already high level of partisan involvement intensified with the overthrow of the monarchy and the aborted attempts at revo-lution that followed Germany's defeat. In the last month of 1918, and the first of 1919, he was a frequent political speaker. At the beginning of this period, he politically endorsed "socialism," not through conviction but for tactical reasons. He apparently hoped to build his credibility and influence among the majority so-cialists who were the most cohesive political force in Germany.[28] He even accepted an invitation to become a member of the Heidelberg Council of Workers and Soldiers, although surely not for the altruistic motives attributed to him by his wife.[29] Many of his speeches in these turbulent months provided heated ex-changes with both left and right. Indeed, a few of these occasions almost resulted in violence."[30]

His "socialism" was short-lived. He soon was supporting the new, very bourgeois German Democratic Party. He gave a large number of campaign speeches on behalf of this party and was almost selected as one of its representatives to parliament. He was seriously considered for a cabinet position, as well as a diplomatic post. He was the only non-legislative member active on the commission that formulated the first draft of what was to become the constitution of the Weimar Republic.[31] In February, 1919, the Heidelberg Association for a Policy Based on Justice was formed in Weber's house at the instigation of the influential former monarch of Baden. Its purpose was to protest the harsh Allied peace terms, and its membership was accordingly drawn from those few notables not compromised during the war by advocating annexations.[32] In May he accompanied the German delegation sent to Versailles to draft the German response to the Allied proposals.

Even before this intensification of his political activity, Weber declared his intention to return to scholarship and avoid politics, and he reaffirmed this intention throughout the hectic period.[33] Yet his actual behavior betrays an unmistakable ambiguity. When opportunities for political involvement beckoned, he obviously found it difficult to resist. Evidence is abundant: his bitterness at not being offered a government position; his decision to go to Versailles despite serious reservations concerning prospects for success; his willingness to accept nomination for political office even though he would do nothing to secure his election.[34]

By the beginning of 1920, however, he finally acted upon his declarations, devoting himself to his new teaching duties and refusing to engage in overt political activity.[35] Yet the gap between declaration and behavior continued. It only became more subtle and probably less conscious. Now his political involvement led to a less explicit, more vicarious form of activity. It was so implicit, and therefore so unlikely to have any consequence for public policy, that Weber was apparently able to delude himself into thinking that he had entirely abjured politics. He had in reality

only renounced participation in the conventionally defined political arena—what contemporary social scientists might call "the
policy making process." But politics is defined by one's orientation to values rather than the context in which it occurs. It is a
type of action. While Weber may have made himself politically
irrelevant to the affairs of his nation, much of his activity continued to be political.

Occasionally this political orientation led to behavior that
completely contradicted his denials of political intent.[36] The
most glaring instance occurred in January, 1920, when the young
murderer of Kurt Eisner, the first prime minister of revolutionary
Bavaria, was pardoned. Although Weber was not among Eisner's
admirers, he objected when right-wing students announced they
would have staged a putsch to prevent the assassin's execution
and subsequently vilified a number of socialist students who dis-
agreed with them. More important than the fact of Weber's ob-
jection is the manner in which he communicated it; he publicly
announced it in his classroom, and he called any participant who
refused to withdraw his accusations against the socialist students
a "son of a bitch" (*Hundsfott*). At his next lecture, right-wing
students packed the hall, drowning his voice whenever he tried to
lecture.

> When Weber calmly remained on the rostrum and laughed at them,
> they became even wilder. His students were just about to hit the oth-
> ers when the lights were turned out and the hall was cleared. Immedi-
> ately afterward Weber attended a rather large social gathering, was
> very animated, and then slept splendidly. Political strife obviously had
> a refreshing effect on him.[37]

The remarkable feature of this incident is Weber's blatant vio-
lation of his own analysis of the impropriety of political pronouncements in the classroom.[38] I will discuss his view of the
proper role of the university teacher in the following pages. For

now I only want to indicate that his behavior in this period was inconsistent with his professed commitment to scholarship and displayed the same sort of ambiguity as before. The affair in the lecture hall is not the only example. Others include his attempt to have published in a newspaper a notice in which he again used the phrase "son of a bitch," this time to describe an anonymous individual who had spread untrue rumors about the Bavarian prime minister. He challenged this person to make himself known and sue Weber for libel.[39] Another is his willingness to debate Oswald Spengler in a public forum on matters that had obvious political implications.[40] Indeed, even his acceptance of the position at Munich after being offered a position especially tailored for him at the more secluded University of Bonn may disclose a yearning to be near a center of political conflict.[41] In any case, he reportedly took full advantage of the opportunities offered by the city to mingle among the politically active.[42]

Such attenuated political activity was apparently sufficient to satisfy Weber's need to involve himself in practical affairs, and his obliviousness to its political nature prevented a recurrence of the psychological ailments that plagued him before the war, especially during the period before 1909. I believe that he was able to achieve this obliviousness because the nature of his scholarly activity changed radically after 1914. During the war, Weber turned to scholarly work only when his efforts at practical activity were frustrated. While waiting for officialdom to find him a meaningful task, he used the superior archival resources in Berlin to extend and elaborate his studies on the different practical ethics entailed in the major religious ideas of the world. Since he already had formulated the structure of his argument in previous work, all that remained was to accumulate additional information and refine his analysis. Consequently, he could easily interrupt and resume this work as his political activity dictated.[43]

This pattern continued after the war. His two major projects, the three volume *Religionssoziologie* and the massive *Wirtschaft und Gesellschaft,* were both conceived before the war, and both required the synthesis and extension of work completed before the summer of 1914. He was filling in the gaps, in effect editing his own past work. All his important ideas were formulated before the war, and none were significantly modified after.[44] Weber's scholarly activity had become "bureaucratic" in that it was largely routine.

He did not, however, become a "bureaucrat" of science. If he had, he might still have had something valuable to contribute. For the scientific equivalent of a bureaucrat is a specialist.[45] Just as the ideal-typical bureaucrat is distinguished from the politician by limited responsibility, so too is the scientific specialist distinguished from the general theorist by limited vision. And according to Weber's own analysis of progress in social science, just as social control requires both leadership and administration, so too does social scientific progress require both specialists and, occasionally, theorists. Yet Weber, as will be seen, conformed to neither type in this final stage of his life.

In his famous essay, "Science as a Vocation," Weber asserted that only the specialist could contribute something of scientific worth given the advanced phase science had entered in modern times.[46] Yet his analysis of change in the social sciences is more complex than this assertion implies. For he presumed that the specialties in social science periodically are rendered obsolete, and at such times the advance of social science is the work of the general theorist. In many respects, this view parallels Thomas Kuhn's analysis of change in natural science articulated in his influential book, *The Structure of Scientific Revolutions.*[47] According to Kuhn, any well-developed science is characterized by a "paradigm," at least one aspect of which is a consensus on a general theoretical framework that defines the subject matter.[48] "Normal science" consists of applying or extending the general theory to various aspects of experience. Consequently, the general theory rationalizes a number of scientific specialties and is not itself subject to scrutiny. Yet these specialties inevitably encounter anomalies that resist all efforts at explanation. These, in turn, may eventually call into question the general theory and prepare the way for a scientific revolution by which a new general theory displaces the old.

Yet any similarity between Kuhn's and Weber's views is superficial.[49] For despite accusations of relativism leveled against Kuhn, his is a theory of theoretical advance by scientific means. An incorrect theory will inevitably produce anomalies, and any rival, if it is to have a realistic chance of being the basis of a new consensus, will have to preserve the accomplishments of the old theory as well as account for its deficiencies.[50] A general theory in cultural science, however, is no more than a comprehensive conceptualization of social reality. Lacking law-like relationships, it can be no more than a code for describing reality. Indeed, since its collective concepts do not even correspond to real entities, theory is no more than a standard by which reality is ordered and assessed. As long as internally consistent, a comprehensive set of collective concepts will provide an adequate basis for understanding any event and need never confront persistent anomalies. "Progress" in such a science can only mean increasing specificity, achieved as specialists cast current and historical events into the idiom of their world view, discerning with increasing detail the patterns of action relevant to the attainment or frustration of their commitments.[51]

Specialists are more important for scientific progress in cultural science than they are in natural science. They are, to be sure, essential for the latter, since the deficiencies of a general theory can be discerned only through efforts to apply its postulates to a diversity of problems. Yet the great advances in natural science occur, according to Kuhn's analysis, when one general theory displaces another by resolving its dilemmas while explaining its successes. Once installed, the new theoretical framework establishes the basis for a new tradition of specialization. The specialists are the drones of science, and Kuhn patronizingly but aptly characterizes their activity as "puzzle-solving." Specialists cannot achieve the next great breakthrough, but only prepare the way by creating the opportunity for the next theoretical giant.

General theorists cannot be scientific giants from Weber's perspective. While a theoretical achievement will have implications for social science, it is not a scientific achievement because general theory cannot claim to be scientific. All social scientists presuppose a general conceptualization of their subject matter, but their scientific activity cannot directly substantiate or discredit these presuppositions. Those who primarily concern themselves with articulating and advocating a particular set of collective concepts for social science can be no more than scientific dilettantes. Indeed, Weber believed that the integrity of a social scientific discipline would be unaffected if specialists reified their most fundamental collective concepts into God-given entities, or even if they lost all awareness that such ideas were presupposed in their work.

> All research in the cultural sciences in an age of specialization, once it is oriented towards a given subject matter through particular settings of problems and has established its methodological principles will consider the analysis of the data as an end in itself. It will discontinue assessing the value of the individual facts in terms of their relationships to ultimate value-ideas. Indeed, it will lose its awareness of its ultimate rootedness in the value-ideas in general. *And it is well that it should be so.* But there comes a moment when the atmosphere changes. The significance of the unreflectively utilized viewpoints becomes uncertain and the road is lost in the twilight. The light of the great cultural problems moves on. Then science too prepares to

change its standpoint and its analytical apparatus and to view the streams of events from the heights of thought.[52]

As discussed in the preceding chapter, a common cultural context is a prerequisite for the establishment of an organized social science. Collective concepts, formulated to focus attention upon "relevant" aspects of social reality, will be meaningful only to those who share a consensus on fundamental values. It is not simply a matter of different perspectives creating obstacles to mutual understanding. Even those who differ fundamentally in outlook might conceivably come to an understanding of one another.[53] That is, it is conceivable if the participants have incentive to communicate. But for social scientists who completely lack common criteria of relevance, the mere fact that they are social scientists does not provide such incentive. For their respective conceptual categories will be mutually irrelevant to their social scientific activity.

Since institutional coherence is derived from cultural context, change in the fundamental concepts of a social science will have to be the result of external rather than internal developments. According to Kuhn, significant change in natural science typically occurs when the advocates of the dominant paradigm encounter problems in trying to explain aspects of experience that, by their own estimate, should be explicable in terms of their theory. In a sense, the paradigm brings itself into question. For reasons already discussed, this state of affairs cannot prevail within cultural science. Fundamental change in conceptualization is to be expected only with the occurrence of a certain type of social conflict. When the society of which it is a part undergoes cultural conflict, so too will social science. Cultural fragmentation will inevitably lead to theoretical dispute and the fragmentation of social scientific organization. Any reintegration, for social science as for society, will have to be the result of political imposition, cultural evolution, or a combination of the two. In any event, the cultural ideas from which a reinterpretation is forged will be the product of general theorizing rather than the work of scientific specialists.[54]

In social science as in natural science, it is the specialists who dominate during normal or tranquil periods. Specialists are usually concerned with the explanation of particular events. Consequently, they are likely to be preoccupied with problems of empirical methodology, almost to the exclusion of abstract theoretical or conceptual questions. As indicated previously, Weber believed that this tendency will usually lead to a situation in which most social scientists are not even aware of their basic conceptual assumptions, and this prospect did not to his mind threaten the viability of social scientific activity. If he himself had become such a specialist, not only would he have continued to engage in meaningful scientific activity, he might also very well have been able to participate to some degree in political affairs. For specialists ignorant of their fundamental assumptions could conceivably compartmentalize their activity, dividing their time between politics and science. Since most self-conceptions, as discussed in Chapter Five, are composed in part of a hierarchy of "functions," the individual would no doubt have to give primacy to one or the other of these mutually incompatible endeavors. But only social scientists aware of their most fundamental conceptual assumptions would seem to be completely incapable of engaging in politics. For one can only be obliged to justify those beliefs of which one is aware. Those that can be taken for granted, whether consciously or unconsciously, would seem to allow for at least some degree of political activity.

It would be farfetched, however, to argue that Weber had become a "bureaucrat" of science if such a designation is identified with the limited theoretical vision of a specialist. Despite his emphasis upon the importance of specialization in science and his own mastery of historical detail, Weber's fame is due largely to his conceptual ideas and methodological arguments. He explicitly postulated his most fundamental conceptual assumptions throughout the pre-war decade. Far from forgetting these comprehensive conceptualizations, or pushing them to the background of consciousness while concentrating attention upon more specific topics, his scholarly efforts in the post-war months were directed toward the systematic elaboration of these previously formulated ideas.[55] Clearly some other explanation must be sought for the diversion of his energies from real inquiry to the routines of scholarship and the hinterlands of politics.

The answer is simply that, despite his emphatic and obviously sincere affirmations, Weber ceased to be a genuine social scientist. He no longer truly felt the necessity of justifying his beliefs to himself. He could go through the motions of scholarship, digging up information relevant to his ideas, refining and relating these ideas into an explicitly coherent structure, but he no longer really entertained the notion that they might be fundamentally misconceived or that patterns of action in society might show little resemblance to his ideal-types. His historical research after 1914 was a search for illustrative materials rather than the confrontation of expectation and reality that makes science meaningful.

Weber surely was aware that he was not really engaging in meaningful scholarship during the war. Then, of course, it did not really matter. One did what one had to do or what one could. If collecting useful information was the closest one could come to real scholarship under the circumstances, then so be it. The activity was, after all, no more than something to occupy his time usefully until he could find the meaningful practical activity that never came. Since he always prefaced his later polemical essays with an explicit disclaimer of their scientific status, we also must assume that he was conscious of the ambiguous role he came to play as the war progressed—the scholar using his expertise to criticize and cajole political authorities into doing what he believed to be in the nation's best interests. Both his wife and Christoph Steding have plausibly argued that he altered his treatment of the old Jewish prophets during this time so that his description of them was, to some extent, a conscious characterization of his own activity.[56] Like them, he did not participate in the politics of partisan advantage but was forced to articulate the doom that awaited his people if they did not heed his message of truth.

Irrespective of the validity of this thesis, such a rationalization could not have outlasted the war. As a matter of fact, Weber ceased to play the prophetic role even before the war ended. As we have seen, he involved himself extensively in partisan politics even to the point, as with his flirtation with socialism, of compromising his public pronouncements. And he attempted, albeit awkwardly and unsuccessfully, to become a political official himself. After the war he eventually carried out, at least as far as he was concerned, his often announced intent to return to scholarship. Accordingly, he largely refrained from the publicist activities that would have been congruent with the prophetic image.

Yet he did not really end the great "trip" that made it possible to suppress the ambiguity within his self-conception. He remained preoccupied with Germany's plight, and this preoccupation continued to be the focal point of his activity. He himself reportedly admitted as much a few months before his death.

When asked [in his seminar] about his political plans, Weber . . . smiled wanly and sadly, then answered: "I have no political plans except to concentrate all my intellectual strength on the one problem, how to get once more for Germany a great General Staff."[57]

Although there is evidence that he had given some thought to this specific problem, it certainly did not absorb his energies in his final months.[58] For this reason I think it is appropriate to consider the statement an effort to epitomize a general task rather than a literal description of an ultimate overriding end.

I believe that Weber formulated this general task in order to reconcile his commitment to scholarship with the needs of his nation. For at one point he feared the latter would make it impossible for him to pursue with a clear conscience the only vocation of which he was capable.

> Next year we will have peace and we will all have to reorient our lives. A peace which none of us, including myself, in all soberness and skepticism had envisioned. . . . One must once more begin the construction of Germany anew, and that we will do. It will be worthwhile even then to be a German. . . . Yet people such as I are now superfluous. . . . Work at which I can accomplish something counts for nothing—and with justice. For the nation will now have to struggle hard for its bread, and it will not have enough for scholarship. . . . "Internally" it will be difficult for me, for my inner "calling" is to scholarly work and scholarly expertise. And even this does not serve the nation now. Thus I will have to try to adapt myself. But how, with what, I do not know, nor even if I can succeed.[59]

Weber resolved this problem by consciously committing himself to incorporate the proper political function of social science within his own behavior. That function, let it be remembered, is to criticize various policy options in light of ultimate cultural values, and thereby to provide that "sense of proportion" necessary for effective politics. As discussed in the preceding chapter, he believed that this function was particularly important in electoral democracies, and this was now the type of government to which Germany aspired.

Germans, however, were ill prepared for the political respon-
sibilities suddenly thrust upon them. Democratic institutions
were established in the wake of military defeat and a series of
aborted revolutions. Political passion and utopian fancy were
rampant. In Weber's opinion, politics was becoming "more and
more the affairs of a madhouse" in this "crazy world."[60] Exas-
perating the situation was the fact that the German middle and
upper classes were particularly susceptible to such irrational in-
fluences. For decades they had cultivated an ideal of a cultural
"*Innerlichkeit*," which discouraged concern for political affairs,
a tendency reinforced by Bismarck's authoritarian political system. According to Fritz Stern, the "German elite tended to become estranged from reality and disdainful of it," losing the ability "to deal with practical matters in practical terms."[61] In
Weber's terminology, Germans tended to lack that personal "distance" necessary for objective appraisal, for a "sense of
proportion."[62]

Even before the end of the monarchy Weber had attacked the
excessive concern among youth for what is now called individual
"self-realization." One cannot really know oneself, one's "ultimate standpoint," without testing commitments against concrete
problems for an extended period. All ultimate questions, he asserted, are conditioned by political events, by the situation of
one's nation in the world.[63] To a well-attended conference of students in 1917, he reportedly posed the question: What good is it
to find yourself if your nation is wretched?[64] Worse than exclusive concern with oneself, however, were the personalization
and consequent romanticizing of politics. He so came to hate any
form of political romanticizing that he resigned from his fraternity because he felt its feudal pretensions inappropriate for the
times.[65] He saw the personalization of events as a major source
of error in German foreign policy. As he put it, "Objective questions are always treated as a *point d'honneur*," and there is then

"talk of 'humiliation' ".[66] Domestically he feared a cycle of revolution and reaction. Only the widespread capacity for honesty with oneself could preclude a self-defeating politics of emotion.[67] Since such honesty is a precondition for meaningful empirical research, an appreciation of social scientific knowledge among political actors would be clearly beneficial from Weber's perspective.

Just as clearly, however, he could not consciously engage in direct efforts to influence political leaders, for such activity would have been too obviously political in nature. How then, could he reconcile his scholarship with national needs? The question would seem especially acute in light of his failure to establish the type of organization for social science conducive to the political function he envisioned for it. His answer was to contribute to the same end through his teaching activity. Future political elites could be given an appreciation of the strengths and limitations of objective social knowledge during their educational experience. They could be forced to clarify their own perspectives and recognize the costs entailed in various policy options.

Above all, Weber wanted to instill in his students the habit of objectivity, to avoid self-delusion.

> The primary task of a useful teacher is to teach his students to recognize "inconvenient" facts—I mean facts that are inconvenient for their party opinions. And for every party opinion there are facts that are extremely inconvenient, for my own opinion no less than for others. I believe the teacher accomplishes more than a mere intellectual task if he compels his audience to accustom itself to the existence of such facts. I would be so immodest as even to apply the expression "moral achievement," though perhaps this may sound too grandiose for something that should go without saying.[68]

In a sense, Weber was attempting to compensate for the absence of a properly organized social science by imparting a degree of objectivity to future political actors. But before students could be accustomed to see inconvenient facts, they must be attuned to facts in general. Consequently, Weber adopted a deliberate policy of minimizing general questions of relevance and personal commitment, focusing his lectures upon historical detail and extensive elaboration and criticism of relatively complex ideal-typical constructions. The effect of this strategy on the exuberance of youthful idealism is predictable.[69] Even in the famous lectures on "Science as a Vocation" and "Politics as a Vocation" he insisted upon first discussing the organizational and financial constraints that affected the chances for a successful career in these fields. He did this despite the knowledge that the students who invited him to speak wanted to hear of the "inward calling" necessary for the meaningful pursuit of these types of activities.[70] Although he eventually turned to these questions, he did so only after attempting to sober his audience with a cold shower of facts.[71]

By compelling students to see the costs of their options, Weber hoped to confront them with the personal responsibility for choosing. In other words, he encouraged his students to develop into responsible politicians capable of arriving at realistic responses to Germany's future domestic and international problems. Through his influence on the next generation of potential political leaders, he could serve his community as well as humanity by increasing the likelihood of meaningful politics. Did he, however, really reconcile his commitments to both scholarship and his nation? He clearly believed that he had. As long as the teacher did not presume the right to take upon himself the responsibility of choosing among policy options, to make the choice for his students on "scientific" grounds, he could remain faithful to his commitment as a scholar.[72]

This latter claim is surely correct. As long as a scholar presents alternative viewpoints and impresses upon his students the inability of evidence to prove the validity of one or the other abso-

lutely, he could continue to maintain a scientific orientation toward his own beliefs.[73] However, the compatibility of teaching
and scholarship is logically beside the point of Weber's effort to
reconcile his scholarly and patriotic commitments. For the latter
was a political commitment, and his attempt to fulfill it by teaching was political activity. Rather than exploring the subject matter for itself, his ultimate aim and justification was to change the
orientation of students in order to help meet Germany's post-war
needs.

The logical difficulty of Weber's resolution becomes apparent
when it is recalled that the political function of social science was
to be achieved spontaneously, without deliberate effort on the
part of social scientists. This function is the criticism of policy
proposals from the perspective of the cultural values that define a
political community. It could be achieved automatically, so to
speak, because social scientists must share a set of cultural values
to have any incentive to organize their endeavors. For meaningful
criticism of one another's work is only likely among those who
share at least some ultimate values or fundamental assumptions.
This mutual criticism will encourage an explicit ranking of ends
and disclose the cultural costs of various proposals. This should
be the result of proper social scientific organization, not the intent of its participants. Their intent must be to test their ideas by
subjecting them to the criticism of colleagues. If they were to set
out deliberately to measure proposals against fundamental beliefs, this would require a completely different orientation toward
fundamentals than that required by science. They would be attempting to implement them socially rather than justify them,
and it would be difficult, if not impossible, to confine this political orientation to fundamental assumptions. Empirical analysis
can only be meaningful insofar as the individual researchers are
primarily motivated by the need to justify their beliefs to themselves. An organization that formally applies an ideological ori-

entation for participation in its proceedings is not likely to be of much use to such an individual.

To have convinced himself that he had successfully reconciled his duties toward scholarship and his nation, Weber evidently identified the former with teaching. Since his teaching duties tended to reinforce his supposed scholarship during this period, this must have been easy enough for him. As we have seen, his scholarship had become largely a matter of codification, and according to his wife, "He noticed that the need to express his sociological categories orally a number of times helped him to formulate it more precisely."[74] Having been able to identify scholarship with teaching and the latter with the political function of social science, the reconciliation must have seemed quite plausible.[75] Since the political function was a function of social science, it could even be considered "social scientific." Such were probably the unreflective and semi-conscious connections that allowed Weber to maintain a sense of personal unity.

I do not begrudge Weber his final months of psychic equilibrium. I only wish to emphasize the costs of its achievement. The purpose of the biographical dimension of this study is to illustrate the intimate connection between personal commitment and scientific integrity. Anyone who engages in political activity is necessarily forced to accept on faith a general view of social reality. Clearly, Weber's performance of what he believed to be the teacher's task presumed the validity of his assessments of Germany's post-war problems and the type of individuals needed to resolve them. These assessments were predicated upon his collective concepts, and these, in turn, were ultimately derived from his view of human nature. To act upon one's conceptions, even in a roundabout or curtailed manner, clearly presumes that they have a high degree of congruence with reality. The "cost" of this reassuring presumption is simply faith. Yet in Weber's case, as in the case of any theoretically conscious social scientist, the cost is much higher. For these individuals, faith is inevitably accompanied by self-delusion.

In a letter of 1908, Weber referred to himself as "religiously unmusical," having "neither need nor ability to erect some sort of spiritual 'edifice' in me."[76] Later, in his lecture on "Science as a Vocation," he presented his audience with a choice between the security of theology and the acceptance of the "disenchantment of the world." The latter he asserted to be the "fate of the times," and he recommended that those unable to accept this fate should quietly return to the "old churches."[77] Yet anyone who considers himself a scientist does not have a choice, for there is an "unbridgeable tension" between science and religion.[78] In effect, Weber was publicly reaffirming his earlier statement. In actuality, however, he had become a "dogmatist" and ceased to be a genuine scientist. This is not to say that he "got religion" in the conventional sense of returning to one of the "old churches" but that he had unknowingly come to accept an edifice of assumptions that he accepted on faith.[79]

His somewhat melancholy conclusion to "Science as a Vocation" is highly indicative of the thought patterns that enabled him to escape recognition of these facts. In his discussion, references to religious commitment alternate between a personal orientation toward belief and a particular type of belief. On the one hand, he repeatedly emphasizes that the "decisive characteristic of the positively religious man" is his capacity for "intellectual sacrifice." On the other, he draws a distinction between the philosophical presuppositions necessary for science and those necessary for theology, asserting that the latter include "a few specific presuppositions for its work and thus for the justification of its existence."[80] These specifically theological axioms are revelatory, and as such they are not "'knowledge' in the usual sense, but rather a possession' ".[81] They are theologically necessary because only through some form of revelation could the meaningfulness of existence be demonstrated.[82]

Revelatory assumptions might very well be taken as the defining characteristic of theology, but it is difficult to understand why they, any more than philosophical presuppositions, should be denied the status of potential "knowledge." In fact, some instances of supposed revelation could conceivably be affirmed or rejected on the basis of historical evidence, something largely precluded for universal, and thus ahistorical, metaphysical postulates. Weber was similarly unjustified in supposing that the message of a revelation was necessarily obligatory or meaningful. Given the analysis of the origin of commitment in Chapter Five, even the audible voice of God would carry no moral weight to those who did not define themselves and humanity in relation to Him. The only essential difference between scientific and religious "virtuosi" is the manner by which they orient their lives toward their fundamental beliefs, not the nature of the beliefs themselves.

Consequently, much of what Weber says about religion and science in these final pages of his essay obscures the nature of the tension between religious belief and scientific activity. Yet the irrelevant distinction between scientific knowledge and theology is suggestive of, for want of a better phrase, the "mental mechanism" by which the nature of his own activity could remain obscure to him. For acceptance of a distinction between the two types of belief imparts a degree of impersonality to both religion and science. If a set of beliefs can be characterized as either "religious" or "scientific," then the organization by which it is propagated and the procedures by which it is formulated and expressed can be similarly characterized. In other words, science can then be given an objective existence quite apart from the individual commitment of those who pursue this kind of knowledge. As an objective phenomenon, it can supply the functional focus for self-identity without requiring the individual to be fully aware of his or her conceptual assumptions or completely consistent in his or her behavior. A person can consider himself or herself a "scientist" simply because of membership in a conventionally defined group or role in an organizational structure. Given such a definition of science, one need not be a "virtuoso" to be a scientist.

The less theoretically sophisticated the scientist, the more likely he or she will be to identify science with its external manifestations. Since under normal circumstances social scientific "progress" is tied to specialization, this can be expected to be the prevailing view within most social scientific communities. Fortunately, however, genuine social science can be a matter of degree in that the ability to question seriously the congruence of highly specific "models" with reality need not be seriously impaired by blind acceptance of fundamentals. A more plausible threat to meaningful inquiry is the possibility that this faulty conception of the nature of science will lead to the confusion of political and scientific ends, to the detriment of both types of activity. But even this is unlikely to pose a significant threat, for most can be expected to compartmentalize these incompatible pursuits. Weber was precluded from such compartmentalizations as a result of his high degree of theoretical awareness. Yet most social scientists will rarely, if ever, reflect upon the political justification or social utility of their endeavor, tending instead to accept as self-evident its contribution to the alleviation of communal woes.

Consequently, the dilemma that haunted Weber and the self-delusion by which he finally escaped it are not of momentous importance to many social scientists. Nor are these matters likely to have tremendous political or social ramifications. For the presumption that the mission or potential of social science is to replace politics as a means of establishing priorities or resolving conflict is the result of either academic conceit or a charmingly antiquated faith in social "progress." Only the virtuosi of social science, those driven beyond the explanation of specific events by the need to understand the larger context in which events occur, are likely to be conscious of their most general conceptual categories. Only they, therefore, will be confronted with the necessity of determining the manner in which they will act upon these assumptions of social science. And only they need be wary of the self-delusion to which Weber fell prey, accepting a "scientific" theory on faith and becoming an absurdity—a scientific politician.

NOTES

CHAPTER ONE
Social Science and Politics

1. See Arthur O. Lovejoy, *The Great Chain of Being* (Cambridge: Harvard University Press, 1936), pp. 24–66. This is the classical conception of natural law. The term is more generally applied to the notion that universal principles of political justice, rooted in human nature, exist. For general surveys, see Paul E. Sigmund, *Natural Law in Political Thought* (Cambridge, Mass.: Winthrop Publishers, 1971), and A. P. D'Entreves, *Natural Law* (New York: Harper & Row, 1965).

2. See Ernst Cassirer, *The Philosophy of the Enlightenement* (Princeton: Princeton University Press, 1951), pp. 7–14, 40–49. Even Carl L. Becker qualifies his controversial thesis that the Philosophs were closer to the Middle Ages in outlook than our own in his recognition that they built their "heavenly city" with up to date materials. *The Heavenly City of the Eighteenth Century Philosophers* (New Haven, Conn.: Yale University Press, 1932), pp. 31, 49.

3. Compare Eric Voegelin, *The New Science of Politics* (Chicago: University of Chicago Press, 1952), pp. 64–68, and Leo Strauss, "Political Philosophy and the Crisis of Our Time," in George J. Graham, Jr., and George W. Carey (eds.), *The Post-Behavioral Era* (New York: David McKay Company, 1972), pp. 217–242.

4. Those of a classical persuasion are, of course, likely to argue not only that politics should be the application of philosophic wisdom, but also that it occasionally is. For instance, see Martin Diamond, "Democracy and *The Federalist*: A Reconsideration of the Framers' Intent," *American Political Science Review* 53 (March, 1959), 52–68. Compare

John P. Roche, "The Founding Fathers: A Reform Caucus in Action," *American Political Science Review* 55 (December, 1961), 799–816.

5. This, of course, was Plato's quandary. The issue was not as acute for Aristotle, since he either doubted that human beings were really capable of philosophy or felt that proper "political" activity was necessary preparation for it. See Terence Ball, "Theory and Practice: An Examination of the Platonic and Aristotelian Conceptions of Political Theory," *Western Political Quarterly* 25 (September, 1972), 534–545.

6. For a general survey, see Robert Bierstedt, "Sociological Thought in the Eighteenth Century," in Tom Bottomore and Robert Nisbet (eds.), *A History of Sociological Analysis* (New York: Basic Books, 1978), pp. 3–38.

7. According to Frank E. Manuel, Saint-Simon even refused to use the term *government. The Prophets of Paris* (Cambridge: Harvard University Press, 1962), p. 122.

8. For instance, see B. F. Skinner, *Beyond Freedom and Dignity* (New York: Bantam Books, 1971), *passim.*

9. John Stuart Mill, *Auguste Comte and Positivism* (Ann Arbor, Mich.: University of Michigan Press, 1961), p. 124.

10. John Stuart Mill, *A System of Logic* (London: Longman, 1970), p. 556. See also Mill, *Auguste Comte*, p. 141.

11. For the different views between the two most influential exponents of this doctrine, compare David Hume, *A Treatise of Human Nature* (London: Oxford University Press, 1888), pp. 470–476, and Alfred Jules Ayer, *Language, Truth and Logic* (New York: Dover Publications, 1952), p. 109.

12. For instance, see W. G. Runciman, *A Critique of Max Weber's Philosophy of Social Science* (London: Cambridge University Press, 1972), p. 49; Leo Strauss, *Natural Right and History* (Chicago: University of Chicago Press, 1953), p. 41. For an engaging discussion of the multifarious debate over his views that began shortly before his death and continue in the present, see Stephen P. Turner and Regis A. Factor, *Max Weber and the Dispute over Reason and Value* (London: Routledge and Kegan Paul, 1984).

13. Joseph Schumpeter, *History of Economic Analysis* (New York: Oxford University Press, 1954), p. 814. See also L. M. Lachmann, *The Legacy of Max Weber* (Berkeley, Calif.: Glendessary Press, 1971), pp. 24–25; Julien Freund, *The Sociology of Max Weber* (New York: Random House, 1968), pp. 37–41.

14. See Vernon Dibble, "Social Science and Political Commitments in the Young Max Weber," *Archives Europeennes de Sociologie* 9 (1968), 92–110.

15. Marianne Weber, *Max Weber: A Biography,* trans. Harry Zohn (New York: John Wiley & Sons, 1975), p. 226.

16. Assuming, of course, that culture is defined in terms of symbolic meaning, as it surely was for Weber. For a more contemporary statement of essentially the same position, see Clifford Geertz, *The Interpretation of Cultures* (New York: Basic Books, 1973), pp. 48–49.

17. For an elementary demonstration of this point, see Irving M. Copi, *Introduction to Logic* (New York: Macmillan, 1953), pp. 417–425. Whether the framework itself is subject to scientific scrutiny has been the subject of much debate. See the essays in Imre Lakatos and Alan Musgrave (eds.), *Criticism and the Growth of Knowledge* (London: Cambridge University Press, 1970); Karl Popper, "The Myth of the Framework," in Eugene Freeman (ed.), *The Abdication of Philosophy* (LaSalle, Ill.: Open Court, 1976), pp. 36–37.

18. The only other attempt to link Weber's personal experience and his methodological thought explicitly rejects the validity of the latter. John Torrance, "Max Weber: Methods and the Man," *European Journal of Sociology* 15 (1974), 127–165.

19. This is, of course, exactly the reverse of the pattern usually sought in psychoanalytical therapy, where the goal is to bring repressed phenomena into consciousness so that they might be in some sense sublimated.

20. Michael Polanyi has intelligently explored another aspect of personal commitment in science. I believe that my analysis is complementary to his. See *Personal Knowledge* (New York: Harper & Row, 1964), pp. 299–316.

CHAPTER TWO
Max Weber Becomes a Scientist

1. The prestige of the university professor persists today, although not to the extent that it did before World War I. Ralf Dahrendorf, *Society and Democracy in Germany* (Garden City, N.Y.: Doubleday, 1967), p. 81.

2. Marianne Weber, *Max Weber: A Biography*, trans. Harry Zohn (New York: John Wiley & Sons, 1975), p. 235; actually, Weber suffered an acute attack of anxiety and exhaustion shortly before this incident. However, after a vacation he had sufficiently recovered to resume his teaching duties and did not believe that it was a serious problem. *Ibid.,* p. 234.

3. See Arthur Mitzman, *The Iron Cage* (New York: Alfred A. Knopf, 1970), pp. 3–163. This simplified outline hardly does justice to Mitzman's analysis. See Marianne Weber, *Max Weber: A Biography*, pp. 230–231, for details of the confrontation between Weber and his father.

4. See Marianne Weber, *Max Weber: A Biography*, p. 232. For Weber's reflections on the incident years later, see the letter to his younger brother, Arthur, probably written in 1919, in *ibid.*, p. 233.

5. See *ibid.*, pp. 195, 207; letter from Weber to Marianne Weber, early 1894, in *ibid.*, p. 196.

6. In fact, Weber's confrontation with his father is apparently the first in a series of aggressive incidents initiated by Weber throughout the rest of his life. Before this confrontation, Weber was not given to expressing strong emotions.

7. Letter from Weber to Lujo Brentano, between 1894 and 1896, in Marianne Weber, *Max Weber: A Biography*, p. 224.

8. He was probably correct in this belief. See Dahrendorf, *Society and Democracy*, pp. 234–235.

9. Marianne Weber, *Max Weber: A Biography*, p. 163. This was not true for his required service as an unpaid legal clerk, which he found extremely boring. *Ibid.*, p. 146.

10. Letter from Weber to Hermann Baumgarten, January 3, 1891, in Eduard Baumgarten, *Max Weber: Werk und Person* (Tuebingen: J. C. B. Mohr, 1964), pp. 74–78; author's translation.

11. See letter from Weber to Alfred Weber, August 5, 1887, in Eduard Baumgarten, *Max Weber,* pp. 59–60. Also letter from Weber to Emmy Baumgarten, July 5, 1887, in Marianne Weber, *Max Weber: A Biography,* pp. 156–157, and letter from Weber to Marianne Schnitger, mid-1893, in *ibid.,* p. 187.

12. See the report on Weber's dissertation defense by Lotz, in *ibid.,* p. 114.

13. Weber explicitly stated that he would "never abandon" the practice of law unless it drove him further from his goal of financial independence and that he might try academics if it seemed the quickest way. Letter from Weber, probably to Emmy Baumgarten, probably late 1890, in Eduard Baumgarten, *Max Weber,* p. 163.

14. See letter from Weber to Hermann Baumgarten, April 30, 1888, in *ibid.* pp. 64–69.

15. Anthony Oberschall, *Empirical Social Research in Germany: 1848–1914* (New York: Basic Books, 1965), p. 4.

16. *Ibid.,* pp. 21–22.

17. Joseph Schumpeter, *History of Economic Analysis* (New York: Oxford University Press, 1954), p. 803.

18. For the most extensive analysis of this issue in English, see Alexander Gerschenkron, *Bread and Democracy in Germany* (Berkeley, Calif.: University of California Press, 1943). The relationship between certain policies and the power of the Junkers was well known at the time. See J. C. G. Roehl, *Germany Without Bismarck* (Berkeley, Calif.: University of California Press, 1967), pp. 57–58.

19. See Franz Boese, *Geschichte des Verein Fuer Sozialpolitik: 1871–1932* (Berlin: Duncker und Humblot, 1939), p. 68.

20. See Wolfgang J. Momnsen, *Max Weber und die Deutsche Politik: 1890–1920, Zweite Auflage* (Tuebingen: J. C. B. Mohr, 1974), p. 23; Boese, *Geschichte,* p. 66; Otto von Zwiedineck-Suedenhorst, "Vom Wirken von Max und Alfred Weber im Verein Fuer Sozialpolitik: Erinnerungen und Eindruecke," in Edgar Salin (ed.), *Synopsis: Festgabe fuer Alfred Weber* (Heidelberg: Verlag Lambert Schneider, 1949) p. 769.

21. Marianne Weber, *Max Weber: A Biography,* p. 200. If Weber had not received the offer from Freiburg, there is little doubt that he would have eventually been offered a position in legal history at Berlin. There is

evidence that Weber might have declined such an opportunity: "Suddenly a great career was opening up to him, but Weber's interests had already shifted too much to the area of political economy. For this reason he did not want to tie himself down to teaching law." *Ibid.*, p. 164.

22. Letter from Weber to Hermann Baumgarten, September 30, 1887, in Max Weber, *Gesammelte Politische Schriften, Erste Auflage* (Munich: Drei Masken, 1921), pp. 270–273.

23. Oberschall, *Empirical Social Research*, p. 138; see also *ibid.*, pp. 68–69; Schumpeter, *History of Economic Analysis*, p. 804. Not only did the Germans lack a social scientific tradition, they even lacked an unambiguous word for *science*. See Fritz Ringer, *The Decline of the German Mandarins: The German Academic Community, 1890–1933* (Cambridge: Harvard University Press, 1969), p. 103.

24. Weber, *Gesammelte Politische Schriften, Dritte Auflage* (Tuebingen: J. C. B. Mohr, 1971), p. 14; author's translation.

25. In fact, the leaders of the *Verein* were among the principal proponents of establishing political economy as a separate academic discipline. See Obserschall, *Empirical Social Research*, p. 69.

26. See Marianne Weber, *Max Weber: A Biography*, pp. 202, 206. Weber did have some trouble with his initial lectures. *Ibid.*, p. 202, and letter from B. Pfister to M. J. Bonn, May 11, 1963, in the Arbeitsstelle und Archiv der Max Weber Gesamtausgabe, Bayerische Akademie der Wissenschaften, Munich.

27. See letter from Weber to Hermann Baumgarten, January 3, 1891, in Eduard Baumgarten, *Max Weber*, pp. 74–78; letter from Weber to Emmy Baumgarten, February 18, 1892, in *ibid.* pp. 79–80; letter from Weber to Marianna Schnitger, mid-1893, in Marianne Weber, *Max Weber: A Biography*, pp. 216–217; Weber lost interest in his major research project on farm workers as soon as other political issues became more current and used the project largely for pedagogical purposes. *Ibid.*, p. 202.

28. Treitschke was famous for his lectures just because of the passion he expressed, but according to Schumpeter, most economists of the time gave lectures that were "horatory in intent." Schumpeter, *History of Economic Analysis*, p. 802. See letter from Weber to Hermann Baumgarten, April 25, 1887, in Baumgarten, *Max Weber*, p. 54. For another

witness of Treitschke's style and effect, see Richard von Kuehlmann, *Erinnerungen* (Heidelberg: Verlag Lambert Schneider, 1948), pp. 72–73.

29. Weber evaluated the reaction to this speech from a political rather than a scholarly perspective and seemed pleased with the result. See letter from Weber to Alfred Weber, May 17, 1895, in Mommsen, *Max Weber und die Deutsche Politik*, p. 39.

30. See Weber, *Gesammelte Politische Schriften*, pp. 12, 17.

31. See Mommsen, *Max Weber und die Deutsch Politik*, p. 20; Marianne Weber, *Max Weber: A Biography*, p. 223; letter from Weber to Hermann Baumgarten, January 3, 1891, in Eduard Baumgarten, *Max Weber*, pp. 74–78; on the Social Union in general and the practical reasons for Weber's participation, see Oberschall, *Empirical Social Research*, pp. 29–30.

32. See Marianne Weber, *Max Weber: A Biography*, p. 135; Mommsen, *Max Weber und die Deutsche Politik*, p. 74. Theodor Heuss claims that Naumann had already moved in a nationalistic direction before Weber's speech and that Weber merely helped to clarify his ideas. *Friedrich Naumann: Der Mann, das Werk, die Zeit, Zweite Auflage* (Stuttgart: Wunderlich, 1949), pp. 137–138; nevertheless, it appears to be generally accepted that Weber's influence was decisive. For instance, see Robert A. Pois, *Friedrich Meinecke and German Politics in the Twentieth Century* (Berkeley, Calif.: University of California Press, 1972), p. 5.

33. See Marianne Weber, *Max Weber: A Biography*, pp. 202, 223. The following letter to his brother Alfred, July 22, 1895, illustrates the political nature of Weber's activity during this period: "In the meantime you will have noticed that the Kreuzeitung did print my article—after sitting on it for one and a half weeks. [Hammerstein] is really incredible. He evidently attributes the Kaiser's change of attitude toward the agrarians to Stumm; as long as it seemed as though the imperial favor was smiling upon the agrarians as well, he kept his hands off the all-powerful one and deemed it 'at this time politically unwise' to take my article, but now he has taken it out of his drawer and flung it in the Kaiser's face! . . . Please watch the Post now, too, so that I can immediately fly at its throat if it opens its mouth." In *ibid.*, p. 219.

34. See letter from Weber to Marianne Weber, November 11, 1896, in *ibid.*, p.198.

35. See Mommsen, *Max Weber und die Deutsche Politik,* p. 81.

36. Letter from Weber to Adolph Hausrath, October 15, 1896, in *ibid.,* p. 136.

37. Marianne Weber, *Max Weber: A Biography,* p. 226. Although it must be admitted that Weber did have reservations about leaving Berlin for this reason. See *ibid.,* 200–201.

38. See Weber, *Gesammelte Politische Schriften, Dritte Auflage,* pp. 26–29; letter from Weber to Marianne Weber, November, 1896, in Marianne Weber, *Max Weber: A Biography,* p. 221; letter from Helene Weber to Ida Baumgarten, October 7, 1896, in Eduard Baumgarten, *Max Weber,* pp. 330–331. A statement by Kurt Eisner, later leader of Bavaria's short-lived revolutionary government at the end of World War I, reveals the seriousness with which Naumann's "national socialism" was viewed. "Eisner compared this to eating sour herring with Schlagsahne [whipped cream] on the dubious gastronomical logic that each tasted good separately, so they must taste good together." Allan Mitchell, *Revolution in Bavaria, 1918–1919: The Eisner Reigme and the Soviet Republic* (Princeton, N.J.: Princeton University Press, 1965), p. 44.

39. Christoph Steding, *Politik und Wissenschaft bei Max Weber* (Breslau: Wilh. Gottl. Korn Verlag, 1932), p. 26; author's translation.

40. In this contention, see letter from Helene Weber to Ida Baumgarten, October 7, 1896, in Eduard Baumgarten, *Max Weber,* pp. 330–331.

41. Mommsen, *Max Weber und die Deutsche Politik,* pp. 37–38.

42. "Next summer he wants to take his doctorate here, and I think that then his other interests will again prevail over this dry-as-dust legal stuff, for which I have no feeling whatever. He is by no means practical and organized enough in his daily doings to be an official; also, he has always been more interested in the historical development of the law than its application." Letter from Helene Weber, probably to Ida Baumgarten, probably early 1886, in Marianne Weber, *Max Weber: A Biography,* p. 106.

43. See Martin Green, *The von Richthofen Sisters: The Triumphant and the Tragic Modes of Love* (New York: Basic Books, 1974), p. 110. We know very little about Max Weber, Sr. In describing the family back-

ground of both parents, Marianne Weber definitely leaves the impression that the Webers were sort of uncomplicated and uninteresting. Her treatment of Max Weber, Sr.'s, youth is almost condescending. Green, *The von Richthofen Sisters,* pp. 24–27.

44. Marianne Weber, *Max Weber: A Biography,* p. 38.

45. See *ibid.,* pp. 37–38. There is evidence that their different orientations began to clash soon after marriage. See letter from Helene Weber to Ida Baumgarten, no date, in *ibid.,* p. 29.

46. See letter from Emily Fallenstein to Fritz Baumgarten, Summer, 1877, in *ibid.,* pp. 60–61; letter from Fritz Baumgarten to Ida Baumgarten, Summer, 1877, in *ibid.,* pp. 48–49.

47. See *ibid.,* pp. 61–62. Also relevant is *ibid.,* p. 30.

48. See letter from Helene Weber, probably to Ida Baumgarten, 1879, in *ibid.,* p. 57.

49. *Ibid.,* p. 49.

50. *Ibid.,* p. 32.

51. See *ibid.,* pp. 48, 60; letter from Helene Weber to Ida Baumgarten, 1879, in *ibid.,* p. 57; "To my joy it now seems to me as though he has somewhat modified his principle of never saying anything sensible to me, and I am now trying to make him stick to this without his being aware of it." Letter from Helene Weber to Ida Baumgarten, 1880, in *ibid.,* p. 60. Also see the newsy and often clever letters Weber wrote his mother when he was between 12 and 14 years of age. They display no intimacy nor disclose any feelings, although they admirably fulfill his duty to write his mother. *Ibid.,* pp. 41–45. Weber's own interpretation of his early relationship with his mother conforms to that offered here: "On top of everything else that is inflicted upon mothers, it is also their fate that as soon as the children's drive for independence awakens and while it is still not sure of itself, it is at first directed purely negatively against the parents and specifically against the mother." Letter from Weber to Helene Weber, April 14, 1902, in *ibid.,* p. 256.

52. See S. N. Eisenstadt, *From Generation to Generation* (New York: Free Press, 1956), Chapter 3, especially pp. 181–182.

53. On the painfulness of the process, see Erik H. Erikson, *Identity, Youth and Crisis* (New York: W. W. Norton, 1968), p. 129.

54. See Murray B. Seidler and Mel Jerome Ravitz, "A Jewish Peer

Group," *American Journal of Sociology* 61 (July, 1955), 11–15. Obviously, the impact of peer groups varies not only with the individual but also with the culture. For instance, see U. Bronfenbrenner, "Response to Pressure from Peers Versus Adults Among Soviet and American School Children," *International Journal of Psychology* 2 (1967), 199–207. Also relevant is Dean Jaros, *Socialization to Politics* (New York: Praeger Publishers, 1973), Chapter 6.

55. Although there is evidence indicating that it is increasingly less likely for parents to be role models as the child matures. See Ruth C. Wylie, *The Self-Concept* (Lincoln, Nebr.: University of Nebraska Press, 1961), pp. 126–137.

56. It may be just as correct to say that his adolescence began early. See Harry Stack Sullivan, *Conceptions of Modern Psychiatry* (New York: W. W. Norton, 1953), p. 58.

57. For the psychological problems this must have caused Weber, see Erik H. Erikson, *Young Man Luther* (New York: W. W. Norton, 1962), pp. 111–112.

58. See Karen Horney, *The Neurotic Personality of Our Time* (New York: W. W. Norton, 1937), p. 84.

59. Also see letter from Emily Fallenstein to Fritz Baumgarten, Summer, 1877, in Marianne Weber, *Max Weber: A Biography*, p. 61, and *ibid.*, pp. 61–62.

60. See *ibid.*, p. 92.

61. See *ibid.*, pp. 106–107; letter from Helene Weber to Ida Baumgarten, approximately 1885, in *ibid.*, p. 96; letter from Weber to Helene Weber, late 1885, in *ibid.*, p. 108; letter from Weber to Emmy Baumgarten, early 1886, in Eduard Baumgarten, *Max Weber*, pp. 50–52.

62. For negative comments about his peers, see letter from Weber to Fritz Baumgarten, 1878, in Marianne Weber, *Max Weber: A Biography*, p. 50; letter from Weber to Helene Weber, July 17, 1882, in Eduard Baumgarten, *Max Weber*, pp. 16–18; and especially letter to Hermann Baumgarten, April 25, 1887, in *ibid.*, p. 54.

63. Marianne Weber, *Max Weber: A Biography*, p. 40.

64. As Mitzman does. *The Iron Cage*, p. 22; Marianne Weber at one

point gives support to Mitzman's interpretation. *Max Weber: A Biography*, p. 62.

65. See Marianne Weber, *Max Weber: A Biography*, pp. 34–35, 42–44.

66. See *Ibid.*, p. 63.

67. Letter from Weber to Fritz Baumgarten, September, 1878, in *ibid.*, pp. 51–52.

68. Letter from Weber to Fritz Baumgarten, December 19, 1879, in *ibid.*, pp. 55–56. A supposed ancient Gallic poet, "Ossian" was the product of a scholarly fraud of the eighteenth century. Weber was not the only victim. Weber also preferred Schiller to Goethe because of a lack of a heroic element in the latter's work. Letter from Weber to Emmy Baumgarten, May 8, 1887, in Eduard Baumgarten, *Max Weber*, p. 53.

69. Letter from Weber to Fritz Baumgarten, September, 1878, in Marianne Weber, *Max Weber: A Biography*, pp. 52–53. Weber never completely lost his linking of politics and heroism. It appears at numerous points in his work, perhaps most forcefully in his inaugural address at Freiburg: "In the full, half conscious, distant urge lies hidden a moment of primitive idealism. Who is not able to decifer it, does not know the magic of freedom. In fact, its spirit seldom moves us in the quiet of the library. The naive, free ideals of our early youth are faded, and many of us are prematurely old, and have become all too clever." Weber, *Gesammelte Dritte Auflage, Politische Schriften*, p. 7; author's translation.

70. See Robert C. Tucker's analysis of Stalin's hero worship and role taking. *Stalin as Revolutionary: 1879–1929* (New York: W. W. Norton, 1973), pp. 126–137.

71. See Marianne Weber, *Max Weber: A Biography*, p. 46.

72. Weber's younger brother, Alfred, seems to have hit upon the same tactic: "He is having a very hard time. This I notice by the vehemence and stubbornness with which he seizes upon every opportunity to prove that every other view has at least the same justification and probability as the Christian religion. Then he cites Strauss's *Das Leben Jesu* and the philosophy of Kant. I stand there and feel sorrowful and sad that I cannot help him because I lack the right words at the right time." Letter

from Helene Weber to Ida Baumgarten, approximately 1880, in *ibid.*, p. 59. Marianne Weber notes immediately after this letter that at least Alfred talked seriously about these matters with her but Max did not.

73. See *ibid.*, pp. 39, 48, 49, 50, 56, 57, 60.

74. See letter to Fritz Baumgarten, approximately 1880, in *ibid.*, p. 58.

75. He concealed his insecurity with clever ridicule and pointed criticism of the social conventions by which youths of the opposite sex interact. For instance, see letter from Weber to Emmy Baumgarten, early 1886, in Eduard Baumgarten, *Max Weber*, pp. 50–52; also in Marianne Weber, *Max Weber: A Biography*, pp. 109–110.

76. H. Rickert recollected that he feared Weber because of his superior knowledge and avoided him for this reason. Review of Marianne Weber, *Max Weber: Ein Lebensbild* (Heidelberg: Verlag Lambert Schneider, 1950), probably 1926, copy in the Arbeitsstelle und Archiv der Max Weber Gesamtausgabe, Bayerische Akademie der Wissenschaften, Munich.

77. See Marianne Weber, *Max Weber: A Biography*, p. 96. The one possible exception would be his cousin, Otto Baumgarten. See Otto Baumgarten, *Meine Lebensgeschichte* (Tuebingen: J. C. B. Mohr, 1929), p. 62.

78. Letter from Weber to Emmy Baumgarten, April 22, 1893, in Marianne Weber, *Max Weber: A Biography*, pp. 182–183; also in Eduard Baumgarten, *Max Weber*, pp. 85–86. For less explicit indications of this resignation, see letter from Weber to Emmy Baumgarten, October, 1887, in *ibid.*, pp. 61–62; letter from Weber to Emmy Baumgarten, February 18, 1892, in *ibid.*, pp. 79–80.

79. For instance, see Erik H. Erikson, *Childhood and Society* (New York: W. W. Norton, 1963), pp. 35, 261–262; R. D. Laing, *The Divided Self* (Baltimore: Penguin Books, 1965), pp. 41–42; Prescott Lecky, *Self-Consistency: A Theory of Personality* (Garden City, N.Y.: Anchor Books, 1961), *passim*; Milton Rokeach, *The Three Christs of Ypsilanti: A Psychological Study* (New York: Alfred A. Knopf, 1964), p. 26; Sullivan, *Modern Psychiatry*, p. 19.

80. See Erikson, *Childhood and Society*, p. 213; Laing, *The Divided Self*, p. 85.

81. See the discussion in Michael Argyle, *The Psychology of Interpersonal Behavior* (Baltimore: Penguin Books, 1972), pp. 155–159.

82. See letter from Weber to Hermann Baumgarten, April 30, 1888, in Eduard Baumgarten, *Max Weber*, pp. 64–69.

83. See Mommsen, *Max Weber und die Deutsche Politik*, pp. 8, 12.

84. Baumgarten believed that politics is "the highest and most difficult profession to which one can devote himself." Quoted in *ibid.*, p. 13. Although Weber referred to Baumgarten at one point as "uniquely a scholar," all the available letters that Weber wrote to him are concerned with contemporary affairs. For the reference, see letter from Weber to Emmy Baumgarten, February 18, 1892, in Eduard Baumgarten, *Max Weber*, pp. 79–80.

85. See Green, *The von Richthofen Sisters*, p. 109; letter from Weber to Helene Weber, September 14, 1892, in Eduard Baumgarten, *Max Weber*, pp. 81–82; Marianne Weber, *Max Weber: A Biography*, pp. 82–83.

86. See letter from Weber to Helene Weber, October 22, 1883, in Eduard Baumgarten, *Max Weber*, pp. 19–20; letter from Weber to Helene Weber, May 3, 1884, in *ibid.*, pp. 26–28.

87. See letter from Weber to Helene Weber, June 8, 1887, in *ibid.*, pp. 29–31.

88. Marianne Weber, *Max Weber: A Biography*, pp. 94–95, 98. Also see the letter from Weber to Helene Weber, April 7, 1884, in Eduard Baumgarten, *Max Weber*, pp. 27–28.

89. Marianne Weber, *Max Weber: A Biography*, p. 70. When his mother saw him for the first time after a year of drinking bouts had increased his girth and a duel had put a scar on his face, "the vigorous woman could think of no other way to express her astonishment and fright than to give him a resounding slap in the face." *Ibid.*, p. 69. See letter from Otto Baumgarten to Hermann Baumgarten, June 19, 1882, in Eduard Baumgarten, *Max Weber*, p. 627.

90. See Marianne Weber, *Max Weber: A Biography*, pp. 141, 145, 149.

91. Mitzman, *The Iron Cage*, p. 47.

92. See, especially, the letter from Weber to Emmy Baumgarten, approximately 1886, in Marianne Weber, *Max Weber: A Biography*, p. 143; also see *ibid.*, pp. 144–145, 153.

93. Letter from Weber to Helene Weber, April 3, 1884, in Eduard Baumgarten, *Max Weber,* pp. 26–28; letter from Weber to Emmy Baumgarten, July 5, 1887, in *ibid.,* pp. 57–59.

94. Marianne Weber, *Max Weber: A Biography,* p. 112. See also *ibid.,* pp. 141–142; letter from Weber to Helene Weber, June 16, 1885, in Eduard Baumgarten, *Max Weber,* pp. 32–33; letter from Weber to Arthur Weber, probably 1919, in *ibid.,* pp. 629–630. In this letter, Weber does relate that a particular incident did "completely alienate" him from his father. But see the letter he wrote to Emmy Baumgarten, October 21, 1887, in *ibid.,* pp. 61–62, where Weber complains about both parents.

95. See letter from Weber to Emmy Baumgarten, October 21, 1887, in Marianne Weber, *Max Weber: A Biography;* letter from Weber to Emmy Baumgarten, probably late 1890, in *ibid.,* p. 163; letter from Weber to Marianne Schnitger, early 1893, *ibid.,* p. 185.

96. See letter to Marianne Weber, late 1892, in *ibid.,* p. 179.

97. See Erikson, *Young Man Luther,* pp. 111–112; Laing, *The Divided Self,* pp. 41–42, 103; Sullivan, *Modern Psychiatry,* p. 47.

98. Letter from Weber to Emmy Baumgarten, Easter, 1887, in Eduard Baumgarten, *Max Weber,* pp. 46–50; translation taken from Marianne Weber, *Max Weber: A Biography,* p. 153.

99. For instance, Mitzman asserts that Weber "put into question his relationship to his mother during his recovery." Mitzman, *The Iron Cage,* p. 179. But according to his mother's own testimony she felt close to him and Marianne for the first time only in the initial years of his recovery, and on previous visits she felt like an "intruder." Marianne Weber, *Max Weber: A Biography,* p. 251. See also *ibid.,* p. 204. The mere fact of hostility in the family does not necessarily result in maladjustment of the child. As Horney points out, "The child's character formation lies not so much in feeling or expressing of protest, but in repressing it." *The Neurotic Personality,* p. 84.

100. In this connection, see C. G. Jung, *Modern Man in Search of a Soul,* trans. W. S. Dell and Cary F. Baynes (New York: Harcourt, Brace and World, 1933), p. 105.

101. Apparently Weber found it difficult to relax and enjoy life even

immediately after his wedding. See Marianne Weber, *Max Weber: A Biography*, pp. 180, 193.

102. See Otto Fenichel, *The Psychoanalytic Theory of Neurosis* (New York: W. W. Norton, 1945), p. 132; Franz Alexander, *Fundamentals of Psychoanalysis* (New York: W. W. Norton, 1963), pp. 245–246.

103. Alexander, *Fundamentals of Psychoanalysis*, pp. 100–101; in this connection, see also Horney, *The Neurotic Personality*, p. 23; Sullivan, *Modern Psychiatry*, p. 23.

104. See Fenichel, *Psychoanalytic Theory*, pp. 168, 187. Fenichel does recognize that trauma caused by external conditions is also a source of neurotic behavior.

105. On the historical and sociological factors that led to the creation of Freudianism, see Franz G. Alexander and Sheldon T. Selesnick, *The History of Psychiatry* (New York: Harper & Row, 1966), p. 271. In this connection, see also Philip Rieff, *Freud: The Mind of the Moralist* (Garden City, N.Y.: Doubleday, 1961), pp. 109–110, and Sigmund Freud, *The History of the Psychoanalytic Movement*, trans. Joan Riviere (New York: Collier Books, 1963), pp. 71–72. Freud denied on numerous occasions that psychoanalysis provided a comprehensive theory of human mentality. See, for instance, *ibid.*, p. 83. On the other hand, he did not consistently hold to this denial. For instance: "The determining cause of all the forms taken by human mental life is, indeed, to be sought in the reciprocal action between innate disposition and accidental experiences." *An Outline of Psycho-Analysis*, trans. James Strachey (New York: W. W. Norton, 1969), p. 40.

106. See Sigmund Freud, *The Ego and the Id*, trans. Joan Riviere (New York: W. W. Norton, 1960), pp. 19–20, 38–39; Fenichel, *Psychoanalytic Theory*, p. 142. Freud and a number of recent psychiatrists have left open the possibility that a good deal of the "superego" might in many cases be considered an "ego-ideal" and be potentially conscious. See Alexander, *Fundamentals of Psychoanalysis*, pp. 82–84; Sigmund Freud, *Psycho-Analysis*, pp. 19, 34. For a denial of this possibility, see Fenichel, *Psychoanalytic Theory*, p. 106.

107. See Alexander, *Fundamentals of Psychoanalysis*, pp. 82–83.

108. See Horney, *The Neurotic Personality*, p. 44; see also Anna

Freud, *The Ego and the Mechanisms of Defense* (London: Hogarth Press, 1942), p. 61.

109. Horney, *The Neurotic Personality*, p. 52. For descriptions of the incredible array of activities that Weber undertook and the constant demands they made on his time in the years before his breakdown, see letter from Weber to Hermann Baumgarten, 1892, in Marianne Weber, *Max Weber: A Biography*, p. 165, and *ibid.*, pp. 195, 202.

110. Letter from Weber to Marianna Schnitger, early 1894, in Marianne Weber, *ibid.*, p. 196; letter from Weber to Marianne Weber, mid-1894, in *ibid.*, pp. 200–201. In the former letter Weber explicitly states that he had been suffering from a nervous disorder for a number of years. Gerhard Hufnagel has emphasized the compulsive nature of work for Weber and, in the author's view, correctly points to the cause of Weber's anxiety. *Kritik als Beruf: Der Kritische Gehalt im Werk Max Webers* (Frankfurt/Main: Propylaeen Verlag, 1971), pp. 22–23.

111. Letter from Weber to Marianne Weber, Fall, 1898, in Marianne Weber, *Max Weber: A Biography*, p. 236; Marianne Weber, *Max Weber: Ein Lebensbild*, p. 271. Weber's reference to "scholarly work" is somewhat inaccurate since his activities, as discussed previously, included many political and journalistic projects. Weber was still hoping to pursue a political career during the first stage of his illness and consciously trying to disengage from academics.

112. For instance, see letter from Weber to Helene Weber, early Summer, 1899, in Marianne Weber, *Max Weber: A Biography*, p. 239, and letter from Weber to Marianne Weber, late 1900, in *ibid.*, p. 245.

113. Fenichel, *Psychoanalytic Theory*, p. 118.

114. Compare *ibid.*, p. 19; Alexander, *Fundamentals of Psychoanalysis*, p. 194; Sullivan, *Modern Psychiatry*, pp. 22, 47.

115. See letter from Weber to Helene Weber, early 1899, in Marianne Weber, *Max Weber: A Biography*, p. 239; letter from Marianne Weber to Helene Weber, Summer, 1899, in *ibid.*, p. 240; letter from Marianne Weber to Helene Weber, Spring, 1899, in *ibid.*, pp. 238–239.

116. See especially letter from Marianne Weber to Helene Weber, July, 1900, in *ibid.*, p. 243; also letter from Marianne Weber to Helene Weber, Spring, 1899, in *ibid.*, p. 237; Helene Weber to Emmy Baumgarten, October 19, 1901, in Eduard Baumgarten, *Max Weber*, pp.

639–641. Weber's excitability occasionally caused sleeplessness for the remainder of his life. At first he took drugs; later he arranged his life in order to avoid anything that might cause excitement late in the day. In Marianne Weber's biography the references of her husband to this daily regimen are too numerous to cite.

117. Marianne Weber is not very specific in describing physical symptoms. The following quote, referring to the Christmas of 1898, is the most detailed reference: "He was so utterly exhausted that his back and arms failed him when he tried to trim the Christmas tree." *Max Weber: A Biography*, p. 237. Weber refers to a strain in his back in a letter to his mother, April 14, 1902, in *ibid.*, pp. 255–257.

118. On anxiety neuroses and its relation to phobia, see Fenichel, *Psychoanalytic Theory*, pp. 194, 210; Alexander, *Fundamentals of Psychoanalysis*, 215–217.

119. Erikson, *Young Man Luther*, pp. 217–218; see also *ibid.*, p. 52.

120. See *ibid.*, pp. 111–112; Laing, *The Divided Self*, p. 42.

121. On "panic," see Sullivan, *Modern Psychiatry*, pp. 134–135.

122. Letter from Marianne Weber to Helene Weber, Spring, 1899, in Marianne Weber, *Max Weber: A Biography*, p. 238. Also see letter from Helene Weber to Emmy Baumgarten and Anne Baumgarten, February 16, 1900, in Eduard Baumgarten, *Max Weber*, p. 639.

CHAPTER THREE
Commitment and Personality

1. Marianne Weber, *Max Weber: A Biography*, trans. Harry Zohn (New York: John Wiley & Sons, 1975), p. 207.

2. Letter from Weber to Helene Weber, probably September, 1897, in *ibid.*, p. 234.

3. See letter from Weber, probably to Marianne Weber, January 3, 1903, in Marianne Weber, *ibid.*, pp. 261–262; see also letter from Marianne Weber to Helene Weber, late 1902, in *ibid.*, p. 210.

4. *Ibid.*, p. 304. Although by one report of dubious validity, some of the natives found his behavior somewhat odd. See *The Daily Oklahomian*, Guthrie, Oklahoma, Thursday, September 29, 1904. Copy at the

Arbeitsstelle und Archiv der Max Weber Gesamtausgabe, Bayerische Akademie der Wissenschaften, Munich.

5. The evidence for this conjecture is, of course, slight. See letter to Helene Weber, April 14, 1902, in Marianne Weber, *Max Weber: A Biography*, pp. 256–257. On the debilitating effect of the neurotic's preoccupation with himself, see Thomas M. French, *Psychoanalytic Interpretations* (Chicago: Quadrangle Books, 1970), pp. 42–43.

6. Letter from Weber to Helene Weber, April 14, 1902, in Marianne Weber, *Max Weber: A Biography*, pp. 255–257.

7. See Fenichel, *The Psychoanalytic Theory of Neurosis.* (New York: W. W. Norton, 1945), p. 185.

8. See Marianne Weber, *Max Weber: A Biography*, pp. 257–258.

9. See letter from Marianne Weber to Helene Weber, Spring, 1899, in *ibid.*, p. 237; letter from Weber to Helene Weber, April 14, 1902, in *ibid.*, p. 256; *ibid.*, pp. 258–259. After 1903, Weber was able to present papers at professional meetings and engage in argument. He read a paper in St. Louis at 1904 and took an active part in some bitter exchanges at the meeting of the *Verein fuer Sozialpolitik* in 1905. See Max Weber, *Gesammelte Aufsaetze zur Soziologie und Sozialpolitik* (Tuebingen: J. C. B. Mohr, 1924), pp. 394–407.

10. In the case of repression, see Franz Alexander, *Fundamentals of Psychoanalysis* (New York: W. W. Norton, 1963), p. 96. Also see in this connection Fenichel, *Psychoanalytic Theory*, p. 210.

11. Marianne Weber, *Max Weber: A Biography*, p. 264; letter from Marianne Weber to Helene Weber, early 1902, in *ibid.*, pp. 252–253; letter from Marianne Weber to Helene Weber, April 1902, in *ibid.*, p. 255; letter from Weber to Marianne Weber, late 1900, in *ibid.*, p. 245.

12. Letter of resignation from Weber to Pan German League, April 22, 1899, in *ibid.*, pp. 224–225.

13. See letter from Marianne Weber to Helene Weber, Spring, 1899, in *ibid.*, pp. 238–239; letter from Marianne Weber to Helene Weber, Fall, 1900, in *ibid.*, p. 246.

14. Letter from Marianne Weber to Helene Weber, July, 1900, in *ibid.*, p. 243.

15. See letters from Marianne Weber to Helene Weber, early 1902, in

ibid., pp. 252–253; from Marianne Weber to Helene Weber, early 1902, *ibid.*, pp. 251–252.

16. Letter from Marianne Weber to Helene Weber, October 10, 1902, in *ibid.*, p. 259.

17. Letter from Marianne Weber to Helene Weber, late 1903 or early 1904, in *ibid.*, pp. 262–263.

18. Letter from Marianne Weber to Helene Weber, early 1902, in *ibid.*, p. 254.

19. Letter from Helene Weber to Emmy Baumgarten, October 19, 1901, in Eduard Baumgarten, *Max Weber: Werk und Person* (Tuebingen: J. C. B. Mohr, 1964), pp. 639–641; author's translation.

20. See Wolfgang J. Mommsen, *Max Weber und die Deutsche Politik: 1890–1920, Zweite Auflage* (Tuebingen: J. C. B. Mohr, 1974), pp. 160–161.

21. *Ibid.*, p. 140. Mommsen suggests that Weber's temperament did not allow him to deal with the drudgery of day to day political activity. As we shall see, day to day administrative work during the war was very therapeutic for Weber, and certainly Mommsen is aware of the drudgery involved in serious scholarship. *Ibid.*, p. 141.

22. The connection between his new methodological interests and his illness is usually not seen, leaving many commentators baffled by the fact that these methodological interests were his first concern once he regained the capacity to work. For instance, see Guy Oakes, "Introductory Essay," in Max Weber, *Roscher and Knies: The Logical Problems of Historical Economics* (New York: Free Press, 1975), p. 5; Arthur Mitzman, *The Iron Cage* (New York: Alfred A. Knopf, 1970), p. 168. Christoph Steding denies that there was a radical break. *Politik und Wissenschaft bei Max Weber* (Breslau: Wilh. Gottl. Korn Verlag, 1932), pp. 17–18. Although the evidence clearly indicates that methodological concerns were the first to occupy Weber in his new phase, he apparently began to develop his ideas on the cultural consequences of Protestantism at about the same time. Compare letter from Marianne Weber to Helene Weber, early 1902, in Marianne Weber, *Max Weber: A Biography*, p. 253; letter from Marianne Weber to Helene Weber, late 1902, in *ibid.*, p. 260; letter from Marianne Weber to Helene Weber, October 10, 1902,

in *ibid.*, p. 259; letter from Weber to Heinrich Rickert, June 14, 1904, in Wolfgang J. Mommsen, *The Age of Bureaucracy* (Oxford: Oxford University Press, 1974), p. 9. On Weber's reluctance to entertain methodological questions seriously and his reason for doing so, see Guy Oakes, "The Verstehen Thesis and the Foundations of Max Weber's Methodology," *History and Theory* 16 (February, 1977), 11–29.

23. Weber, *Roscher and Knies;* Max Weber, *The Protestant Ethic and the Spirit of Capitalism,* trans. Talcott Parsons (New York: Charles Scribner's Sons, 1958).

24. Max Weber, *Gesammelte Aufsaetze zur Wissenschaftslehre, Dritte Auflage* (Tuebingen: J. C. B. Mohr, 1956), p. 132; author's translation.

25. Compare Prescott Lecky, *Self-Consistency: A Theory of Personality* (Garden City, N.Y.: Anchor Books, 1961).

26. Wolfgang J. Mommsen, "Max Weber's Political Sociology and His Philosophy of World History," *International Social Science Journal* 7 (1965), 28.

27. Not even, apparently, to his wife. See letter from Marianne Weber to Helene Weber, October 10, 1902, in Marianne Weber, *Max Weber: A Biography,* p. 59; her concern for his academic career only exacerbated his problems and indicates how little she knew of their origin. It was apparently a source of irritation to Weber. See letter from Marianne Weber to Helene Weber, very late 1902, in *ibid.*, p. 261; letter from Marianne Weber to Helene Weber, April, 1902, in *ibid.*, p. 255; letter from Marianne Weber to Helene Weber, early 1902, in *ibid.*, pp. 252–253.

28. In this connection, see Weber, *Wissenschaftslehre,* pp. 88–89, 115–116.

29. See Weber, *Wissenschaftslehre,* pp. 12–13, 180, 430; Max Weber, *Wirtschaft und Gesellschaft, Vierte Auflage,* ed. Johannes Winkelmann (Tuebingen: J. C. B. Mohr, 1956), p. 1. It is only in his later methodological writings that Weber places the emphasis on action. However, from the earliest essays he emphasizes the *interpreting* of social phenomena in terms of *means* and *ends*. Only his terminology changed. Unlike Tenbruck, I believe that the fundamental tenets of Weber's methodological thought are present in his earliest essays, and

only modified slightly, if at all, in his later work. Friedrich H. Tenbruck, "Die Genesis der Methodologie Max Webers," *Koelner Zeitschrift fuer Soziologie und Sozialpsychologie* 11 (1959), 573–630. Since the primary goals of this study are theoretical rather than historical, I draw upon both early and late works to support my interpretations of Weber's thought. However, I have taken care to insure adequate reference to his early works in this chapter in order to allay any doubts concerning his intentions in undertaking these questions.

30. See Weber, *Wirtschaft,* pp. 4–5; Weber, *Wissenschaftslehre,* p. 227.

31. Weber, *Wissenschaftslehre,* pp. 50, 70, 198, 430–431, 503; Weber, *Wirtschaft* pp. 8–9. See Susan J. Hekman, "Weber's Concept of Causality and the Modern Critique," *Sociological Inquiry* 49 (1976), 67–76.

32. Weber, *Wissenschaftslehre,* pp. 64–65, 137, 221–222.

33. Weber, *Wissenschaftslehre,* pp. 70, 134–135, 174, 180; Weber, *Wirtschaft,* p. 118. Weber *Gesammelte Autsaetze zur Soziologie,* pp. 244–247, 249. See Richard Herbert Howe, "Max Weber's Elective Affinities: Sociology Within the Bounds of Pure Reason," *American Journal of Sociology* 84 (1978), 366–385.

34. See Weber, *Wissenschaftslehre,* pp. 12–13, 68–69; Weber, *Wirtschaft,* pp. 127, 180.

35. See Weber, *Wissenschaftslehre,* pp. 50, 68.

36. Weber, *Wirtschaft,* p. 14; see also Weber, *Wissenschaftslehre,* pp. 127, 180.

37. See Weber, *Wissenschaftslehre,* pp. 112–113, 127, 175–176, 349, 452.

38. See Weber, *Wissenschaftslehre,* pp. 150, 180, 183–184.

39. Weber, *Wirtschaft,* p. 16; see also *ibid.,* p. 182; Weber, *Wissenschaftslehre,* p. 504; Max Weber, *Gesammelte Aufsaetze zur Religionssoziologie, I* (Tuebingen: J. C. B. Mohr, 1924), p. 252.

40. See Weber, *Wirtschaft,* pp. 294, 549; Weber, *Religionssoziologie,* p. 242.

41. Weber, *Wissenschaftslehre,* p. 180; Max Weber, *Methodology of the Social Sciences,* trans. Edward A. Shils and Henry A. Finch (Glencoe, Ill.: Free Press, 1949), p. 81.

42. See Weber, *Religionssoziologie,* pp. 259–261; Weber, *Wirtschaft,* pp. 259, 307–308.

43. Weber emphasized both the importance and the complexity of this interaction. Compare Weber, *Wirtschaft,* p. 275, *ibid.,* p. 349, and Weber, *Religionssoziologie,* pp. 252–253.

44. See Weber, *Religionssoziologie,* p. 549.

45. See, especially, *ibid.,* pp. 63–69.

46. *Ibid.,* p. 117; translation taken from Weber, *Protestant Ethic,* p. 119.

47. In this connection, see Weber, *Wirtschaft,* pp. 288, 298–299.

48. Weber, *Religionssoziologie,* p. 204; Weber, *Protestant Ethic,* p. 182.

49. See Weber, *Wissenschaftslehre,* pp. 132–133.

50. *Ibid.,* pp. 170–171; see also *ibid.,* p. 103.

51. *Ibid.,* p. 107; translation taken from Weber, *Roscher and Knies,* p. 116; see also *ibid.,* p. 104.

52. Weber, *Wissenschaftslehre,* p. 180; translation taken from Weber, *Methodology,* p. 178.

53. See, especially, Weber, *Wissenschaftslehre,* pp. 88–89. Also see *ibid.,* pp. 73, 80, 115.

54. This was the essential point of disagreement between Simmel and Weber. Compare Max Weber, "George Simmel as Sociologist," trans. Donald N. Levine, *Social Research* 39 (Spring, 1972), pp. 158–163, with Donald N. Levine, ed., *George Simmel on Individuality and Social Forms* (Chicago: University of Chicago Press, 1971), pp. 6–22.

55. "The 'interpretation' of 'Faust' or of 'Puritanism' or of some specific aspect of 'Greek culture' in *this* sense is an inquiry into those 'values' which 'we' *can* find 'embodied' in these objects. It is an inquiry into the invariably concrete 'form' that constitutes these 'entities' as objects of 'historical explanation.'" Weber, *Wissenschaftslehre,* p. 112; Weber, *Roscher and Knies,* p. 181. See also *ibid.,* pp. 86, 161, 174, 245–246.

56. Weber was quite explicit on this point. See Weber, *Religionssoziologie,* p. 30.

57. In this regard, see Weber, *Wissenschaftslehre,* p. 180.

58. In one context or another Weber used the term *ideal-type* to indicate almost any instance of intellectual construction, and it is probably

futile to attempt to discern its "real" meaning in his thought. Compare
Weber, *Wirtschaft,* pp. 9–11, Weber, *Wissenschaftslehre,* pp. 196–197,
534–535; and letter to H. Rickert, June 14, 1904, reprinted in Mommsen, *Age of Bureaucracy,* p. 9. Talcott Parsons was quite generous in
finding only three distinct uses of the term. *The Structure of Social Action* (New York: Free Press, 1968), pp. 604–605. My use of the term is
intended to correspond to what Weber must have had in mind when he
asserted the absolute necessity of the ideal-typical concepts in social science. See Weber, *Wissenschaftslehre,* p. 195; H. H. Bruun, *Science, Values and Politics in Max Weber's Methodology* (Copenhagen: Munksgaard, 1972), p. 206.

59. See Weber, *Wirtschaft,* p. 6; also Weber, *Wissenschaftslehre,* pp.
290, 439. "If I am now a sociologist (according to my official position),
then it is so that I can put an end to the ghostly enterprise of those who
work with collective concepts. In other words, even sociology can only
be pursued by proceeding from the action of one or more, whether a few
or many individuals. It is, therefore, strictly 'individualistic' in method."
Letter to Robert Lietmann, March 9, 1920; quoted in Brunn, *Science,
Values and Politics,* pp. 38–39; author's translation.

60. Weber, *Wissenschaftslehre,* p. 396; translation taken from Max
Weber, "Marginal Utility Theory and the Fundamental Law of Psychophysics," trans. Louis Schneider, *Social Science Quarterly* 56 (1975),
34.

61. Weber, *Wissenschaftslehre,* pp. 190–191; Weber, *Methodology,*
p. 90. See also *ibid.,* pp. 196–198; Weber, *Wirtschaft,* pp. 10–11.

62. See Weber, *Wissenschaftslehre,* pp. 194, 436, 534–535.

63. *Ibid.,* p. 124; Weber, *Roscher and Knies,* p. 183.

64. Weber, *Wissenschaftslehre,* p. 47; see also *ibid.,* p. 152.

65. Weber, *Wirtschaft,* p. 3; Weber, *Wissenschaftslehre,* p. 227.

66. Weber, *Wissenschaftslehre,* pp. 67, 226–227; Weber, *Wirtschaft,*
p. 6.

67. Weber, *Wissenschaftslehre,* p. 132.

68. See *ibid.,* pp. 67, 132–133, 226–227.

69. See letter from Weber to Edgar Jaffe, September 13, 1907, in
Marianne Weber, *Max Weber: A Biography,* p. 377; Weber, *Protestant
Ethic,* p. 119; Weber, *Wissenschaftslehre,* p. 517.

70. Weber, *Wissenschaftslehre*, p. 494; Weber, *Methodology*, pp. 5–6; see also *ibid.*, p. 591.

71. "I have become convinced from long experience as well as conviction that only through the testing of one's supposed 'ultimate' opinions in relationship to crucial concrete problems does his own real will become clear to the individual." Letter to Erich Trummber, January 17, 1918, in Weber, *Gesammelte Politische Schriften, Erste Auflage.* (Munich: Drei Masken, 1921), pp. 474–475; author's translation.

72. Letter from Weber to Lilli Schaefer, September 8, 1914, in Eduard Baumgarten, *Max Weber*, pp. 492–493.

73. In this connection, see Edward B. Portis, "Society and Political Choice: Social Science in Emile Durkheim's Sociology," *Sociological Analysis and Theory* 7 (June, 1977), 117–133.

CHAPTER FOUR
The Scientific Personality

1. Professor Martin B. Spencer has argued that a general process of social and cultural determination of character is implied in Weber's discussions of such social roles. "Ideas, Character and Conduct: An Inquiry into Weber's Sociology of Religions." Paper presented at Max Weber Colloquium, November, 1977.

2. See Weber, *Wirtschaft und Gesellschaft, Vierte Auflage*, ed. Johannes Winkelmann (Tuebingen: J. C. B. Mohr, 1956), pp. 207, 298–299.

3. *Ibid.*, pp. 237, 239, 252, 254. Weber, *Gesammelte Aufsaetze zur Wissenschaftslehre, Dritte Auflage,* ed. Johannes Winkelmann (Tuebingen: J. C. B. Mohr, 1956), p. 455.

4. Weber, *Wirtschaft*, pp. 298–299. Translation taken from Weber, *Economy and Society*, ed. Guenther Roth and Claus Wittich (New York: Bedminster Press, 1968), pp. 490–491; see also Weber, *Gesammelte Politische Schriften, Dritte Auflage*, ed. Johannes Winkelmann (Tuebingen: J. C. B. Mohr, 1971), pp. 270, 282.

5. See Weber, *Wirtschaft*, pp. 560–561, 566; Weber, *Gesammelte Politische Schriften, Dritte Auflage*, pp. 516–517.

6. Weber implied that many such individuals need not even be aware

of the cultural values that ultimately confer status, and thereby self-esteem, upon them. See Weber *Wirtschaft*, p. 314; Max Weber, *The Protestant Ethic and the Spirit of Capitalism*, trans. Talcott Parsons (New York: Charles Scribner's Sons, 1958), pp. 181–182. He also noted, however, that when such elites lose their status they tend to raise questions about ultimate worth. See Weber, *Wirtschaft*, p. 305.

7. Letter from Weber to Edgar Jaffe, September 13, 1907, in Marianne Weber, *Max Weber: A Biography*, trans. Harry Zohn (New York: John Wiley & Sons, 1975), pp. 278–289. See also Weber, *Wirtschaft*, pp. 307–308.

8. The only category mentioned is that of "artist." See Weber, *Wissenschaftslehre*, pp. 590–591.

9. See Weber, *Gesammelte Politische Schriften, Dritte Auflage*, pp. 16–17; Weber, *Wissenschaftslehre*, pp. 157, 598–599.

10. See Weber, *Gesammelte Politische Schriften, Dritte Auflage*, pp. 14, 17.

11. For instance, see Arnold Brecht, *Political Theory* (Princeton, N.J.: Princeton University Press, 1959), p. 114.

12. Weber, *Wissenschaftslehre*, pp. 170–171; Weber, *Methodology of the Social Sciences*, trans. Edward A. Shils and Henry A. Finch (Glencoe, Ill.: Free Press, 1949), p. 72; see also *ibid.*, pp. 161, 166, 177–178, 251; Weber, *Gesammelte Aufsaetze zur Soziologie und Sozialpolitik*, ed. Marianne Weber (Tuebingen: J. C. B. Mohr, 1924), p. 420.

13. See Weber, *Wissenschaftslehre*, pp. 279, 534–535.

14. *Ibid.*, p. 155. Also see Weber, *Gesammelte Aufsaetze zur Soziologie*, pp. 419–420.

15. This problem has been well publicized in the polemics concerning Thomas S. Kuhn's book, *The Structure of Scientific Revolutions* (Chicago: University of Chicago Press, 1962). See Israel Scheffler, *Science and Subjectivity* (Indianapolis: Bobbs-Merrill Company, 1967); and the essays in Imre Lakatos and Alan Musgrave (eds.), *Criticism and the Growth of Knowledge* (London: Cambridge University Press, 1970). Paradoxically, Lakatos, a critic of Kuhn, attempts to save the integrity of science in a manner very similar to Michael Polanyi, who is sympathetic with Kuhn. See *ibid.*, pp. 91–195; Michael Polanyi, *Science, Faith and Society* (Chicago: University of Chicago Press, 1964), pp. 7–62.

16. A good survey, complete with examples, of the literature on the problem of operational validity in social science can be found in Derek L. Phillips, *Knowledge from What?* (Chicago: Rand McNally, 1971), pp. 12–49.

17. For an excellent statement of this thesis, see Richard Rudner, "Value Judgments in Scientific Validation," *Scientific Monthly* 79 (September, 1954), 151–153.

18. See Weber's striking statement on the cultural determination of the problems and conceptual categories of social science. Weber, *Wissenschaftslehre*, p. 214.

19. Weber's translators have often simply assumed that he accepted the "fact-value dichotomy." To assume this, however, one must assume that Weber was very casual about the words he employed. For instance, Shils and Finch at one point render "prinzipielle Scheidung" as "logical distinction," instead of "fundamental distinction" (even more literal would be "separation"). Weber, *Methodology*, p. 51; Weber, *Wissenschaftslehre*, p. 148. H. H. Bruun, in his very thorough study, makes the same mistake. *Science, Values, and Politics in Max Weber's Methodology* (Copenhagen: Munksgaard, 1972), pp. 23–24.

20. Weber, *Wissenschaftslehre*, pp. 153, 214.

21. *Ibid.*, p. 156; Weber, *Methodology*, p. 59. See also the note Weber made to himself while reading Richert's *Grenzen*, quoted by Bruun, *Science, Values, and Politics*, p. 132.

22. Weber, *Wissenschaftslehre*, p. 215; Weber, *Methodology*, p. 111.

23. *Ibid.*, pp. 152.

24. As Weber himself implicitly stated in a footnote. See *ibid.*, p. 92. Felix E. Oppenheim asserts that Weber was a "value-noncognitivist" and presents several supporting quotes. These quotes, however, refer to science, not to values. Since Weber does not discuss the nature of values, there seems to be no explicit basis upon which to classify him as either a "cognitivist" or "noncognitivist" in regard to them. *Moral Principles in Political Philosophy* (New York: Random House, 1968), p. 164.

25. For instance, see Weber, *Wissenschaftslehre*, p. 152, 154, 492, 598–599.

26. Letter of 1908 to Toennis, reprinted in Eduard Baumgarten, *Max Weber: Werk und Person* (Tuebingen: J. C. B. Mohr, 1964), p. 339. For

an interesting discussion of the implications of this view of scientific knowledge for political science, see Avery Leiserson, "Charles Merriam, Max Weber, and the Search for Synthesis in Political Science," *The American Political Science Review* 69 (March, 1975), 175–185.

27. See Weber, *Wissenschaftslehre,* pp. 593–594; Weber, *Protestant Ethic,* pp. 24–25.

28. See Weber, *Wissenschaftslehre,* pp. 104, 230; one must do this even when reflecting on one's own past actions and experiences. *Ibid.,* p. 280.

29. See *ibid.,* pp. 4–5, 221, 232, 537. In this connection, see Bertrand Russell, *Mysticism and Logic and Other Essays* (New York: Longman, 1918), p. 155.

30. See Weber, *Wissenschaftslehre,* pp. 4, 262. It may be that Weber had what is now an old-fashioned Newtonian view of natural science. Yet his analysis would apply just as well to Albert Einstein's conception of the purpose of science. See "The Method of Science" in Edward H. Madden (ed.), *The Structure of Scientific Thought* (Boston: Houghton Mifflin Company, 1960), pp. 80–84.

31. See Weber, *Wirtschaft,* p. 7; Weber, *Wissenschaftslehre,* p. 176. Also see R. B. Braithwaite, *Scientific Explanation* (Cambridge: Cambridge University Press, 1953), p. 79.

32. See Weber, *Protestant Ethic,* p. 47; Weber, *Wissenschaftslehre,* pp. 170–171, 174–176, 178, 180; Weber, *Wirtschaft, p.* 7.

33. *See* Weber, *Wissenschaftslehre,* p. 115, 140, 260; Weber, *Wirtschaft,* pp. 2–5.

34. See Weber, *Wissenschaftslehre,* pp. 122, 124, 508.

35. See letter of June 14, 1904, to Richert, reprinted in Wolfgang J. Mommsen, *The Age of Bureaucracy* (Oxford: Oxford University Press, 1974), p. 9.

36. Weber, *Wissenschaftslehre,* p. 252.

37. See *Wissenschaftslehre,* p. 489; Weber, *Gesammelte Aufsaetze zur Soziologie,* p. 420; Brunn, *Science, Values, and Politics,* p. 28.

38. See Weber, *Wissenschaftslehre,* pp. 179–180, 537.

39. See *ibid.,* p. 428. Also see *ibid.,* pp. 115–116, 122, 198.

40. *Ibid.,* p. 194; translated from Weber, *Methodology,* p. 93. See also *ibid.,* pp. 436, 534–535.

41. *Ibid.*, p. 194; translation taken from Weber, *Methodology*, p. 93. See also in this connection Weber, *Wissenschaftslehre*, pp. 86, 131. Thomas Burger correctly identifies the nature of ideal-typical concepts but inexplicably depreciates their importance in Weber's conception of social science. *Max Weber's Theory of Concept Formation* (Durham, N.C.: Duke University Press, 1976), p. 116. Compare Stephen P. Turner and Regis A. Factor, "Objective Possibility and Adequate Causation in Weber's Methodological Writings," *The Sociological Review* 29 (1981), 16–18.

42. See Weber, *Wissenschaftslehre*, pp. 170–171, 212–213, 433, 537, 603; Max Weber, *Gesammelte Aufsaetze zur Soziologie*, p. 432. Brunn errs in asserting that Weber demanded the elimination of all "valuational elements" from social scientific concepts. *Science, Values, and Politics*, p. 38. As will be seen, Weber only demanded that science be free of "value judgments." As Brunn himself points out, not all valuational elements are value judgments for Weber.

43. See Weber, *Wissenschaftslehre*, p. 505; Weber, *Gesammelte Politische Schriften, Dritte Auflage*, pp. 144–145. Fragment of a manuscript discovered by W. J. Mommsen, reprinted in Eduard Baumgarten, *Max Weber*, pp. 394–400.

44. Weber, *Gesammelte Politische Schriften, Dritte Auflage*, pp. 550–551.

45. *Ibid.*, p. 347; Weber, *Wissenschaftslehre*, p. 517.

46. See Leo Tolstoy, *Selected Essays,* trans. Aylmer Maude (New York: Modern Library, 1964), pp. 330–338. Weber's wife disclosed that he had planned to devote an entire volume to Tolstoy, although he never found the time. Marianne Weber, *Max Weber: A Biography,* p. 466.

47. "Radical doubt is the father of knowledge." Weber, *Wissenschaftslehre,* p. 496.

48. See Weber, *Wirtschaft,* p. 666.

49. In this connection, see *ibid.,* p. 188.

50. "The objective validity of all empirical knowledge rests exclusively upon the ordering of given reality according to categories which are *subjective* in a specific sense, namely, in that they present the presuppositions of our knowledge and are based on the *presupposition* of the *value* of those truths which empirical knowledge alone is able to

give us. . . . It should be remembered that the belief in the value of scientific truth is the product of certain cultures and is not a product of man's original nature." Weber, *Wissenschaftslehre*, pp. 212–213; Weber, *Methodology*, p. 110; see also *ibid.*, p. 278.

51. "Whoever lacks the capacity to put on blinders, so to speak, and to come up to the idea that the fate of his soul depends upon whether or not he makes the correct conjecture at this passage of the manuscript may as well stay away from science." Weber, *Wissenschaftslehre*, p. 589; translation taken from Weber, *From Max Weber*, (New York: Oxford University Press, 1946), p. 135.

52. "The politician shall and must make compromises . . . the *scholar dare* not make compromises nor cloak any nonsense. I definitely cannot do this. . . . If I [did], I would regard myself as a criminal to my profession." Letter of April 14, 1920, to Carl Peterson, Bruce B. Frye, "A Letter from Max Weber," *The Journal of Modern History* 39 (1967), 123.

53. See Milton Rokeach, *The Three Christs of Ypsilanti: A Psychological Study* (New York: Alfred A. Knopf, 1964), p. 26; Robert J. Lifton, *Thought Reform and the Psychology of Totalism* (New York: W. W. Norton, 1961), p. 467.

54. Weber, *Wissenschaftslehre*, pp. 591–592.

55. Weber, *Gesammelte Politische Schriften, Dritte Auflage*, p. 546.

56. *Ibid.*, pp. 545–546.

CHAPTER FIVE
Personality Identity and Social Theory

1. See Marianne Weber, *Max Weber: A Biography*, trans. Harry Zohn (New York: John Wiley & Sons, 1975), pp. 360–361.

2. *Ibid.*, pp. 479–480.

3. See letter to L. Brentano, February 28, 1906, in *ibid.*, p. 358. Also *ibid.*, pp. 359, 368, 413.

4. On the daily regimen that the Webers followed in order to minimize exhaustion and excitation, see *ibid.*, pp. 471–473. Weber was obviously subject to extreme irritability, as indicated by the ridiculous lengths to which he pursued a number of public and legal disputes. Even

Marianne Weber must be somewhat apologetic in relating these events. See *ibid.*, pp. 429–448.

5. *Ibid.*, p. 517.

6. See Max Weber, *Gesammelte Politische Schriften, Dritte Auflage,* ed. Johannes Winkelmann (Tuebingen: J. C. B. Mohr, 1971).

7. See letter to Sombart, August 20, 1906, in Marianne Weber, *Max Weber: A Biography,* p. 361.

8. *Ibid.*, p. 328.

9. *Ibid.*, p. 360.

10. See letter to Naumann, December 14, 1906, in Max Weber, *Gesammelte Politische Schriften, Erste Auflage* (Munich: Drei Masken, 1921), pp. 451–452; translation taken from Marianne Weber, *Max Weber: A Biography,* pp. 398–400.

11. In his history of Weber's political activity, Mommsen has almost nothing to say about, or cite, from these years. See Wolfgang J. Mommsen, *Max Weber und die Deutsche Politik: 1890–1920, Zweite Auflage* (Tuebingen: J. C. B. Mohr 1974). Marianne Weber also does not refer to any political activity during these years. *Max Weber: A Biography.*

12. See C. G. Jung, *Modern Man in Search of a Soul,* trans. W. S. Dell and Cary F. Baynes (New York: Harcourt, Brace and World, 1933), p. 101.

13. As discussed in previous chapters, Weber tried unsuccessfully to make a choice. During the dark days of his illness, apparently any suggestion that "will power" was the solution to his problems agitated him greatly. See letters from Marianne to Helene Weber, Spring, Summer, 1894, Marianne Weber, *Max Weber: A Biography,* pp. 277, 240.

14. See Richard Taylor, *Action and Purpose* (Englewood Cliffs, N.J.: Prentice-Hall, 1966), p. 109. But William Heard Kilpatrick is obviously correct in asserting that cultural development is historically associated with the development of more complex self-conceptions. *Selfhood and Civilization* (New York: Macmillan, 1941), pp. 35–39.

15. See Sigmund Freud, *The Ego and the Id,* trans. by Joan Riviere (New York: W. W. Norton, 1960), p. 15. Gordon W. Allport, however, has pointed out that the term has a variety of meanings among psychologists. *Personality and Social Encounter* (Boston: Beacon Press, 1960), pp. 73–77.

16. See Thomas M. French, *Psychoanalytic Interpretations* (Chicago: Quandrangle Books, 1970), pp. 172–173.

17. See Erik H. Erikson, *Childhood and Society* (New York: W. W. Norton, 1963), p. 194.

18. Repression is generally recognized in psychoanalytical theory as a necessary condition of the ego's functioning. See Sigmund Freud, *The Psychopathology of Everyday Life,* trans. Alan Tyson (New York: W. W. Norton, 1965), p. 14; see also Franz Alexander, *Fundamentals of Psychoanalysis* (New York: W. W. Norton, 1963), p. 26.

19. Alexander, *Fundamentals of Psychoanalysis,* p. 96. See also Sigmund Freud, *Ego and Id,* p. 7.

20. See Karen Horney, *The Neurotic Personality of Our Time* (New York: W. W. Norton, 1937), pp. 76–77.

21. See Harry Stack Sullivan, *Conceptions of Modern Psychiatry* (New York: W. W. Norton and Company, 1953), pp. 19, 23; Ernest Hilgard, "Human Motives and the Concept of the Self," *The American Psychologist* 4 (1949), 374–382; Gregory Rochlin, *Manic Aggression: The Defense of the Self* (Boston: Gambit, 1973), p. 21.

22. Jean Piaget, *The Moral Judgment of the Child* (New York: Free Press, 1965), pp. 95–96; see also Jean Piaget, *Six Psychological Studies* (New York: Random House, 1967), pp. 12–13, 54–55.

23. For further examples of empirical evidence, see Dana Bramel, "A Dissonance Theory Approach to Defensive Projection," *Journal of Abnormal and Social Psychology* 64 (1962), 121–129; Philip W. Blumstein, "Identity Bargaining and Self-Conception," *Social Forces* 53 (March, 1975), 476–485. Also relevant is Calvin S. Hall, "What People Dream About," *Scientific American* 184 (May, 1951), 62; Allport, *Personality,* p. 88; M. Brewster Smith, "The Self and Cognitive Consistency," in Robert P. Abelson et al. (eds.), *Theories of Cognitive Consistency: A Sourcebook* (Chicago: Rand McNally, 1968), pp. 368–369.

24. See Allport, *Personality,* p. 88; Jung, *Modern Man,* pp. 98–99; Hilgard, "Human Motives," p. 375, and Terrence Penelham, "Self-Identity and Self-Regard," in Amelie Rorty (ed.), *The Identities of Persons* (Berkeley, Calif.: University of California Press, 1976), p. 256.

25. See George H. Mead, *Mind, Self and Society* (Chicago: University of Chicago Press, 1934), pp. 67, 73. Stuart Hampshire would even

say that an animal without the means to reflect upon and announce its own future behavior could not have intentions. *Thought and Action* (London: Chatto and Windus, 1959), pp. 98–99.

26. Mead, *Mind, Self and Society,* p. 139.

27. *Ibid.,* p. 47.

28. Piaget, *Six Studies,* p. 40.

29. See Henry A. Murray, *Explorations in Personality* (Oxford and London: Oxford University Press, 1938), p. 61; Gilbert Ryle, *The Concept of Mind* (New York: Barnes and Noble, 1949), p. 110.

30. See Sigmund Freud, *Ego and Id,* pp. 19–20; Otto Fenichel, *The Psychoanalytic Theory of Neurosis* (New York: W. W. Norton, 1948), pp. 105, 134.

31. See Fenichel, *Psychoanalytic Theory,* p. 106; Alexander, *Fundamentals of Psychoanalysis,* p. 84; Edith Jacobson, *The Self and the Object World* (New York: International Universities Press, 1964), p. 119.

32. See Alfred Schutz, *Collected Papers, The Problem of Social Reality,* Vol. I (The Hague, Netherlands: Martinus Nijhoff, 1971), pp. 68–69, 72–73.

33. In this connection, see Hampshire, *Thought and Action,* p. 170; Taylor, *Action and Purpose,* p. 115.

34. See Alfred Schutz, *The Phenomenology of the Social World,* trans. George Walsh and Frederick Lehnert (Evanston, Ill.: Northwestern University Press, 1957), p. 64; see also Hampshire, *Thought and Action,* p. 126; French, *Psychoanalytic Interpretations,* pp. 166–167.

35. See Hampshire, *Thought and Action,* p. 97.

36. See William James, *Psychology: The Briefer Course* (New York: Henry Holt and Company, 1910), p. 205.

37. For instance, see Ryle, *Concept of Mind,* pp. 196–197; Taylor, *Action and Purpose,* pp. 134–137. For efforts to avoid the problem, see Shelley Duval and Robert A. Wicklund, *A Theory of Objective Self-Awareness* (New York: Academic Press, 1972), p. 33, Mead, *Mind, Self and Society,* p. 178.

38. Ralph H. Turner, "The Self-Conception in Social Interaction," in Chad Gordon and Kenneth J. Gergen (eds.), *The Self in Social Interaction* (New York: John Wiley & Sons, 1968), p. 97. In this connection, compare Immanuel Kant, *Critique of Pure Reason,* trans. Norman

Kemp Smith (New York: St. Martin's Press, 1929), p. 169; David Bohm, "Human Nature as the Product of Our Mental Models," in Jonathan Benthall (ed.), *The Limits of Human Nature* (London: Institute of Contemporary Arts, 1973), p. 102; Seymour Epstein, "The Self-Concept Revisited: Or a Theory of a Theory," *American Psychologist* 28 (May 1973), 404–416, 407.

39. Consequently, the use of the term that implies that the self can be evaluated and found wanting is incorrect. For instances, see James, *Psychology*, p. 140; Duval and Wicklund, *Objective Self-Awareness*, pp. 3–4. Erikson's use of the term, on the other hand, is consistent with the analysis presented here. *Childhood and Society*, p. 235. For a general survey of the scientific literature, see L. Edward Wells and Gerald Maxwell, *Self-Esteem* (Beverly Hills, Calif.: Sage Publications, 1976). Also relevant are Helen Merrell Lynd's impressionistic but often insightful reflections, *On Shame and the Search for Identity* (New York: Harcourt, Brace, and Company, 1958).

40. See the essays in Erik H. Erikson, *Identity, Youth and Crisis* (New York: W. W. Norton, 1968).

41. Mead, *Mind, Self and Society*, pp. 142–143.

42. See Flora Rleta Schreiber, *Sybil* (New York: Warner Books, 1973); Hilgard, *Human Motives*, p. 375.

43. That self-conception necessarily involves a core of basic beliefs that are relatively stable, see Smith, "The Self," p. 367; Epstein, "Self-Concept," p. 409; Blumstein, "Identity Bargaining," p. 483; Abner Cohen, *Two-Dimensional Man* (Berkeley, Calif.: University of California Press, 1974), pp. 54–56.

44. Philosophers have occupied themselves at length with the question of whether body or memory is "the" criterion for personal identity. Sydney Shoemaker points out that we employ both as criteria in practice and implies that neither, therefore, could be the "essence" of identity. "Personal Identity and Memory," in John Perry (ed.), *Personal Identity* (Berkeley, Calif.: University of California Press, 1975), pp. 128, 131. See also Hampshire, *Thought and Action*, p. 75.

45. As Paul Schilder points out, one's "body image" is not a mere sensation but involves projection. *The Image and Appearance of the Human Body* (New York: International Universities Press, 1935), p. 11.

46. See R. D. Laing, *The Divided Self* (Baltimore: Penguin Books, 1965). p. 85; Erikson, *Childhood and Society*, pp. 261–262.

47. Piaget, *Moral Judgment*, p. 93.

48. Mead, *Mind, Self and Society*, p. 139.

49. See *ibid.*, pp. 162–163; George J. McCall and J. L. Simmons, *Identities and Interactions*, 2nd ed. (New York: Free Press, 1978), p. 66.

50. See McCall and Simmons, *Identities and Interactions*, pp. 73–79; Howard S. Bech and James Casper, "The Development of Identification with an Occupation." *American Journal of Sociology* 61 (1956), 289–298.

51. Mead, *Mind, Self and Society*, pp. 167–168; see also *ibid.*, p. 140.

52. Compare Turner, "Self-Conception," p. 97; Mead, *Mind, Self and Society*, pp. 142–143; James, *Psychology*, p. 190; Chad Gordon, "Self Conception: Configurations of Content," in Chad Gordon and Kenneth J. Gergen (eds.), *The Self in Social Interaction* (New York: John Wiley & Sons, 1968), pp. 115–135.

53. According to Duval and Wicklund, this lack of attention to one's self-conception is essential for effective interaction with the external world. *Objective Self-Awareness*, pp. 22–23. See also Laing, *The Divided Self*, p. 113.

54. Milton Rokeach, *The Three Christs of Ypsilanti: A Psychological Study* (New York: Alfred A. Knopf, 1964), p. 20. See also Hampshire, *Thought and Action*, pp. 100–101.

55. In this connection, compare Turner, "Self-Conception," p. 97; Rokeach, *Three Christs*, p. 310; Hilgard, "Human Motives," p. 373; Rochlin, *Manic Aggression*, pp. 21–22. For a divergent view of the importance of identity problems to most cases of neurosis, see Jacobson, *The Self*, p. 29.

56. According to his wife, Weber was once asked "what his scholarship meant to him." He replied, "I want to see how much I can stand." Marianne did not pretend to know what he meant by this response. Marianne Weber, *Max Weber: A Biography*, p. 678.

57. See Turner, "Self-Conception," p. 94; Jacobson, *The Self*, p. 20.

58. See Fred R. Dallmayr, "Empirical Political Theory and the Image of Man," *Polity* 2 (Spring, 1970), 443–478.

59. On the difficulty of defining human nature in terms of "needs," see Marvin Zetterbaum, "Equality and Human Need," *American Political Science Review* 71 (September 1977), pp. 983–998.

60. In this connection, see Marvin Zetterbaum, "Human Nature and History," in J. Roland Pennock and John W. Chapman (eds.), *Human Nature in Politics* (New York: New York University Press, 1977), pp. 225–249.

CHAPTER SIX
The Political Function of Social Science

1. For instance, see Fred M. Frohock, "Notes on the Concept of Politics: Weber, Easton, Strauss," *Journal of Politics* 36 (May, 1974), 381; Robert A. Dahl, *Modern Political Analysis* (Englewood Cliffs, N.J.: Prentice-Hall, 1964), p. 5.

2. Groups that attempt to influence political organizations are called "politically oriented groups." Max Weber, *Wirtschaft und Gesellschaft, Vierte Auflage*, ed. Johannes Winkelmann (Tuebingen: J. C. B. Mohr, 1956), pp. 29–30. See also *ibid.*, pp. 184–185.

3. Max Weber, *Gesammelte Politische Schriften, Dritte Auflage* (Tuebingen: J. C. B. Mohr, 1971), p. 505. Immediately following this definition he moves on to characterize political institutions and organizations.

4. Max Weber, *Gesammelte Aufsaetze zur Wissenschaftslehre, Dritte Auflage* (Tuebingen: J. C. B. Mohr, 1956), p. 517; translation taken from Weber, *Methodology of the Social Sciences*, trans. Edward A. Shils and Henry A. Finch (Glencoe, Ill.: Free Press, 1949), pp. 26–27.

5. Weber, *Gesammelte Politische Schriften, Dritte Auflage*, p. 347.

6. For instance, see *ibid.*, pp. 336–337; letters from Weber to Naumann, November 12, 1908, and November 18, 1908, reprinted in Max Weber, *Gesammelte Politische Schriften, Erste Auflage* (Munich: Drei Masken, 1921), pp. 455–458.

7. See *Gesammelte Politiche Schriften, Dritte Auflage*, pp. 343, 351–352, 392–393, 516–517, 524–525.

8. In this connection, see J. C. G. Roehl, *Germany Without Bismarck* (Berkeley, Calif.: University of California Press, 1967), p. 147.

9. Wolfgang J. Mommsen, "Max Weber's Political Sociology and His Philosophy of World History," *International Social Science Journal* 7 (1965), 40.

10. Weber, *Wissenschaftslehre*, p. 589. See also Weber, *Gesammelte Politische Schriften, Dritte Auflage*, pp. 24–25.

11. Weber, *Wissenschaftslehre*, p. 180.

12. Note especially his occasional remarks on the need for individuals to feel "justified in life." Weber, *Wirtschaft*, pp. 299, 549; Max Weber, *Gesammelte Aufsaetze zur Religionssoziologie, I* (Tuebingen: J. C. B. Mohr, 1920), p. 242.

13. See Weber, *Wissenschaftslehre*, p. 505; fragment of a manuscript found in Merseburger Staats archive by W. Mommsen, 1912, in Eduard Baumgarten, *Max Weber: Werk und Person* (Tuebingen: J. C. B. Mohr, 1964), pp. 399–400.

14. Letter to Dr. Henrich Simon, Fall, 1911, quoted in Marianne Weber, *Max Weber: A Biography*, trans. Harry Zohn (New York: John Wiley & Sons, 1975), p. 412; see also Weber, *Gesammelte Politische Schriften, Dritte Auflage*, pp. 144–145.

15. Weber, *Wissenschaftslehre*, p. 589; translation taken from Weber, *From Max Weber*, trans. H. H. Gerth and C. Wright Mills (New York: Oxford University Press, 1946), p. 135.

16. Weber, *Gesammelte Politische Schriften, Dritte Auflage*, p. 545; translation taken from Weber, *From Max Weber*, p. 115. (Emphasis added.) See also *ibid.*, p. 513.

17. In this connection, see Wolfgang J. Mommsen, *Max Weber and die Deutsche Politik: 1890–1920, Zweite Auflage* (Tuebingen: J. C. B. Mohr, 1974), p. 140.

18. See, especially, Weber, *Gesammelte Politische Schriften, Dritte Auflage*, p. 546.

19. In a conversation with Paul Honigsheim, Marianne intimated that Weber would have liked to teach a "value-free political science." Honigsheim, *On Max Weber*, trans. Joan Rytina (East Lansing, Mich.: Michigan State University, 1968), p. 62. Although no one, to my knowledge, has realized the extent to which Weber's thought is unified by his concern for politics, many have directly or indirectly noted its importance in different parts of his work. For instance, see H. H. Brunn, *Sci-*

ence, Values, and Politics in Max Weber's Methodology (Copenhagen: Munksgaard, 1972), pp. 37, 54; Karl Loewenstein, *Max Weber's Political Ideas in the Perspective of Our Time,* trans. Richard and Clara Winston (Amherst, Mass.: University of Massachusetts Press, 1966), pp. 26–27; Wolfgang J. Mommsen, *The Age of Bureaucracy* (Oxford: Oxford University Press, 1974), p. 20; Arthur Mitzman, *The Iron Cage* (New York: Alfred A. Knopf, 1970), p. 8; Alexander von Schelting, *Max Weber's Wissenschaftslehre* (Tuebingen: J. C. B. Mohr, 1934), p. 58. Often Weber's diverse works are not considered sufficiently coherent to be labeled a social or political "theory." For instance, see Ilse Dronberger, *The Political Thought of Max Weber* (New York: Appleton-Century-Crofts, 1971), p. 317. On the other hand, see Karl Loewith, *Gesammelte Abhandlungen* (Stuttgart: W. Kohlhammer Verlag, 1960), p. 4; Mommsen, "Max Weber's Political Sociology," p. 29; Lawrence A. Scaff, "Max Weber's Politics and Political Education," *American Political Science Review* 67 (March, 1973), 128–141.

20. Weber does not really present a single definition of the concept. See Weber, *Religionssoziologie,* p. 266; Weber, *Gesammelte Politische Schriften, Dritte Auflage,* p. 322; Weber, *Wissenschaftslehre,* p. 473, 593–594; Weber, *Wirtschaft,* pp. 33, 42, 569–571. For an interesting, insightful discussion of the various types and manifestations of this cultural process in Weber's thought, see Steven Kalberg, "Max Weber's Types of Rationality: Cornerstones for the Analysis of Rationalization Processes in History," *American Journal of Sociology* 85 (1980), 1145–1178.

21. "One of the fundamental elements of the spirit of modern capitalism, and not only of that but of all modern culture: rational conduct on the basis of the ideal of the calling, was born—that is what this discussion has sought to demonstrate—from the spirit of Christian ascetism." Weber, *Religionssoziologie,* p. 202; translation taken from Weber, *The Protestant Ethic and the Spirit of Capitalism,* trans. Talcott Parsons (New York: Charles Scribner's Sons, 1958), p. 180. In this connection, also see Anthony Giddens, *Politics and Society in the Thought of Max Weber* (London: Macmillan, 1972), p. 36.

22. According to Weber, the "bourgeois classes . . . have seldom before" the Reformation, "and never since displayed heroism." *Re-*

ligionssoziologie, pp. 20–21; translation taken from Weber, *Protestant Ethic*, p. 37. He ends this famous essay with an emphasis upon the inevitable restraints that have been placed on individual initiative.

23. See Wolfgang Schluchter, *The Rise of Western Rationalism: Max Weber's Developmental History*, trans. Guenther Roth (Berkeley, Calif.: University of California Press, 1981), pp. 10–11, 31–32; Juergen Habermas, *The Theory of Communicative Action*, Vol. I, trans. Thomas McCarthy (Boston: Beacon Press, 1984), pp. 143–271, especially pp. 145, 270–271. For a lucid summary and critique of Habermas's treatment of Weber, see Susan J. Hekman, *Weber, the Ideal Type, and Contemporary Social Theory* (Notre Dame, Ind.: University of Notre Dame Press, 1983), pp. 136–145. Schluchter cites two letters from Weber to his publisher, Paul Siebeck, written on January 23 and December 30, 1913, which indicate that his contribution to the project that led to *Economy and Society* was to have been a "sociological theory of the state" and that he eventually broadened his work to relate "major social groups to the economy" because of the failure of a collaborator to adequately analyze the "developmental states." *Western Rationalism*, pp. 82–83.

24. See Mommsen, *Max Weber und die Deutsche Politik*, p. 51; J. P. Mayer, *Max Weber and German Politics* (London: Faber and Faber, 1956), p. 87; Mitzman, *The Iron Cage*, p. 51. Other scholars, especially those who ere personally acquainted with Weber, deny that his nationalism was either absolute or his ultimate value. See Honigsheim, *On Max Weber*, p. 9; Karl Jaspers, *Three Essays*, trans. Ralph Manheim (New York: Harcourt, Brace and World, 1964), p. 220; Loewenstein, *Political Ideas*, p. xii. For examples of explicit affirmations of his nationalism, see Weber, *Gesammelte Politische Schriften, Dritte Auflage*, pp. 11, 309.

25. More recently Mommsen has stressed "individualism" as Weber's ultimate value. See, especially, Wolfgang J. Mommsen, *Max Weber: Gesellschaft, Politik und Geschichte* (Frankfurt am Main: Suhrkamp Verlag, 1974), pp. 83, 86. In this connection, see also Fred H. Blum, "Max Weber's Postulate of 'Freedom' from Value Judgments," *American Journal of Sociology* 50 (1944), 51. Much of his "individualism" can be explained by Weber's concern for politics. It is, after all, defined in terms

of individual initiative. However, Beetham's assertion that Weber's political thought is "bourgeois" has a number of problems. David Beetham, *Max Weber and the Theory of Modern Politics* (London: George Allen and Unwin, 1974), pp. 55–59. For one, Weber did not believe that individual autonomy could mean very much in modern society. See Weber, *Gesammelte Politische Schriften, Dritte Auflage*, p. 544; Weber, *Wirtschaft*, p. 575. Just for this reason, he argued, all classes ought to be given political rights in the interests of social peace and efficiency. See Weber, *Gesammelte Politische Schriften, Dritte Auflage*, pp. 246, 251. Whether Weber's thought is a manifestation of class interests is an empirical question. It should be noted, however, that Weber occasionally expressed contempt for the bourgeoisie. See *ibid.*, pp. 245, 252. Also see note 22.

26. *Ibid.*, p. 14; author's translation.

27. Jaspers, *Three Essays*, p. 190.

28. See, especially, Weber *Gesammelte Politische Schriften, Dritte Auflage* pp. 284, 353–379, 441. Also see letter to Graf Keyserling, June 21, 1911, in Eduard Baumgarten, *Max Weber*, p. 429.

29. In this connection, see Weber, *Gesammelte Politische Schriften, Dritte Auflage*, p. 246. See also *ibid.*, pp. 142–143.

30. *Ibid.*, p. 547; translation taken from Weber, *From Max Weber*, pp. 116–117. Assertions that Weber glorified power politics are obviously incorrect. See Mayer, *Max Weber*, p. 58; Raymond Aron, "Max Weber and Power-Politics," in Otto Stammer (ed.), *Max Weber and Sociology Today* (New York: Harper & Row, 1971), p. 84. For other statements of an idealism incompatible with such a claim, see *Verhandlungen des evangelisch-sozialen Kongress*, 1984, p. 80, quoted in Mommsen, *Max Weber und die Deutsche Politik*, p. 108; letter to Adolph V. Harnack, January 12, 1905, quoted in Mommsen, *Max Weber: Gesellschaft*, p. 76; letter to Toennies, 1908, quoted in Eduard Baumgarten, *Max Weber*, p. 670; letter to Graf Keyserling, June 21, 1911, in *ibid.*, p. 429.

31. Even though direct influence is difficult to demonstrate, I think Weber's analysis could be considered a political interpretation of Nietzsche's approach to meaning. Although he sees a distinct affinity, Robert Eden has recently argued that Weber sought "to meet the dangers

of . . . Nietzschean politics" but at the cost of "conceding considerable ground to Nietzsche's creative and destructive nihilism." *Political Leadership and Nihilism: A Study of Weber and Nietzsche* (Tampa: University of South Florida Press, 1983), p. 193. Our different interpretations of Weber are probably less fundamental than our respective understandings of Nietzsche. Mine can be found in Edward B. Portis, "Nietzsche and Social Commitment," *GPSA Journal* 4 (1976), 55–67. For a more sophisticated analysis, see Mark Warren, "The Politics of Nietzsche's Philosophy: Nihilism, Culture and Power," *Political Studies* 33 (1985), 418–438.

32. Weber, *Gesammelte Politische Schriften, Dritte Auflage*, p. 440; author's translation. For similar statements, see *ibid.*, pp. 12–13; report of a speech delivered August 1, 1916, official Akten Reichskanzlei, quoted in Mommsen, *Max Weber und die Deutsche Politik*, p. 259.

33. Weber, *Gesammelte Politische Schriften, Dritte Auflage*, p. 442; author's translation.

34. On the political servility of Germans during this period and some of its causes, see *ibid.*, p. 441; letter to Harnack, February 5, 1906, in Mommsen, *Max Weber: Gesellschaft*, pp. 83–84; Erich Eyck, *Bismarck and the German Empire* (New York: W. W. Norton and Company, 1958), pp. 177–178; Peter Gay, *Weimar Culture* (New York: Harper & Row, 1968), p. 90.

35. See Weber, *Wirtschaft*, p. 647.

36. In a rather confused discussion, Mommsen correctly points out that Weber did not identify the nation only with cultural values but ultimately with a simple feeling of belongingness in a political sense. *Max Weber und die Deutsche Politik*, pp. 55–57. As such, the nation is a communal value in itself. Mommsen also insightfully points out that Weber felt the separation of nationalism from cultural ideals was the main weakness of German social thought in the years before the war. *Ibid.*, pp. 70–71.

37. Weber listed two other types of action, but he noted that they were on the "borderline" that divides action from mere behavior. Weber, *Wirtschaft*, pp. 12–13. Weber's definitions of goal- and value-rational action are not clear; for a different interpretation of his meaning, see Raymond Aron, *Main Currents in Sociological Thought*, Vol. II (Garden City, N.Y.: Anchor Books, 1970), p. 221. Although Weber's wording

gives some support to Aron's interpretation, I believe that it leads to an illogical classification. Weber's discussion of "formal" and "substantive" rationality gives some support to my interpretation. Weber, *Wirtschaft*, p. 44. W. G. Runciman thinks that the distinction between goal- and value-rational action is superfluous because it can be expressed simply "in terms of means and ends." *A Critique of Max Weber's Philosophy of Social Science* (London: Cambridge University Press, 1972), p. 14. Since all action by Weber's account contains, by definition, both means and ends, Runciman has obviously missed Weber's point.

38. Weber, *Wirtschaft*, p. 1; translation taken from Max Weber, *Economy and Society*, ed. Guenther Roth and Claus Wittich (New York: Bedminster Press, 1968), p. 4.

39. On the two types of social relationships, see *ibid.*, pp. 21, 239, 534–535; Weber, *Wissenschaftslehre*, p. 452.

40. Weber, *Wirtschaft*, p. 15; author's translation. Talcott Parsons has effectively hidden Weber's negative connotation in the last clause of this passage. His translation is reprinted in Weber, *Economy and Society*, p. 30. See also Weber, *Religionssoziologie*, p. 61.

41. See Weber, *Wissenschaftslehre*, p. 461.

42. See Weber, *Gesammelte Politische Schriften, Dritte Auflage*, p. 332; Weber, *Wirtschaft*, pp. 560–561, 569–571, 578.

43. Peter M. Blau and W. Richard Scott, *Formal Organizations: A Comparative Approach* (Scranton, Pa.: Chandler Publishing Co., 1962), p. 34; see also James G. March and Herbert A. Simon, *Organizations* (New York: John Wiley & Sons, 1958), p. 36.

44. See Martin Albrow, *Bureaucracy* (New York: Praeger Publishers, 1970), pp. 63–64. Also relevant is Robert D. Cuff, "Wilson and Weber: Bourgeois Critics in an Organizational Age," *Public Administration Review* 39 (May/June, 1978), 240–244.

45. For instance, see Blau and Scott, *Formal Organizations*, pp. 34–35; Robert K. Merton, *Social Theory and Social Structure*, 2nd ed. (Glencoe, Ill.: Free Press, 1957), pp. 50–54; Carl J. Friedrich, "Some Observations on Weber's Analysis of Bureaucracy," in Robert K. Merton et al. (eds.), *Reader in Bureaucracy* (Glencoe, Ill.: Free Press, 1952), pp. 27–33.

46. See Weber, *Wirtschaft*, p. 118.

47. See, especially, *ibid.*, p. 578; Weber, *Gesammelte Politische Schriften, Dritte Auflage* pp. 351–353, 516–517. Also see Weber, *Wirtschaft,* pp. 125, 127, 560.

48. Weber, *Wirtschaft,* p. 566; Max Weber, *Gesammelte Aufsaetze zur Soziologie und Sozialpolitik* (Tuebingen: J. C. B. Mohr, 1924), p. 414.

49. See Weber, *Gesammelte Politische Schriften, Dritte Auflage,* p. 326; Weber, *Wirtschaft,* pp. 130, 538–539.

50. In this connection, see Weber, *Wirtschaft,* pp. 128–129; Weber, *Gesammelte Politische Schriften, Dritte Auflage,* p. 364.

51. See Weber, *Religionssoziologie,* p. 204.

52. See Weber, *Wirtschaft,* pp. 690–691, 695.

53. See Weber, *Gesammelte Politische Schriften, Dritte Auflage,* p. 441; Weber, *Wissenschaftslehre,* p. 473.

54. See Weber, *Religionssoziologie,* p. 204, where Weber uses Nietzsche's phrase, "die letzten Menschen."

55. Weber, *Gesammelte Politische Schriften, Dritte Auflage,* p. 332; author's translation.

56. Weber, *Wirtschaft,* p. 665; Weber, *Gesammelte Politische Schriften, Dritte Auflage,* p. 508.

57. Glen D. Paige thinks that Weber's concept included both factors. *The Scientific Study of Political Leadership* (New York: Free Press, 1977), p. 85.

58. James MacGregor Burns believes that Weber's language was ambiguous on this point. *Leadership* (New York: Harper & Row, 1978), p. 243. Yet Robert C. Tucker asserts, correctly I think, that Weber "stresses the response of the followers as the crucial test." "The Theory of Charismatic Leadership," in Dankwart A. Rustow (ed.), *Philosophers and Kings: Studies in Leadership* (New York: George Braziller, 1970), p. 75.

59. William A. Welsh, *Leaders and Elites* (New York: Holt, Rinehart and Winston, 1979), p. 17.

60. Carl J. Friedrich, "Political Leadership and the Problem of the Charismatic Power," *Journal of Politics* 23 (1961), 15.

61. Weber, *Wirtschaft,* p. 665; Weber, *Gesammelte Politische Schriften, Dritte Auflage,* p. 508.

62. See Weber, *Wirtschaft,* p. 122, 542.

63. Weber, *Gesammelte Politische Schriften, Dritte Auflage*, p. 268. See also Weber, *Wirtschaft*, p. 514.

64. See Weber, *Wirtschaft*, p. 290.

65. See *ibid.*, p. 662; Weber, *Gesammelte Politische Schriften, Dritte Auflage*, pp. 351–352, 392–393; Weber, *Gesammelte Aufsaetze zur Soziologie*, p. 414.

66. See Weber, *Gesammelte Politische Schriften, Dritte Auflage*, pp. 334, 524; Weber, *Wirtschaft*, p. 127.

67. Weber, *Wirtschaft*, p. 154.

68. See Weber, *Gesammelte Politische Schriften, Dritte Auflage*, pp. 340–341, 541–543.

69. Weber, *Wirtschaft*, pp. 142, 361; Mommsen, *Age of Bureaucracy*, p. 20.

70. Weber, *Wirtschaft*, p. 665; Weber, *Economy and Society*, p. 116.

71. See Weber, *Wissenschaftslehre*, p. 514; Mommsen, "Max Weber's Political Sociology," p. 29. The original title Weber gave to *Economy and Society* was, "The Economy and the Arena of Normative and defacto Powers," Guenther Roth and Wolfgang Schluchter, *Max Weber's Vision of History: Ethics and Methods* (Berkeley, Calif.: University of California Press, 1979), p. 174. His lectures of 1918, the first he was able to deliver after his recovery, were entitled "Economy and Society: Positive Critique of the Materialist Conception of History." Official announcement of the Summer semester, 1918, University of Vienna. Copy in the Arbeitsstelle und Archiv der Max Weber Gesamtausgabe, Bayerische Akademie der Wissenschaften, Munich.

72. Weber's work on the origins of capitalism and the social implications of the major religious ethics was primarily intended to explain the nature and growth of cultural rationalism. See Weber, *Gesammelte Politische Schriften, Dritte Auflage*, p. 322; Weber, *Wirtschaft*, p. 259.

73. See Weber, *Gesammelte Politische Schriften, Dritte Auflage*, pp. 287, 336; Albrow, *Bureaucracy*, pp. 48–49; Mommsen, "Max Weber's Political Sociology," p. 39.

74. See Weber, *Gesammelte Politische Schriften, Dritte Auflage*, pp. 401, 544; Weber, *Wirtschaft*, pp. 155–156.

75. See Weber, *Gesammelte Politische Schriften, Dritte Auflage*, pp. 291, 318–319, 441; Scaff, "Max Weber's Politics."

76. See Weber, *Gesammelte Politische Schriften, Dritte Auflage*, pp. 340–341, 395, 403, 532–533.

77. *Ibid.*, pp. 251–266, 268, 291.

78. See *ibid.*, pp. 326, 339–340, 389–390.

79. See *ibid.*, pp. 403, 544.

80. See *ibid.*, pp. 401, 525.

81. See *ibid.*, pp. 399–400; Mommsen, "Max Weber's Political Sociology," p. 39; Loewenstein, *Political Ideas*, p. 23; Lawrence A. Scaff, "Max Weber and Robert Michels," *American Journal of Sociology* 86 (1981), 1269–1286.

82. See Weber, *Gesammelte Politische Schriften, Dritte Auflage*, pp. 348–349.

83. Weber, *Wissenschaftslehre*, pp. 517–518; translation taken from Weber, *Methology*, p. 27.

84. See Weber, *Gesammelte Politische Schriften, Dritte Auflage*, pp. 336, 349.

85. *Ibid.*, pp. 339–340, 353, 349.

86. *Ibid.*, pp. 403–404; translation taken from Weber, *Economy and Society*, pp. 1459–1460.

87. Weber was very concerned that the influence of non-intellectual considerations in academic appointments would undermine the "moral authority of the faculties," with the result that the "university will be incapable of offering any resistance to public opinion or to the government." Max Weber, *Max Weber on Universities*, trans. and ed. Edward Shils (Chicago: University of Chicago Press, 1974), p. 6.

88. Franz Boese, *Geschichte des Verein fuer Sozialpolitik: 1871–1932* (Berlin: Duncker und Humblot, 1939), pp. 147–148.

89. Weber, *Wissenschaftslehre*, pp. 146–214.

90. Boese, *Geschichte*, p. 113.

91. It is mistaken to assume, as does Theodor Heuss, that Weber was primarily concerned with defending the honor of a friend. *Friedrich Naumann: Der Mann, das Werk, die Zeit: Zweite Auflage* (Stuttgart: Wunderlich, 1949), pp. 317–318. As Schmoller himself pointed out, Weber's efforts persisted long after Naumann had declared himself satisfied with Schmoller's public clarification of his intent and meaning. Letter from Schmoller to Lujo Brentano, October 26, 1905, reprinted in Boese, *Geschichte*, p. 118.

92. See Mommsen, *Max Weber und die Deutsche Politik*, p. 142; letter from Weber to Lujo Brentano, October 26, 1905; letter to Brentano, November 24, 1905, both letters in Brentano's Papers, Bundesarchiv, Koblenz.

93. Letter from Schmoller to Brentano, October 29, 1905, in Boese, *Geschichte*, pp. 116–120.

94. T. S. Simey is clearly mistaken in asserting that Weber started arguing for freedom from value judgments only because his own value position had been rejected. "Max Weber: Man of Affairs or Theoretical Sociologist?" *Sociological Review* 14 (November, 1966), 303–327. His protest was occasioned by the difficulty in having his proposals seriously considered. It should be noted that he advocated the same orientation for universities and their professors—they should not be committed to teaching only one "outlook." See Weber, *Max Weber on Universities*, pp. 21–22.

95. Weber, *Wirtschaft*, p. 164; translation from Weber, *Economy and Society*, p. 280.

96. See Wolfgang Schluchter's insightful remarks on the type of leadership appropriate for scientific, bureaucratic, and political organizations. Roth and Schluchter, *Max Weber's Vision*, pp. 105–106. In 1905, Weber recommended four different offices to replace the one held by Schmoller. Letter to Brentano, November 11, 1905, Brentano Papers, Bundesarchiv, Koblenz.

97. "The more inconsiderable and colorless the [officer] is, so much the better." Letter to Brentano, November 24, 1905, in Brentano Papers, Bundesarchiv, Koblenz. See also letter to W. Windelband, 1909, in Marianne Weber, *Max Weber: A Biography*, p. 425; Weber, *Gesammelte Aufsaetze zur Soziologie*, p. 432.

98. This was also the task, according to Weber, of the university teacher. "He must make his chair into a forum where the understanding of ultimate standpoints—alien to and diverging from his own—is fostered, rather than into an arena where he propagates his own ideals." Weber, *Max Weber on Universities*, p. 22.

99. Weber, *Wissenschaftslehre*, p. 184; translation from Weber, *Methodology*, p. 84.

100. See *ibid.*, pp. 157, 166, 207–208.

101. In this connection, see *ibid.*, p. 399.

102. *Ibid.*, p. 213; translation from Weber, *Methodology*, p. 111.

103. See *ibid.*, pp. 161, 514.

104. See Christoph Steding, *Politik und Wissenschaft bei Max Weber* (Breslau: Wilh. Gottl. Korn Verlag, 1932), pp. 22–23; Weber, *Wissenschaftslehre*, p. 603.

105. See Weber, *Wissenschaftslehre*, pp. 150–151; Roth and Schluchter, *Max Weber's Vision*, p. 103.

106. See Weber, *Max Weber on Universities*, p. 33. The Prussian Minister of Education, Althoff, was severely critizized for bureaucratizing the universities, which led to a decline of scholarship as a factor determining personnel decisions. See *ibid.*, pp. 27–28. Lujo Brentano reached the same conclusion concerning Althoff. *Mein Leben* (Jena: Eugen Diederichs Verlag, 1931), p. 218.

107. Weber, *Gesammelte Aufsaetze zur Soziologie*, pp. 431–432. Ferdinand Toennies apparently took the initiative in establishing this organization. Fritz Ringer, *The Decline of the German Mandarins: The German Academic Community, 1890–1933* (Cambridge, Mass.: Harvard University Press, 1969), p. 103.

108. Letters to Brentano, July 1, 1912; July 3, 1912, Brentano Papers, Bundesarchiv, Koblenz.

109. "An die Herren Teilnehmer der Leipziger Besprechung," reprinted in Bernhard Schaefer, "Ein Rundschreiben Max Webers zur Sozialpolitik," *Sozial Welt* 18 (1967), 265.

110. Letter to Brentano, end of August, 1912, Brentano Papers, Bundesarchiv, Koblenz.

111. Mommsen mistakenly attributes this motive to Weber and claims that the two were unable to collaborate because of Weber's greater sense of political tactics. *Max Weber und die Deutsche Politik*, pp. 127–128.

112. Letter to Brentano, September 11, 1912, Brentano Papers, Bundesarchiv, Koblenz.

113. Letter to Brentano, end of August, 1912, Brentano Papers, Bundesarchiv, Koblenz.

114. Letter to Brentano, September 16, 1912, Brentano Papers, Bundesarchiv, Koblenz.

115. Weber's draft of the announcement for the prospective meeting;

author's translation. Brentano Papers, Bundesarchiv, Koblenz. See also "An die Herren Teilnehmer," pp. 268–69.

116. See Weber, *Gesammelte Aufsaetze zur Soziologie*, pp. 2–3; Anthony Oberschall, *Empirical Social Research in Germany, 1848–1914* (New York: Basic Books, 1965), p. 114; Otto von Zwiedineck-Suedenhorst, "Vom Wirken von Max und Alfred Weber im Verein Fuer Sozialpolitik: Erinnerungen und Eindruecke," in Edgar Salin (ed.), *Synopsis: Festgabe fuer Alfred Weber* (Heidelberg: Verlag Lambert Schneider, 1949), p. 784.

117. Boese, *Geschichte*, p. 147; Ringer, *German Mandarins*, p. 162.

118. Letter to unknown recipient, quoted in Marianne Weber, *Max Weber: A Biography*, pp. 424–425.

CHAPTER SEVEN
Max Weber Becomes a Politician

1. On the cultural impact of World War I, see Paul Fussell, *The Great War and Modern Memory* (London: Oxford University Press, 1975).

2. In addition to the fact that he could now engage in the previously forbidden activities, there are numerous statements by both Weber and his wife indicating recovery. See Marianne Weber, *Max Weber: A Biography*, trans. Harry Zohn (New York: John Wiley & Sons, 1975), pp. 525, 575–576, 692–695; letter from Marianne to Max Weber, April 20, 1920, in Eduard Baumgarten, *Max Weber: Werk und Person* (Tuebingen: J. C. B. Mohr, 1964), p. 633.

3. There was a brief period of melancholia in his last year. See Marianne Weber, *Max Weber: A Biography*, pp. 689–690. This might have been caused in part by the suicide of his sister.

4. See *ibid.*, p. 519. Differences over the war caused Weber to break with two old friends, Troeltsch and Michels. See *ibid.*, pp. 524–525; letter from Ernst Troeltsch to Paul Honigsheim, July 6, 1917, in Eduard Baumgarten, *Max Weber*, p. 489.

5. Letter from Weber to Toennies, October 15, 1914; letter from Weber to Helene Weber, April 13, 1915; both in Marianne Weber, *Max Weber: A Biography*, pp. 521–522.

6. See *ibid.*, p. 667.

7. See *ibid.*, pp. 645, 672.

8. See *ibid.*, pp. 689–690; Henrich Rickert's review of Marianne Weber, *Max Weber: Ein Lebensbild,* of July 14, 1926, probably in the *Frankfurter Zeitung,* copy in the Arbeitsstelle und Archiv der Max Weber Gesamtausgabe, Bayerische Akademie der Wissenschaften, Munich.

9. See Wolfgang J. Mommsen, *The Age of Bureaucracy* (New York: Harper & Row, 1974), p. 23; Martin Green, *The von Richthofen Sisters* (New York: Basic Books, 1974), p. 28; letter from Else Jaffe to Miss Brentano, July 24, 1952, Nachlass Brentano, Bundesarchiv, Koblenz; letter from Marianne Weber to Paul Honigsheim, September 1, 1947, in Arbeitsstelle und Archiv der Max Weber Gesamtausgabe, Bayerische Akademie der Wissenschaften, Munich.

10. For instance, see Erich von Kahler, *Der Beruf der Wissenschaft* (Berlin: Georg Bondi, 1920), p. 8; Theodor Heuss, *Erinnerungen, 1905–1933* (Tuebingen: Rainer, Wunderlich Verlag, 1963), pp. 225–226; Karl Loewenstein, *Max Weber's Political Ideas in the Perspective of Our Time,* trans. Richard and Clara Winston (Amherst, Mass.: University of Massachusetts Press, 1966), p. 102; report in the *Frankischen Tagespost,* August 2, 1916, quoted in Wolfgang J. Mommsen, *Max Weber und die Deutsche Politik* (Tuebingen: J. C. B. Mohr, 1974), p. 259; letter from Dr. Dora Busch to Johannes Winckelmann, August 22, 1962, in the Arbeitsstelle und Archiv der Max Weber Gesamtausgabe, Bayerische Akademie der Wissenschaften, Munich. Also see the poem, "Max Weber," by Friedrich Gundolf in his *Gedichte* (Berlin: Bandi, 1930), p. 23.

11. See letter from Weber to Jaffe, early 1915, in Marianne Weber, *Max Weber: A Biography,* p. 535.

12. See letter from Weber to Mina Tobler, August 28, 1915, in Eduard Baumgarten, *Max Weber,* pp. 493–494; also in Marianne Weber, *Max Weber: A Biography,* p. 535.

13. It was just as well that nothing came of this prospect. Von Bissing, the head of the German occupation of Belgium, wanted annexation and saw these studies as preparatory for this goal. Weber was against almost all annexations. See Mommsen, *Max Weber und die Deutsche Politik,*

pp. 216–218. Marianne Weber simply refers to the object of the study as a "social policy project." *Max Weber: A Biography,* p. 536.

14. See Mommsen, *Max Weber und die Deutsche Politik,* p. 224; Marianne Weber, *Max Weber: A Biography,* p. 554.

15. Marianne Weber, *Max Weber: A Biography,* pp. 555, 572; Mommsen, *Max Weber und die Deutsche Politik,* pp. 235–236, 244.

16. But he certainly did not give up hope that he might still be offered a position. See letter from Weber to Helene Weber, April 17, 1916, in Marianne Weber, *Max Weber: A Biography,* pp. 571–572.

17. *Ibid.,* p. 563. The foreign secretary urged him, for political reasons, to circulate the memorandum more broadly. This was done. Mommsen, *Max Weber und die Deutsche Politik,* pp. 249–250.

18. Hans W. Gatzke, *Germany's Drive to the West* (Baltimore: Johns Hopkins University Press, 1950), p. 17.

19. See *ibid.,* pp. 26, 170–175. Officially, the Pan-German League was not affiliated with any party, but its membership was drawn exclusively from the right. See Mildred S. Wertheimer, *The Pan-German League, 1890–1914* (New York: Octagon Books, 1971), pp. 132–159.

20. *Ibid.,* p. 133.

21. Mommsen, *Max Weber und die Deutsche Politik,* p. 215.

22. Letter from Weber to the editor of the *Frankfurter Zeitung,* December, 1915, in Weber, *Gesammelte Politische Schriften, Erste Auflage.* 1st ed. (Munich: Drei Masken, 1921), p. 459.

23. See Mommsen, *Max Weber und die Deutsche Politik,* pp. 224, 255, 257.

24. *Ibid.,* p. 260; Marianne Weber, *Max Weber: A Biography,* p. 580.

25. See letters from Weber to Naumann, February 2, 1917, and April 12, 1917, and to the editor of the *Frankfurter Zeitung,* July 27, 1916, and August 20, 1916. All reprinted in Weber, *Gesammelte Politische Schriften, Erste Auflage.* 1st ed.

26. See Mommsen, *Max Weber und die Deutsche Politiik,* p. 265.

27. See *ibid.,* pp. 273–274, 278.

28. See *ibid.,* pp. 320–322.

29. Marianne Weber, *Max Weber: A Biography,* p. 632.

30. See *ibid.,* pp. 627–628, 642; Allan Mitchell, *Revolution in Ba-*

varia, 1918–1919: The Eisner Regime and the Soviet Republic (Princeton: Princeton University Press, 1965), p. 174; Richard Grunberger, *Red Rising in Bavaria* (London: Arthur Barker, 1973), p. 44. Weber's rhetoric was at times extremely provocative. See Mommsen, *Max Weber und die Deutsche Politik*, p. 327.

31. See Mommsen, *Max Weber und die Deutsche Politik*, pp. 380, 397; Marianne Weber, *Max Weber: A Biography*, p. 61. Mommsen makes a very plausible argument that Weber's influence on the final product has been overemphasized. pp. 377–379.

32. On this affair see Mommsen, *Max Weber und die Deutsche Politik*, pp. 338–339; Marianne Weber, *Max Weber: A Biography*, pp. 646–647.

33. See letters from Weber to Baden Ministry of Education, August 8, 1917, in Marianne Weber, *Max Weber: A Biography*, pp. 592–593; to Marianne Weber, July 1, 1919, *ibid.*, p. 658; to Klara Mommsen, early 1920, *ibid.*, p. 689; to editor of the *Frankfurter Zeitung*, February 9, 1919, Weber, *Gesmmelte Politische Schriften, Erste Auflage*. 1st ed., pp. 485–486.

34. On these instances, see Mommsen, *Max Weber und die Deutsche Politik*, pp. 324–325, 328–329, 331–334; Marianne Weber, *Max Weber: A Biography*, pp. 634, 643. Another instance of seemingly ambiguous behavior is Weber's refusal to support the German Democratic party openly when it was first formed. He agreed with its leadership on fundamentals, but it advocated the complete abolition of monarchy, a position he had politically opposed. Yet he apparently had few qualms about publicly advocating "socialism" for tactical reasons. See letter from Weber to Else Jaffe, mid-November, 1918, in Eduard Baumgarten, *Max Weber*, pp. 531–532; Marianne Weber, *Max Weber: A Biography*, pp. 641–642.

35. See Bruce B. Frye, "A Letter from Max Weber," *The Journal of Modern History* 39 (1967), 119–125; Mommsen, *Max Weber und die Deutsche Politik*, p. 334.

36. Apparently it also made him a difficult person to deal with generally. One of his former junior colleagues at Munich commented that Weber seemed to lack "harmony" in his "life, thought and writings" and

that this imbalance led to occasional outbursts that were botn unattractive and uncontrolled—although impressive. He concluded that it was probably good for Weber that "he only temporarily submerged himself in politics." Letter from Professor B. Pfister to Professor M. J. Bonn, May 11, 1963, Arbeitsstelle und Archiv der Max Weber Gesamtausgabe, Bayerische Akademie der Wissenschaften, Munich.

37. Marianne Weber, *Max Weber: A Biography*, p. 673. For other descriptions of the incident, see letter from F. J. Berber to unknown recipient, March 31, 1963; letter from Dr. Georg Schenk to Alfred Kroewer, December 11, 1964; letter from E. Baumgarten to Dr. Schenk, January 5, 1965. All in Arbeitstelle und Archiv der Max Weber Gesamtausgabe, Bayerische Akademie der Wissenschaften, Munich.

38. In fact, the Munich Student's Association publically criticized *both* Weber and the agitators for introducing politics into the classroom. *Frankfurter Zeitung*, January 31, 1920, p. 2.

39. Notice is reprinted in Marianne Weber, *Max Weber: A Biography*, p. 688. The newspaper refused to print the challenge.

40. See *ibid.*, p. 674.

41. See *ibid.*, p. 645–655. In fact, Weber was publically cautioned that he could not make a sharp distinction between the tasks of the professor and the politician at Munich in a newspaper article by one Immanuel Birnbaum. "Max Weber in Muenchen," *Sueddeutsche Freiheit*, March 24, 1919.

42. See report reprinted in Guenther Roth and Wolfgang Schluchter, *Max Weber's Vision of History: Ethics and Methods* (Berkeley, Calif.: University of California Press, 1979), p. 116.

43. See Marianne Weber, *Max Weber: A Biography*, pp. 560, 574, 583–584; letter from Weber to Marianne, early 1916, *ibid.*, p. 570; letter from Marianne to Weber, early 1916, *ibid.*, p. 571; letters from Weber to Mina Tobler, August 8, 1915; July, 1916; September 4, 1916; Autumn, 1916; May 7, 1917; August 9, 1917, May 1918; all in Eduard Baumgarten, *Max Weber*, pp. 491–503.

44. See Marianne Weber, *Max Weber: A Biography*, pp. 551–552, 593, 664, 675–676; Roth and Schluchter, *Max Weber's Vision*, p. 62.

45. Weber himself once used this terminology. See Max Weber,

Gesammelte Aufsaetze zur Wissenschaftslehre, Dritte Auflage (Tuebingen: J. C. B. Mohr, 1956), p. 278. See also in this connection, *ibid.*, pp. 590–591.

46. *Ibid.*, p. 588. See also Max Weber, *Gesammelte Aufsaetze zur Religionssoziologie, I* (Tuebingen: J. C. B. Mohr, 1920), pp. 13–14.

47. Thomas S. Kuhn, *The Structure of Scientific Revolutions* (Chicago: University of Chicago Press, 1962).

48. Kuhn admits that his use of the word *paradigm* has been ambiguous. Margaret Masterman has asserted that he uses the term in twenty-two different ways. "The Nature of a Paradigm," in Imre Lakatos and Alan Musgrave (eds.), *Criticism and the Growth of Knowledge* (Cambridge: Cambridge University Press, 1970), pp. 59–89. Kuhn seems to de-emphasize the theoretical aspect of his concept in later writings. Thomas S. Kuhn, *The Essential Tension* (Chicago: University of Chicago Press, 1977), pp. 293–319.

49. Kuhn himself made no claim that his analysis was applicable to the social sciences. *Scientific Revolutions*, p. 15.

50. See *ibid.*, p. 168; Karl R. Popper, "The Rationality of Scientific Revolutions," in Ron Harre (ed.), *Problems of Scientific Revolution* (London: Oxford University Press, 1975), p. 83.

51. See Weber, *Wissenschaftslehre*, p. 251.

52. *Ibid.*, p. 214; translation taken from Weber, *Methodology of the Social Sciences*, trans. Edward A. Shils and Henry A. Finch (Glencoe, Ill.: Free Press, 1949), p. 112. (Emphasis added.)

53. In this connection, see Karl R. Popper, "The Myth of the Framework," in Eugene Freeman (ed.), *The Abdication of Philosophy* (LaSalle, Ill.: Open Court, 1976).

54. See Weber, *Wissenschaftslehre*, pp. 206–208, 262.

55. It is sometimes asserted that Weber's approach to "ideal-types" changed shortly before the war. After this change they supposedly ceased to be instruments of inquiry and became the object or end of research. See, for example, Mommsen, *Age of Bureaucracy*, p. 14; H. Stuart Hughes, *Consciousness and Society* (New York: Random House, 1958), p. 324. I think this is misconceived, but the focus of this activity certainly did change. Christoph Steding noted the irony of Weber's emphasis upon specialization in science, given the comprehensivness of his

own work. *Politik und Wissenschaft bei Max Weber* (Breslau: Wilh. Gottl. Korn Verlag, 1932), p. 30.

56. Marianne Weber, *Max Weber: A Biography,* p. 593; Steding, *Politik,* pp. 31, 34, 47.

57. Gustav Stolper, *This Age of Fable* (New York: Reynaland Hitchcock, 1942), p. 318. Stolper was a student in Weber's last seminar.

58. Letter from Weber to Delbruck, October 8, 1919, quoted in Mommsen, *Max Weber und die Deutsche Politik,* p. 351.

59. Letter from Weber, October 10, 1918, quoted in *ibid.,* p. 308; recipient not disclosed.

60. Letter from Weber to Else Jaffe, January, 1919, Arbeitsstelle und Archiv der Max Weber Gesamtausgabe, Bayerische Akademie der Wissenschaften, Munich.

61. Fritz Stern, *The Politics of Cultural Despair* (Berkeley, Calif.: University of California Press, 1961), p. 17.

62. In this connection see the letter from Weber to Karl Loewenstein, February 10, 1917, in Eduard Baumgarten, *Max Weber,* pp. 497–498.

63. See letter from Weber to Erich Trummler, January 17, 1918, Weber, *Gesammelte Politische Schriften, Erste Auflage,* 1st ed., pp. 474–475.

64. Ernst Toller, *Eine Jugend im Deutschland* (Amsterdam: Querido Verlag, 1933), p. 57.

65. Letter from Weber to Fritz Keller, Chairman of the Philiser Commission der Allemania, October 17, 1918, in Mommsen, *Max Weber und die Deutsche Politik,* p. 336. Also see Toller, *Ein Jugend,* p. 57.

66. Letter from Weber, probably to Marianne, February 27, 1916, in Marianne Weber, *Max Weber: A Biography,* pp. 561–562.

67. See letter from Weber, recipient unknown, November 18, 1918, in *ibid.,* p. 633; letter from Weber to Friedrich Crusins, November 24, 1918, in *ibid.,* p. 637.

68. Weber, *Wissenschaftslehre,* p. 603; translation from Max Weber, *From Max Weber,* trans. H. H. Gerth and C. Wright Mills (New York: Oxford University Press, 1946), p. 147.

69. Weber announced his intentions at the beginning of the semester. Marianne Weber, *Max Weber: A Biography,* p. 662. Max Horkheimer, whom Weber might have considered a hopeless case, still remembered

his own disappointment after half a century. "Discussion," in *Max Weber and Society Today,* ed. Otto Stammer (New York: Harper & Row, 1971), p. 51.

70. Weber, *Wissenschaftslehre,* p. 588; translation taken from Weber, *From Max Weber,* p. 134.

71. In fact, Weber was publicly criticized on this point. Kahler, *Der Beruf,* pp. 9–10. On the events that led Weber to present these lectures and the students sponsoring them, see Roth and Schluchter, *Max Weber's Vision,* p. 115. See also Robert Eden, "Doing Without Liberalism: Max Weber's Regime Politics," *Political Theory* 10 (1982), 385–396.

72. Weber, *Wissenschaftslehre,* pp. 607–609.

73. Weber himself did not always see it this way. As mentioned in Chapter 2, he originally enjoyed teaching because he considered it practical activity. When he first began teaching in 1918, he continued to draw a distinction between scholarship and teaching. See Marianne Weber, *Max Weber: A Biography,* pp. 612, 613. Once he found that he was capable of fulfilling his academic duties, and even achieved some acclaim for it, he apparently changed his mind.

74. *Ibid.,* p. 664. Also see p. 671.

75. In this connection, see Lawrence A. Scaff's analysis of the role of education in Weber's political thought. "Max Weber's Politics and Political Education," *American Political Science Review* 67 (March, 1973), 128–141.

76. Letter from Weber to Toennis, 1908, in Eduard Baumgarten, *Max Weber,* p. 670.

77. Weber, *Wissenschaftslehre,* p. 612.

78. *Ibid.,* p. 611.

79. Although his wife believed that he had reconciled himself with God in the delirium of his deathbed. Marianne Weber, *Max Weber: A Biography,* p. 667. Weber himself at one point drew a contrast between the "dogmatist" and the scientist. Weber, *Wissenschaftslehre,* pp. 306–307.

80. Weber, *Wissenschaftslehre,* p. 610; Weber, *From Max Weber,* p. 153. Weber, of course, realized that science must have presuppositions that it cannot demonstrate. He classifies these presuppositions as "re-

ligious-philosophical." *Ibid.*, p. 611. Perhaps he uses this terminology because he does not believe that all religions develop theologies, but it would appear to conflict with the sharp distinction he draws between religion and science.

81. *Ibid.*, p. 611; Weber, *From Max Weber*, p. 154.

82. See also *ibid.*, p. 154.

BIBLIOGRAPHY

Albrow, Martin. *Bureaucracy.* New York: Praeger Publishers, 1970.

Alexander, Franz. *Fundamentals of Psychoanalysis.* New York: W. W. Norton, 1963.

_____ and Sheldon T. Selesnick. *The History of Psychiatry.* New York: Harper & Row, 1966.

Allport, Gordon W. *Personality and Social Encounter.* Boston: Beacon Press, 1960.

Argyle, Michael. *The Psychology of Interpersonal Behavior.* Baltimore: Penguin Books, 1972.

Aron, Raymond. *Main Currents in Sociological Thought,* Vol. II. Garden City, N.Y.: Anchor Books, 1970.

_____. "Max Weber and Power Politics." In *Max Weber and Sociology Today,* edited by Otto Stammer. New York: Harper & Row, 1971.

Ayer, Alfred Jules. *Language, Truth and Logic.* New York: Dover Publications, 1952.

Ball, Terence. "Theory and Practice: An Examination of the Platonic and Aristotelian Conceptions of Political Theory." *Western Political Quarterly* 25 (1972).

Baumgarten, Eduard. *Max Weber: Werk und Person.* Tuebingen: J. C. B. Mohr, 1964.

Baumgarten, Otto. *Meine Lebensgeschichte.* Tuebingen: J. C. B. Mohr, 1929.

Bech, Howard S., and James Casper. "The Development of Identification with an Occupation." *American Journal of Sociology* 61 (1956).

Becker, Carl L. *The Heavenly City of the Eighteenth Century Philosophers.* New Haven, Conn.: Yale University Press, 1932.

Beetham, David. *Max Weber and the Theory of Modern Politics.* London: George Allen and Unwin, 1974.

Bierstedt, Robert. "Sociological Thought in the Eighteenth Century." In *A History of Sociological Analysis,* edited by Tom Bottomore and Robert Nisbet. New York: Basic Books, 1978.

Birnbaum, Immanuel. "Max Weber in Muenchen." In *Sueddeutsche Freiheit.* March 24, 1919.

Blau, Peter M., and W. Richard Scott. *Formal Organizations: A Comparative Approach.* Scranton, Pa.: Chandler Publishing Co., 1962.

Blum, Fred H. "Max Weber's Postulate of 'Freedom' from Value Judgments." *American Journal of Sociology* 50 (**1944**).

Blumstein, Philip W. "Identity Bargaining and Self-Conception." *Social Forces* 53 (1975).

Boese, Franz. *Geschichte des Verein Fuer Sozialpolitik: 1871–1932.* Berlin: Duncker und Humblot, 1939.

———. *Geschichte des Verein Fuer Sozialpolitik: 1890–1920, Zweite Auflage.* Tuebingen: J. C. B. Mohr, 1974.

Bohm, David. "Human Nature as the Product of Our Mental Models." In *The Limits of Human Nature,* edited by Jonathan Benthall. London: Institute of Contemporary Arts, 1973.

Braithwaite, R. B. *Scientific Explanation.* Cambridge: Cambridge University Press, 1953.

Bramel, Dana. "A Dissonance Theory Approach to Defensive Projection." *Journal of Abnormal and Social Psychology* 64 (1962).

Brecht, Arnold. *Political Theory.* Princeton, N.J.: Princeton University Press, 1959.

Brentano, Lujo. *Mein Leben.* Jena: Eugen Diederichs Verlag, 1931.

Bronfenbrenner, U. "Response to Pressure from Peers Versus Adults Among Soviet and American School Children." *International Journal of Psychology* 2 (1967).

Bruun, H. H. *Science, Values, and Politics in Max Weber's Methodology.* Copenhagen: Munksgaard, 1972.

Burger, Thomas. *Max Weber's Theory of Concept Formation.* Durham, N.C.: Duke University Press, 1976.

Burns, James MacGregor. *Leadership.* New York: Harper & Row, 1978.

Cassirer, Ernest. *The Philosophy of the Enlightenment.* Princeton, N.J.: Princeton University Press, 1951.

Cohen, Abner. *Two-Dimensional Man.* Berkeley, Calif.: University of California Press, 1974.

Copi, Irving M. *Introduction to Logic*. New York: Macmillan, 1953.

Cuff, Robert D. "Wilson and Weber: Bourgeois Critics in an Organizational Age." *Public Administration Review* 39 (1978).

Dahl, Robert. *Modern Political Analysis*. Englewood Cliffs, N.J.: Prentice-Hall, 1964.

Dahrendorf, Ralf. *Society and Democracy in Germany*. New York: Doubleday, 1967.

Dallmayr, Fred R. "Empirical Political Theory and the Image of Man." *Polity* 2 (1970).

Diamond, Martin. "Democracy and *The Federalist:* A Reconsideration of the Framers' Intent." *American Political Science Review* 53 (1959).

Dibble, Vernon. "Social Science and Political Commitments in the Young Max Weber." *Archives Europeennes des Sociologie* 9 (1968).

Dronberger, Ilse. *The Political Thought of Max Weber*. New York: Appleton-Century-Crofts, 1971.

Duval, Shelley, and Robert A. Wicklund. *A Theory of Objective Self-Awareness*. New York: Academic Press, 1972.

Eden, Robert. "Doing Without Liberalism: Max Weber's Regime Politics." *Political Theory* 10 (1982).

_____. *Political Leadership and Nihilism: A Study of Weber and Nietzsche*. Tampa: University of South Florida Press, 1983.

Eisenstadt, S. N. *From Generation to Generation*. New York: Free Press, 1956.

Epstein, Seymour. "The Self-Concept Revisited: Or a Theory of a Theory." *American Psychologist* 28 (1973).

Erikson, Erik H. *Childhood and Society*. New York: W. W. Norton, 1963.

_____. *Identity, Youth and Crisis*. New York: W. W. Norton, 1968.

_____. *Young Man Luther*. New York: W. W. Norton, 1962.

Eyck, Erich. *Bismarck and the German Empire*. New York: W. W. Norton, 1958.

Fenichel, Otto. *The Psychoanalytic Theory of Neurosis*. New York: W. W. Norton, 1945.

French, Thomas M. *Psychoanalytic Interpretations*. Chicago: Quadrangle Books, 1970.

Freud, Anna. *The Ego and the Mechanisms of Defense*. London: Hogarth Press, 1942.

Freud, Sigmund. *The Ego and the Id,* translated by Joan Riviere. New York: W. W. Norton, 1960.

———. *The History of the Psychoanalytic Movement,* translated by Joan Riviere. New York: Collier Books, 1963.

———. *An Outline of Psycho-Analysis,* translated by James Strachey. New York: W. W. Norton, 1969.

———. *The Psychopathology of Everyday Life,* translated by Alan Tyson. New York: W. W. Norton, 1965.

Freund, Julien. *The Sociology of Max Weber.* New York: Random House, 1968.

Friedrich, Carl J. "Political Leadership and the Problem of the Charismatic Power." *Journal of Politics* 23 (1961).

———. "Some Observations on Weber's Analysis of Bureaucracy." In *Reader in Bureaucracy,* edited by Robert K. Merton et al. Glencoe, Ill.: Free Press, 1952.

Frohock, Fred M. "Notes on the Concept of Politics: Weber, Easton, Strauss." *Journal of Politics* 36 (1974).

Frye, Bruce B. "A Letter from Max Weber." *The Journal of Modern History* 39 (1967).

Fussell, Paul. *The Great War and Modern Memory.* London: Oxford University Press, 1975.

Gatzke, Hans W. *Germany's Drive to the West.* Baltimore: Johns Hopkins University Press, 1950.

Gay, Peter. *Weimar Culture.* New York: Harper & Row, 1968.

Geertz, Clifford. *The Interpretation of Cultures.* New York: Basic Books, 1973.

Gerschenkron, Alexander. *Bread and Democracy in Germany.* Berkeley, Calif.: University of California Press, 1943.

Giddens, Anthony. *Politics and Society in the Thought of Max Weber.* London: Macmillan, 1972.

Gordon, Chad. "Self Conception: Configurations of Content." In *The Self in Social Interaction,* edited by Chad Gordon and Kenneth J. Gergen. New York: John Wiley & Sons, 1968.

Green, Martin. *The von Richthofen Sisters: The Triumphant and the Tragic Modes of Love.* New York: Basic Books, 1974.

Grunberger, Richard. *Red Rising in Bavaria.* London: Arthur Barker, 1973.

Gundolf, Friedrich. *Gedichte*. Berlin: Bandi, 1930.

Habermas, Juergen. *The Theory of Communicative Action,* Vol. I, translated by Thomas McCarthy. Boston: Beacon Press, 1984.

Hall, Calvin S. "What People Dream About." *Scientific American* 184 (1951).

Hampshire, Stuart. *Thought and Action*. London: Chatton and Windus, 1959.

Hekman, Susan J. "Weber's Concept of Causality and the Modern Critique." *Sociological Inquiry* 49 (1979).

_____. *Weber, the Ideal Type, and Contemporary Social Theory*. Notre Dame, Ind: University of Notre Dame Press, 1983.

Heuss, Theodor. *Erinnerungen, 1905–1933*. Tuebingen: Rainer, Wunderlich, 1963.

_____. *Friedrich Naumann: Der Mann, das Werk, die Zeit, Zweite Auflage*. Stuttgart: Wunderlich, 1949.

Hilgard, Ernest. "Human Motives and the Concept of the Self." *The American Psychologist* 4 (1949).

Honigsheim, Paul. *On Max Weber,* translated by Joan Rytina. East Lansing, Mich.: Michigan State University Press, 1968.

Horkheimer, Max. "Discussion." In *Max Weber and Society Today,* edited by Otto Stammer. New York: Harper & Row, 1971.

Horney, Karen. *The Neurotic Personality of Our Time*. New York: W. W. Norton, 1937.

Howe, Richard Herbert. "Max Weber's Elective Affinities: Sociology Within the Bounds of Pure Reason." *American Journal of Sociology* 84 (1978).

Hufnagel, Gerhard. *Kritik als Beruf: Der Kritische Gehalt im Werk Max Webers*. Frankfurt am Main: Propylaeen Verlag, 1971.

Hughes, Stuart. *Consciousness and Society*. New York: Random House, 1958.

Hume, David. *A Treatise of Human Nature*. London: Oxford University Press, 1888.

Jacobson, Edith. *The Self and the Object World*. New York: International Universities Press, 1964.

James, William. *Psychology: The Briefer Course*. New York: Henry Holt and Company, 1910.

Jaros, Dean. *Socialization to Politics.* New York: Praeger Publishers, 1973.

Jaspers, Karl. *Three Essays,* translated by Ralph Manheim. New York: Harcourt, Brace and World, 1964.

Jung, C. G. *Modern Man in Search of a Soul,* translated by W. S. Dell and Cary F. Baynes. New York: Harcourt, Brace and World, 1933.

Kahler, Erich von. *Der Beruf der Wissenschaft.* Berlin: Georg Bondi, 1920.

Kalberg, Steven. "Max Weber's Types of Rationality: Cornerstones for the Analysis of Rationalization Processes in History." *American Journal of Sociology* 85 (1980).

Kant, Immanuel. *Critique of Pure Reason,* translated by Norman Kemp Smith. New York: St. Martin's Press, 1929.

Kilpatrick, William Heard. *Selfhood and Civilization.* New York: Macmillan, 1941.

Kuehlmann, Richard von. *Erinnerungen.* Heidelberg: Verlag Lambert Schneider, 1948.

Kuhn, Thomas S. *The Essential Tension.* Chicago: University of Chicago Press, 1977.

———. *The Structure of Scientific Revolutions.* Chicago: University of Chicago Press, 1962.

Lachmann, L. M. *The Legacy of Max Weber.* Berkeley, Calif.: Glendessary Press, 1971.

Laing, R. D. *The Divided Self.* Baltimore: Penguin Books, 1965.

Lakatos, Imre, and Alan Musgrave, eds. *Criticism and the Growth of Knowledge.* London: Cambridge University Press, 1970.

Lecky, Prescott. *Self-Consistency: A Theory of Personality.* Garden City, N.Y.: Anchor Books, 1961.

Leiserson, Avery. "Charles Merriam, Max Weber, and the Search for Synthesis in Political Science." *The American Political Science Review* 69 (1975).

Levine, Donald N., ed. *George Simmel on Individuality and Social Forms.* Chicago: University of Chicago Press, 1971.

Lifton, Robert J. *Thought Reform and the Psychology of Totalism.* New York: W. W. Norton, 1961.

Loewenstein, Karl. *Max Weber's Political Ideas in the Perspective of Our*

Time, translated by Richard and Clara Winston. Amherst, Mass.: University of Massachusetts Press, 1966.

Loewith, Karl. *Gesammelte Abhandlungnen.* Stuttgart: W. Kohlhammer Verlag, 1960.

Lovejoy, Arthur O. *The Great Chain of Being.* Cambridge: Harvard University Press, 1936.

Lynd, Helen Merrell. *On Shame and the Search for Identity.* New York: Harcourt, Brace, and Company, 1958.

Madden, Edward H., ed. *The Structure of Scientific Thought.* Boston: Houghton Mifflin, 1960.

Manuel, Frank E. *The Prophets of Paris.* Cambridge: Harvard University Press, 1962.

March, James G., and Herbert A. Simon. *Organizations.* New York: John Wiley & Sons, 1958.

Masterman, Margaret. "The Nature of a Paradigm." In *Criticism and the Growth of Knowledge,* edited by Imre Lakatos and Alan Musgrave. Cambridge: Cambridge University Press, 1970.

Mayer, J. P. *Max Weber and German Politics.* London: Faber and Faber, 1956.

McCall, George J., and J. L. Simmons. *Identities and Interactions.* 2nd ed. New York: Free Press, 1978.

Mead, George H. *Mind, Self and Society.* Chicago: University of Chicago Press, 1934.

Merton, Robert K. *Social Theory and Social Structure.* 2nd ed. Glencoe, Ill.: Free Press, 1957.

Mill, John Stuart. *Auguste Comte and Positivism.* Ann Arbor, Mich.: University of Michigan Press, 1961.

——. *A System of Logic.* London: Longman, 1970.

Mitchell, Allan. *Revolution in Bavaria, 1918–1919: The Eisner Regime and the Soviet Republic.* Princeton, N.J.: Princeton University Press, 1965.

Mitzman, Arthur. *The Iron Cage.* New York: Alfred A. Knopf, 1970.

Mommsen, Wolfgang J. *The Age of Bureaucracy.* Oxford: Oxford University Press, 1974.

——. *Max Weber: Gesellschaft, Politik und Geschichte.* Frankfurt am Main: Suhrkamp Verlag, 1974.

_____. *Max Weber und die Deutsche Politik: 1890–1920, Zweite Auflage*. Tuebingen: J. C. B. Mohr, 1974.

_____. "Max Weber's Political Sociology and His Philosophy of World History." *International Social Science Journal* 7 (1965).

Murray, Henry A. *Explorations in Personality*. Oxford and London: Oxford University Press, 1938.

Oakes, Guy. "Introductory Essay." In Max Weber, *Roscher and Knies: The Logical Problems of Historical Economics*. New York: Free Press. 1975.

_____. "The Verstehen Thesis and the Foundations of Max Weber's Methodólogy." *History and Theory* 16 (1977).

Oberschall, Anthony. *Empirical Social Research in Germany: 1848–1914*. New York: Basic Books, 1965.

Oppenheim, Felix E. *Moral Principles in Political Philosophy*. New York: Random House, 1968.

Paige, Glen D. *The Scientific Study of Political Leadership*. New York: Free Press, 1977.

Parsons, Talcott. *The Structure of Social Action*. New York: Free Press, 1968.

Penelham, Terrence. "Self-Identity and Self-Regard." In *The Identities of Persons*, edited by Amelie Rorty. Berkeley, Calif.: University of California Press, 1976.

Perry, John. "Personal Identity." In *Personal Identity*, edited by John Perry. Berkeley, Calif.: University of California Press, 1975.

Phillips, Derek L. *Knowledge from What?* Chicago: Rand McNally, 1971.

Piaget, Jean. *The Moral Judgement of the Child*. New York: Free Press, 1965.

_____. *Six Psychological Studies*. New York: Random House, 1967.

Pois, Robert A. *Friedrich Meinecke and Germany Politics in the Twentieth Century*. Berkeley, Calif.: University of California Press, 1972.

Polanyi, Michael. *Personal Knowledge*. New York: Harper & Row, 1964.

_____. *Science, Faith and Society*. Chicago: University of Chicago Press, 1964.

Popper, Karl. "The Myth of the Framework." In *The Abdication of Philosophy,* edited by Eugene Freeman. LaSalle, Ill.: Open Court, 1976.

———. "The Rationality of Scientific Revolutions." In *Problems of Scientific Revolutions,* edited by Ron Harre. London: Oxford University Press, 1975.

Portis, Edward B. "Nietzsche and Social Commitment." *GPSA Journal* 4 (1976).

———. "Society and Political Choice: Social Science in Emile Durkheim's Sociology." *Sociological Analysis and Theory* 7 (1977).

Rieff, Philip. *Freud: The Mind of the Moralist.* Garden City, N.Y.: Doubleday, 1961.

Ringer, Fritz. *The Decline of the German Mandarins: The German Academic Community, 1890–1933.* Cambridge: Harvard University Press, 1969.

Roche, John P. "The Founding Fathers: A Reform Caucus in Action." *American Political Science Review* 55 (1961).

Rochlin, Gregory. *Manic Aggression: The Defense of the Self.* Boston: Gambit, 1973.

Roehl, J. C. G. *Germany Without Bismarck.* Berkeley, Calif.: University of California Press, 1967.

Rokeach, Milton. *The Three Christs of Ypsilanti: A Psychological Study.* New York: Alfred A. Knopf, 1964.

Roth, Guenther, and Wolfgang Schluchter, *Max Weber's Vision of History: Ethics and Methods.* Berkeley, Calif.: University of California Press, 1979.

Rudner, Richard. "Value Judgments in Scientific Validation." *Scientific Monthly* 79 (1954).

Runciman, W. G. *A Critique of Max Weber's Philosophy of Social Science.* London: Cambridge University Press, 1972.

Russell, Bertrand. *Mysticism and Logic and Other Essays.* New York: Longman, 1918.

Ryle, Gilbert. *The Concept of Mind.* New York: Barnes and Noble, 1949.

Scaff, Lawrence A. "Max Weber and Robert Michels." *American Journal of Sociology* 86 (1981).

————. "Max Weber's Politics and Political Education." *American Political Science Review* 67 (1973).

Schaefer, Bernhard. "Ein Rundschreiben Max Webers zur Sozialpolitik." *Sozial Welt* 18 (1967).

Scheffler, Israel. *Science and Subjectivity.* Indianapolis: Bobbs-Merrill Company, 1967.

Schelting, Alexander von. *Max Weber's Wissenschaftslehre.* Tuebingen: J. C. B. Mohr, 1934.

Schilder, Paul. *The Image and Appearance of the Human Body.* New York: International Universities Press, 1935.

Schluchter, Wolfgang. *The Rise of Western Rationalism: Max Weber's Developmental History,* translated by Guenther Roth. Berkeley, Calif.: University of California Press, 1981.

Schreiber, Flora Rleta. *Sybil.* New York: Warner Books, 1973.

Schumpeter, Joseph. *History of Economic Analysis.* New York: Oxford University Press, 1954.

Schutz, Alfred. *Collected Papers. The Problem of Social Reality,* Vol. I. The Hague, Netherlands: Martinus Nijhoff, 1971.

————. *The Phenomonology of the Social World,* translated by George Walsh and Frederick Lehnert. Evanston, Ill.: Northwestern University Press, 1957.

Seidler, Murray, B., and Mel Jerome Ravitz. "A Jewish Peer Group." *American Journal of Sociology* 61 (1955).

Shoemaker, Sydney. "Personal Identity and Memory." In *Personal Identity,* edited by John Perry. Berkeley, Calif.: University of California Press, 1975.

Sigmund, Paul E. *Natural Law in Political Thought.* Cambridge, Mass.: Winthrop Publishers, 1971.

Simey, T. S. "Max Weber: Man of Affairs or Theoretical Sociologist?" *Sociological Review* 14 (1966).

Skinner, B. F. *Beyond Freedom and Dignity.* New York: Bantam Books, 1971.

Smith, M. Brewster. "The Self and Cognitive Consistency." In *Theories of Cognitive Consistency: A Sourcebook,* edited by Robert P. Abelson et al. Chicago: Rand McNally, 1968.

Steding, Christoph. *Politik und Wissenschaft bei Max Weber.* Breslau: Wilh. Gottl. Korn Verlag, 1932.

Stern, Fritz. *The Politics of Cultural Despair.* Berkeley, Calif.: University of California Press, 1961.

Stolper, Gustav. *This Age of Fable.* New York: Reynal and Hitchcock, 1942.

Strauss, Leo. *Natural Right and History.* Chicago: University of Chicago Press, 1953.

_____. "Political Philosophy and the Crisis of Our Time." In *The Post-Behavioral Era,* edited by George J. Graham, Jr., and George W. Carey. New York: David McKay Company, 1972.

Sullivan, Harry Stack. *Conceptions of Modern Psychiatry.* New York: W. W. Norton, 1953.

Taylor, Richard. *Action and Purpose.* Englewood Cliffs, N.J.: Prentice-Hall, 1966.

Tenbruck, Friedrich H. "Die Genesis der Methodologie Max Webers," *Koelner Zeitschrift fuer Soziologie und Sozialpsychologie* 11 (1959).

Toller, Ernst. *Eine Jugend im Deutschland.* Amsterdam: Querido Verlag, 1933.

Tolstoy, Leo. *Selected Essays,* translated by Aylmer Maude. New York: Modern Library, 1964.

Torrance, John, "Max Weber: Methods and the Man." *European Journal of Sociology* 15 (1974).

Tucker, Robert C. *Stalin as Revolutionary: 1879–1929.* New York: W. W. Norton, 1973.

_____. "The Theory of Charismatic Leadership." In *Philosophers and Kings: Studies in Leadership,* edited by Dankwart A. Rustow. New York: George Braziller, 1970.

Turner, Ralph H. "The Self-Conception in Social Interaction." In *The Self in Social Interaction,* edited by Chad Gordon and Kenneth J. Gergen. New York: John Wiley & Sons, 1968.

Turner, Stephen P., and Regis A. Factor. "Objective Possibility and Adequate Causation in Weber's Methodological Writings." *The Sociological Review* 29 (1981).

_____. *Max Weber and the Dispute over Reason and Value*. London: Routledge and Kegan Paul, 1984.

Voegelin, Eric. *The New Science of Politics*. Chicago: University of Chicago Press, 1952.

Warren, Mark. "The Politics of Nietzsche's Philosophy: Nihilism, Culture and Power." *Political Studies* 33 (1985).

Weber, Marianne. *Max Weber: A Biography*, translated by Harry Zohn. New York: John Wiley & Sons, 1975.

_____. *Max Weber: Ein Lebensbild*. Heidelberg: Verlag Lambert Schneider, 1950.

Weber, Max. *Economy and Society*, edited by Guenther Roth and Claus Wittich. New York: Bedminster Press, 1968.

_____. *From Max Weber*, translated by H. H. Gerth and C. Wright Mills. New York: Oxford University Press, 1946.

_____. "George Simmel as Sociologist," translated by Donald N. Levine. *Social Research* 39 (1972).

_____. *Gesammelte Aufsaetze zur Religionssoziologie, I*. Tuebingen: J. C. B. Mohr, 1920.

_____. *Gesammelte Aufsaetze zur Soziologie und Sozialpolitik*, edited by Marianne Weber. Tuebingen: J. C. B. Mohr, 1924.

_____. *Gesammelte Aufsaetze zur Wissenschaftslehre, Dritte Auflage*, edited by Johannes Winkelmann. Tuebingen: J. C. B. Mohr, 1956.

_____. *Gesammelte Politische Schriften, Dritte Auflage*, edited by Johannes Winkelmann. Tuebingen: J. C. B. Mohr, 1971.

_____. *Gesammelte Politische Schriften, Erste Auflage*. Munich: Drei Masken, 1921.

_____. "Marginal Utility Theory and the Fundamental Law of Psychophysics," translated by Louis Schneider. *Social Science Quarterly* 56 (1975).

_____. *Max Weber on Universities*, edited by Edward Shils. Chicago: University of Chicago Press, 1974.

_____. *Methodology of the Social Sciences*, translated by Edward A. Shils and Henry A. Finch. Glencoe, Ill.: Free Press, 1949.

_____. *The Protestant Ethic and the Spirit of Capitalism*, translated by Talcott Parsons. New York: Charles Scribner's Sons, 1958.

————. *Wirtschaft und Gesellschaft, Vierte Auglage,* edited by Johannes Winkelmann. Tuebingen: J. C. B. Mohr, 1956.

Wells, L. Edward, and Gerald Maxwell, *Self-Esteem.* Beverly Hills, Calif.: Sage Publications, 1976.

Welsh, William A. *Leaders and Elites.* New York: Holt, Rinehart and Winston, 1979.

Wertheimer, Mildred S. *The Pan-German League, 1890–1914.* New York: Octagon Books, 1971.

Wylie, Ruth C. *The Self-Concept.* Lincoln, Nebr.: University of Nebraska Press, 1961.

Zetterbaum, Marvin. "Equality and Human Need." *American Political Science Review* 71 (1977).

————. "Human Nature and History." In *Human Nature in Politics,* edited by J. Poland Pennock and John W. Chapman. New York: New York University Press, 1977.

Zwiedineck-Suedenhorst, Otto von. "Vom Wirken von Max und Alfred Weber im Verein Fuer Sozialpolitik: Erinnerungen und Eindruecke." In *Synopsis: Festgabe fuer Alfred Weber,* edited by Edgar Salin. Heidelberg: Verlag Lambert Schneider, 1949.

INDEX

Action, 95, 97, 99–101, 190n29; goal rational, 128, 124, 210n37; political, 152, 165; social, 124; value-rational, 124, 210n37

Allport, Gordon W., 200n15

Althoff, Friedrich, 216n106

Archiv für Sozialwissenschaft und Sozialpolitik, 54

Aristotle, 172n5

Aron, Raymond, 210n37

Ayer, Alfred Jules, 172n11

Baumgarten, Emmy, 39–40

Baumgarten, Fritz, 32

Baumgarten, Hermann, 38, 183n84

Baumgarten, Ida, 31, 39

Baumgarten, Otto, 39, 182n77

Becker, Carl L., 171n2

Beetham, David, 208n25

Birnbaum, Immanuel, 221n41

Bismarck, Otto von, 38, 162

Brentano, Lujo, 141–42, 216n106

Brunn, H. H., 198n42

Bureaucratic organization, 116–17; and cultural rationalization, 125–29; and political leadership, 131–33

Burger, Thomas, 198n41

Burns, James MacGregor, 212n58

Calling. *See* Personality

Charismatic leadership, and cultural rationalization, 129–33

Cicero, 35

Collective concepts. *See* Ideal-types

Comte, Auguste, 7–8

Condorcet, Marquis de, 6

Copi, Irving M., 173n17

Culture, 14, 59–60, 63, 68–69, 80, 99, 110–11, 139, 194n6; and scientific change, 157–58; and social scientific organization, 140, 157; as subjective meaning, 173n16. *See also* Rationalization, cultural

Determinism, 7, 59

Durkheim, Emile, 67

Duval, Shelley, 204n53

241

Eden, Robert, 209n31
Einstein, Albert, 197n30
Eisner, Kurt, 152, 178n38
Enlightenment, 3, 6
Erikson, Erik H., 47, 48
Ethic of pure intentions, 82
Ethic of responsibility, 82
Ethical virtuoso, 60, 70, 109,
    168, 170. *See also* Hero ethics;
    Self-concept
Ethnic honor, 68
Evangelical Social Union, 27–28

Fact-value dichotomy, 8–9, 71,
    74, 75, 94, 110
Factor, Regis A., 172n12
Fenichel, Otto, 46
Frankfurt Times, 149, 150
Freud, Sigmund, 44, 67,
    185n105, 185n106. *See also*
    Freudean orthodoxy;
    Psychoanalytic theory
Freudean orthodoxy, 22–23, 43–
    45, 94, 185n105. *See also*
    Freud; Psychoanalytic theory
Friedrich, Carl J., 130

Geertz, Clifford, 173n16
German Democratic Party, 150,
    220n34
German National Committee,
    149
German Sociological Association,
    141, 144
Gerschenkron, Alexander,
    175n18

Goethe, Johann Wolfgang von,
    181n68

Habermas, Juergen, 121, 208n23
Hampshire, Stuart, 201n25
Heidelberg Association for a
    Policy Based on Justice, 151
Heidelberg Council of Workers
    and Soldiers, 150
Hekman, Susan J., 208n23
Hero ethics, 70. *See also* Ethical
    virtuoso; Personality; Weber,
    Max
Heuss, Theodor, 177n32, 214n91
Homer, 35
Honigsheim, Paul, 206n19
Horkheimer, Max, 223n69
Horney, Karen, 184n99
Hufnagel, Gerhard, 186n110
Human nature, 111–12; and self-
    concept, 16, 112. *See also*
    Weber, Max
Hume, David, 172n11

Ideal-types, 63–65, 67, 78, 80–
    81, 114, 120, 134, 136, 138–
    39, 155, 198n41; and social
    evaluation, 134–35; variety of
    Weber's definitions, 192n58,
    222n55
Individualism, 7; Weber's,
    207n22, 208n25; Weber's
    methological, 193n59
Intersubjectivity. *See* Social
    science

Jacobson, Edith, 204n55
Jaffe, Edgar, 54
Junkers, 25

Kaiser, Wilhelm II, 92, 116
Kalberg, Steven, 207n20
Kant, Immanuel, 63
Kilpatrick, William Heard, 200n14
Kuhn, Thomas S., 154–57, 195n15, 222n48

Laing, R. D., 48
Lakatos, Irme, 195n15
Leiserson, Avery, 196n26
Lynd, Helen Merrell, 203n39

Machiavelli, Niccolo, 93
Marx, Karl, 18
Masterman, Margaret, 222n48
Mead, George Herbert, 97, 101, 104, 106
Meaning, 77–78; subjective, 56–57, 58, 62, 65, 67, 68, 198n50. See also Action; Self-concept
Menger, Carl, 11
Methodenstreit, 11–12
Michels, Robert, 217n4
Mill, John Stuart, 7–8
Mitzman, Arthur, 174n3, 180n64, 184n99
Mommsen, Wolfgang J., 30, 55, 117, 121, 189n21, 200n11, 208n25, 210n36, 216n111, 220n31

Moroccan Affair, 92
Munich Student's Association, 221n38

National Socialist Association, 28, 29–30
Natural law, 3–4, 5, 10, 171n1
Naumann, Freidrich, 27–29, 42, 53, 92, 137, 148, 177n32, 178n38, 209n31, 214n91

Oakes, Guy, 189n22
Objectivity: political, 5, 86, 162–63; social scientific, 4, 9, 17, 71, 79, 80–81, 84, 136. See also Personality; Social science
Oppenheim, Felix E., 196n24
Ossian, 35, 181n68

Paige, Glen D., 212n57
Pan German League, 149, 150, 219n19
Parsons, Talcott, 192n58
Personal identity. See Self-concept
Personality: artistic, 195n8; political, 41, 70, 82–83, 86–87, 115, 118, 141, 164; saintly, 79, 82–83, 118; scientific, 17, 70, 71, 74, 83–87, 118, 140, 199nn51, 52. See also Objectivity; Self-concept
Phillips, Derek L., 196n16
Piaget, Jean, 96, 98, 101
Plato, 172n5

Polanyi, Michael, 173n20, 195n15

Positive law, 3–4, 5, 10, 57–58, 155

Post-Enlightenment ideologues of social science, 6–7

Pragmatism, scientific, 79

Psycho-biography, 18

Psychoanalytic theory, 44–47, 95–96, 99, 173n19, 185n106, 201n18. *See also* Freud; Freudean orthodoxy

Puritanism, 60–62

Rationalization, cultural, 76, 120–21, 123–25, 207n20, 213n72. *See also* Social science

Rickert, Heinrich, 182n76, 196n21

Rokeach, Milton, 108

Rudner, Richard, 196n17

Runciman, W. G., 210n37

Saint-Simon, Claude Henri de, 172n7

Scaff, Lawrence A., 224n75

Schilder, Paul, 203n45

Schiller, Friedrich, 181n68

Schluchter, Wolfgang, 121, 208n23, 215n96

Schmoller, Gustav, 137, 214n91

Schnitger, Marianne. *See* Weber, Marianne

Schutz, Alfred, 100

Self-concept, 14, 101–02, 104; and communication, 97–98; and deliberation, 98; and memory, 97; and mental pathology, 19; and ultimate commitments, 15–16, 94, 98–103; change in, 103–04, 108; components of, 16, 105–06, 203n43; in early adolescence, 38; necessity of, 15, 94–98; relation to social thought, 16–17, 94, 106–07, 110. *See also* Personality; Weber, Max; Self-esteem

Self-esteem, 99, 103, 203n39

Self-image, 38. *See also* Self-concept

Shoemaker, Sidney, 203n44

Simey, T. S., 215n94

Simmel, Georg, 192n54

Social science: and cultural rationalization, 76, 140; general theory, 155–56; interpretation, 78, 80, 190n29; intersubjectivity, 20, 72, 86; objectivity, 72–74; organizational principles, 13, 136–43; progress, 6–7, 155; specialization and progress, 154–58, 169. *See also* Objectivity; Personality; Pragmatism; Weber, Max

Social theory, and political commitment, 17, 111

Sombart, Werner, 54

Spencer, Martin B., 194n1

Spengler, Oswald, 153

Stalin, 181n70
Status honor, 68–69
Steding, Christoph, 189n22, 222n55
Stern, Fritz, 162
Stolper, Gustav, 223n57
Subjectivity, 8–9, 10, 20, 74, 78, 86, 101. *See also* Culture; Meaning; Social science

Tenbruck, Freidrich H., 190n29
Toennies, Ferdinand, 216n107
Tolstoy, Leo, 83, 198n46
Torrance, John, 173n18
Treitschke, Heinrich von, 176n28
Troeltsch, Ernst, 217n4
Tucker, Robert C., 181n70, 212n58
Turner, Stephen P., 172n12

Verein für Sozialpolitik, 24–26, 136–38, 142, 143, 176n25
Versailles peace negotiations, 151
Vienna, university, 145
Virgil, 35

Weber, Alfred, 34, 54, 181n72
Weber, Helene, 35–36, 40, 179n51, 184n99; early relationship with sons, 30–32, 181n72; later relationship with Max, 183n89
Weber, Marianne, 41, 53, 91, 146, 178n43, 180n64, 187n117, 190n27, 199n4, 200n11, 204n56, 224n79

Weber, Max: concept of action, 56, 210n37; study of agrarian workers, 25–26, 176n27; on disenchantment of the world, 167; *Economy and Society,* 121, 154, 208n23, 213n71; and fact-value dichotomy, 9; move to Heidelberg, 42; view of human nature, 16, 112, 117–19; inaugural address, 27, 71, 181n69; first scholarly interests after breakdown, 189n22; and Jewish prophets, 160; early relationship with Mother, 35–36, 179n51; nationalism, 108, 121–23, 208n24; nervous disorders, 12–13, 19, 47, 50–52, 90–93, 174n2, 174n6, 186n110, 186n116, 187n117, 199n4, 200n13, 217n2, 217n3; concept of personality, 13–14, 55, 61, 62, 89, 95, 109–10, 194n71, 207n21; plebiscitary democracy, 133–36; political activity, 27–28, 54, 91–92, 148–52, 177n29, 177n33, 218n13, 219n16, 219n17, 220n34; political science, 206n19; concept of politics, 114–17, 122–23; "Politics as a Vocation," 164; and power politics, 209n30; *The Protestant Ethic and the Spirit of Capitalism,* 120; religion and science, 167–68, 224n79,

Weber, Max (*cont.*)
224n80; *Religionssoziologie,*
154; essays on Russian
revolution (1905), 91; "Science
as a Vocation," 85, 154, 164,
167; self-concept, 16, 19, 34,
38, 94, 108–09, 111; concept
of social causation, 57–59;
political benefits of social
science, 136, 139–41; "Social
Scientific 'Objectivity' and
Social/Political Knowledge,"
136; on teaching, 152, 163–
64, 215n98, 224n73; travel as
therapy, 49–50, 90, 92;
typology of personalities, 70,
81; on values in social science,
71–82. *See also* Ideal-types;
Individualism; Weber, Helene
Weber, Max, Sr., 22–23, 30–31,
34, 49, 178n43
Weimar Republic, 151
Wicklund, Robert A., 204n53

Zetterbaum, Marvin, 205n59